A Decade of Transition:
Achievements and Challenges

A DECADE OF TRANSITION: ACHIEVEMENTS AND CHALLENGES

Editors

Oleh Havrylyshyn
Saleh M. Nsouli

IMF Institute
International Monetary Fund
Washington, D.C.

Production: IMF Graphics Section
Cover design: Sanaa Elaroussi
Typesetting: Joseph A. Kumar

Library of Congress Cataloging-in-Publication Data

A Decade of Transition: Achievements and Challenges/Oleh
Havrylyshyn, Saleh M. Nsouli, editors.—Washington, D.C. :
International Monetary Fund, IMF Institute, 2001.

    p. cm.

    "Selected papers presented at an IMF conference in Washing-
ton, D.C., February 1–3, 1999, sponsored by the European I
and II Departments and the IMF Institute."

    Includes bibliographical references.
    ISBN 1-58906-013-X

1. Economic stabilization—Europe, Central—Congresses.
2. Economic stabilization—Europe, Eastern—Congresses.
3. Economic stabilization—Former Soviet republic—Congresses.
4. Deflation   (Finance)—Europe,   Central—Congresses.
5. Deflation   (Finance)—Europe,   Eastern—Congresses.
6. Deflation (Finance)—Former Soviet republics—Congresses.
7. Europe, Central—Economic condition—1989—Congresses.
8. Europe, Eastern—Economic conditions—1989—Congresses.
9. Former Soviet republics—Economic conditions—1991—
Congresses. I. Havrylyshyn, Oli. II. Nsouli, Saleh M. III. International Monetary Fund.

HB3782.9.D32 2001

Price: $26.00

Address orders to:
International Monetary Fund, Publication Services
700 19th Street, N.W., Washington, D.C., 20431, U.S.A.
Tel.: (202) 623-7430   Telefax: (202) 623-7201
E-mail: publications@imf.org

Contents

Foreword

A decade of experience in the transformation of former centrally planned economies to market-oriented economies has produced important lessons. To identify the lessons from the experience of 25 non-Asian transition countries, the IMF held a conference, "A Decade of Transition: Achievements and Challenges," on February 1–3, 1999, in Washington, D.C. The conference brought together senior government officials, staff from the European Bank for Reconstruction and Development, the IMF, the World Bank, and academics to answer three questions: How far has the transition progressed in different countries? What factors explain the differences in progress and in economic performance? And what remains to be done?

The contributions in this volume cover a broad range of issues relevant to transition: financial stabilization, growth recovery, privatization, banking reform, income inequality, and the changing role of government. The conference discussions raised at least as many questions as they answered. The discussions, and the papers in this volume, provide some answers to the three questions posed above. First, transition countries have made substantial progress in financial stabilization, but progress with structural reforms and institutional development has been distinctly greater in Central Europe and the Baltics than in countries farther to the east. Second, although financial stabilization is essential for renewed economic growth, it is not enough: structural reforms and the development of market institutions must also be sufficiently advanced. Third, while in the next phase of transition the consolidation of stabilization will need to continue, the emphasis will need to shift to several other tasks: carrying through the unfinished structural agenda (especially in lagging countries), accelerating institutional development, addressing egregious cases of income inequality, and dealing firmly with corruption and the growth of vested interests.

I believe that this volume will contribute to deepening the understanding of the challenges still facing the transition economies and the policies needed to address them. The tasks that remain are great, requiring continued determined effort by the countries concerned.

Horst Köhler
Managing Director

Acknowledgments

Many people contributed to the success of the conference, A Decade of Transition: Achievements and Challenges, and to the ensuing book. We wish to express our appreciation to all the conference participants whose presentations and interventions made for a lively discussion, and to the authors of a comprehensive and insightful set of papers that appear in this volume. We are grateful to the three organizing departments, the European I and II Departments and the IMF Institute, and in particular to their Directors, Michael Deppler, Mohsin S. Khan, and John Odling-Smee, for their encouragement and support. Further, we want to thank Deirdre Clark, Gabriele Monnett, and Chris Withee of the Administrative Division of the IMF Institute for their valuable assistance in organizing the conference, as well as Joan Campayne of the European II Department, who contributed tirelessly from the inception stage to the final preparation of this volume. We also want to thank Farah Ebrahimi, who, along with Mike Treadway, edited the volume and saw it through production; Frank Welffens, for editorial assistance; and Marie Therese Culp for her thoroughness and hard work in preparing the final manuscript.

A Decade of Transition   1

Oleh Havrylyshyn and Saleh M. Nsouli

Since the fall of the Berlin Wall nearly a decade ago, the former centrally planned economies of Central and Eastern Europe and the Baltics, Russia, and other former Soviet Union countries have made major strides in moving toward market-based economies. Initially, this historic transformation was accompanied by considerable price and output instability. In many countries, stabilization programs supported by the IMF and the World Bank helped contain this instability and bolstered the momentum for structural reforms. Yet by 1998, only countries in Central Europe had achieved sustained growth and recovery from the recession that followed the transition. And even in that region, Albania, Bulgaria, and Romania suffered setbacks during 1996–97. The crisis that beset Russia in 1998 not only exacerbated the recession in the region, it highlighted the key challenge of transition: achieving sustained economic growth.

To take stock of the accomplishments of the transition economies over the past 10 years and identify the challenges ahead, in February 1999 the IMF organized a conference for senior officials from transition countries, academics, and staff of international organizations. This volume contains the papers presented at the conference. The chapters explore a broad set of issues in the transition process—from the overarching macroeconomic problems of achieving stabilization and sustained growth to the microeconomic building blocks of the transformation. Specifically, the chapters examine private sector development, financial sector evolution, external sector relations, social protection, and most important, the proper role of government, the rule of law, and the effective functioning of market-friendly institutions.

In his opening remarks, former IMF Managing Director Michel Camdessus set the tone of the IMF conference. He pointed to the progress made, but cautioned that important challenges remained, reminding participants that most countries now had to turn to the much more difficult and time-consuming task of implementing second-generation reforms, at the heart of which is: "enforcing the rule of law and fostering a culture that respects and welcomes a framework of law, regulation, and codes of good practice."

1

Achievements, Shortfalls, and Lessons

The non-Asian transition economies have generally achieved considerable inflation control, and many have begun to grow. The economic literature on the transition process has grappled with two critical questions on disinflation. First, how rapid has disinflation been during transition? Second, what effect has disinflation had on output? Carlo Cottarelli and Peter Doyle, whose chapter explores the record on disinflation, found that many transition countries achieved rapid disinflation. The median inflation rate in the CEE countries dropped from 84 percent in 1992 to about 9 percent in 1995. Disinflation was achieved even more quickly in the Baltics, Russia, and other former Soviet Union countries, where the median inflation rate fell from 1,210 percent in 1992 to 60 percent in 1995. The two groups of countries converged to a median inflation rate of about 11–12 percent by 1997. But the reduction in inflation has not always been sustained, and inflation has resurged in some countries.

Despite the rapid disinflation, the authors found no evidence that disinflation had a role in depressing output. Four factors played a key role in limiting the impact of disinflation on output: first, there was considerable political support for disinflation and price liberalization; second, stabilization policies were introduced early; third, in several countries comprehensive fiscal consolidation underpinned disinflation; and fourth, the monetary frameworks were appropriately flexible. Rather than depressing output, the resulting moderate- and low-inflation environment had an eventual positive impact on growth. Although few participants disagreed with these views, some emphasized that inflation control, while necessary, was not enough to increase output and had to be made sustainable, primarily by controlling the fiscal situation.

Nonetheless, in the early years of transition virtually every country in the region experienced a substantial decline in recorded output. According to Oleh Havrylyshyn and Thomas Wolf, although long time lags were inevitable in reallocating resources to more efficient uses in a decentralized system, the initial loss in output reflected the collapse of the highly centralized and inefficient production and distribution network of the command economy. Moreover, differences in the conditions and policies of the transition economies had different effects on output. These differences led to a much greater decline at the beginning of transition in the Baltics, Russia, and other former Soviet Union countries than in the Central and Eastern European countries. But after about three years of decline, output began to grow in many countries, although Albania, Bulgaria, and Romania suffered setbacks during 1996–97 because of failure to undertake some important structural reforms. Moreover, Kazakhstan, Moldova, Russia, Tajikistan, Turkmenistan, and Ukraine have registered little or no growth after eight years of transition, primarily because of civil conflict, weak policies, and the decline in world oil prices. And as already mentioned, the spillover effects of the Russian crisis in 1998—which itself reflects political uncertainties and an unfinished structural reform agenda—further exacerbated the recession in these countries.

Havrylyshyn and Wolf, using econometric analysis, demonstrated that after accounting for differences in initial conditions, variations in growth performance by country was attributable primarily to the ability of the more successful economies to quickly control inflation and to progress with such structural reforms as privatization, market liberalization, private sector development, and the establishment of financial and legal frameworks. Although conference participants generally agreed with this finding, some were concerned about the effect of underground activity on measuring growth. Others thought that the econometrics could be strengthened to emphasize the study's conclusions and to show such missing factors as reverse causality. Some participants wanted to extend the discussion to a key future issue: how to "starve" the rent-seekers who in some countries have captured the policymaking process, slowing reform and hurting growth performance.

In contrast to the experience of the Baltics, Russia, and other former Soviet Union countries, the experience of the East Asian transition countries—notably, China—was considerably different in both growth and inflation. Sanjay Kalra and Torsten Sløk observe that the stronger performance of the East Asian countries reflects not only more favorable initial conditions but also far-reaching reforms in several areas—agriculture, in particular—undertaken early in the process. They warned that the lessons of Asian economies—which are still highly agricultural—are not easily transferable to other transition economies.

Promoting the Private Sector

Nicholas Stern noted that the reform of the public enterprise sector has often been patchy and inconsistent in transition economies. As a result, unprofitable enterprises have continued to operate. Furthermore, as John Nellis pointed out, in Russia and elsewhere, too much was promised of privatization. Several conference participants suggested setting clear, but limited goals for privatization, as opposed to the broad objective of creating a good market environment for all private sector activity, including new start-ups. Nellis underscores that some policymakers had incorrectly viewed privatization as a sufficient condition to bring about a new liberal order. Privatization was often pursued without due attention to whether the necessary supporting systems for private enterprises were in place, to the time it would take to establish such systems, or to the likely consequences of privatization in their absence. The poor record of privatization evoked considerable debate on the proper role of government and the political economy of interest group struggles. On balance, however, there was wide consensus for the view that any mistakes in privatization should not be corrected by going back, but by ensuring the development of a proper hard budget and competitive environment for efficient private sector operation.

According to former Prime Minister Yegor Gaidar, at the heart of Russia's difficulties and setbacks during transition has been its inability to move effectively from a system of "soft" budget constraints with "hard" administrative constraints to the decentralized market system of hard budget constraints with little administrative and political interference. In Russia today both the budget and the administrative constraints have become soft. Even when privatized, enterprises are subjected to hard budget constraints owing to institutional weaknesses. Consequently, the opportunities for rent-seeking (that is, socially unproductive profit-seeking) are in place, but incentives for enhancing efficiency are not. The key to reducing corruption and enhancing efficiency is market discipline under hard macroeconomic constraints. Gaidar emphasizes, however, that macroeconomic discipline has been absent in Russia, and the resulting lax fiscal and monetary policies have proved unsustainable.

Some of the transition countries have large underground economies. According to Simon Johnson and Daniel Kaufmann, overregulation, corruption, and weak legal systems are what drive businesses underground. Aggregate data and microsurveys show that in Russia and Ukraine, unofficial output constitutes 40 to 50 percent of total GDP, whereas in most of Eastern Europe it is under 20 percent. The difference across countries is due primarily to variations in the degree of institutional weaknesses and government corruption. As a result of the growing underground economy, tax revenues have fallen and the quality of public administration has declined accordingly, further reducing firms' incentives to be "official." The authors' main recommendation is to move on with privatization and regulatory and legal reforms in order to provide opportunities and incentives for firms to operate in the official sector.

Social Impact of Transition and the Role of Government

The transition from a planned to a market economy has been accompanied by one of the biggest and fastest increases in income inequality ever recorded. Branko Milanovic showed that, on average, inequality in Eastern Europe, the Baltics, Russia, and other former Soviet Union countries increased rapidly, as measured by a rise in the Gini coefficient from 25–28 to 35–38 in less than 10 years. (The Gini coefficient is a measure of the inequality of income distribution in a country, with 0 representing absolute equality.) In some countries, such as Bulgaria, Russia, and Ukraine, the increase in inequality was even more dramatic, outpacing by three to four times the yearly rate of increase in the Gini coefficient in the United Kingdom and the United States in the 1980s. What were the factors driving this growing inequality? First, wage inequality is greater in the new private sector than in the old, relatively egalitarian state sector. Second, income from self-employment and property, both of which are fairly unequal sources of income, have grown during the transition. And third, the incomes of former state sector workers who are now unemployed have declined, contributing to a "hollowing out" of the middle class.

Some of the commentators wondered whether the calculations might not have overstated the deterioration, given the distorted prices of the earlier period and the existence of shortages, but in general participants agreed that inequality had increased significantly. The implication drawn by the author and shared by most conference participants was clear: the transition governments must make more effort to offset the falling-out effect and to provide support for the neediest and most adversely affected, or risk losing social support for reforms. Nevertheless, some participants cautioned against going too far and undoing the part of the growing inequality that is an inherent outcome of the transition process.

Tanzi and Tsibouris, in examining the proper role of government, outlined the considerable changes made in the fiscal functions (tax collection and budget expenditures), especially in the tax systems. Nevertheless, they consider these structural improvements a beginning of the major changes needed—a beginning that in many instances had caused a sharp deterioration in revenue collections. They argue that, in the long run, transition economies need to develop governments that support but that do not distort markets, that provide the discipline of rule of law, that establish an efficient bureaucracy, and that meet their fiscal obligations and promises.

This view became virtually the identifying theme of the conference. It had relevance to every session and was forcefully echoed in the closing panel. A number of participants emphasized that, despite reforms, the state remained too large in many countries. They agreed that the transformation of the role of government was at the heart of the transition process. Others noted that although much had been achieved in institution building (especially in key agencies like central banks, finance ministries, and regulatory agencies for countries more likely to be integrated into the European Union) continued strengthening of institutions was an essential part of the integration process.

The Support Roles of Financial Sector and External Capital

Following external and internal liberalization, the transition economies had large and growing current account deficits, which were financed largely by capital inflows. Garibaldi and others (1999),[1] in their study of capital flows to 25 transition economies between 1991 and 1997, showed sizable net capital inflows to transition economies during the 1990s. On a per capita basis, the inflows were similar to those to the Latin American countries and to the more advanced Asian economies, and much higher than those to other developing regions. The distribution of inflows across countries, however, was not uniform. The more advanced transition countries—Central Europe and the Baltics—generally received much higher net inflows, whereas Russia was a net capital exporter. The econometric analysis demonstrated the importance of perceptions of country risk and institutional obstacles (such as government red tape) in determining foreign direct investment flows.

Generally, capital inflows at the beginning of the transition period consisted largely of exceptional financing, but later their composition shifted to favor foreign direct investment and other private capital. This suggests that official and private debt relief did indeed help the transition economies to adjust and reform.

Lajos Bokros's survey of banking sector reforms in the Baltics and Eastern Europe shows that competition, corporate governance, and prudential regulation and supervision play a critical role in the transition to a market economy. Of particular importance to their performance were effective foreign and domestic bank entry and exit regulations, which facilitated the entry of foreign banks, thereby fostering competition, increasing the sophistication of the financial products available, and strengthening the domestic banking system. In contrast, the financial sectors in the weak performers lacked competition and sector-specific expertise; had low-quality assets, significant state ownership, and low levels of corporate lending; and operated in an unsta-

---

[1]Pietro Garibaldi, Nada Mora, Ratna Sahay, and Jeromin Zettelmeyer, 1999, "What Moves Capital to Transition Economies?" (unpublished; Washington: International Monetary Fund). This paper was presented at the conference but is not included in this volume.

ble macroeconomic environment. Those with the least progress in bank restructuring were countries with inappropriate incentive structures that encouraged the accumulation of risky assets in pursuit of quick profits.

The Challenges Ahead

The record of the last decade in the transition of countries to a market economy is one of progress, but also of challenges ahead, as pointed out by IMF Deputy Managing Director Shigemitsu Sugisaki in his concluding remarks. Although these countries have generally managed to reduce inflation and to renew output growth, their situation remains fragile. Resurgence of inflation, a weakening of output performance, and an intensification of external sector pressures are all possible. In this regard, the conference identified the main challenges facing these countries:

- *First, the role of government needs to be radically transformed.* As pointed out by Vito Tanzi, to function well, market economies need governments that are efficient and evenhanded in establishing and enforcing essential rules for promoting widely shared social objectives, for raising revenues to finance public sector activities, for spending these revenues productively, for bringing required corrections to and controls over the working of the private sector, and for enforcing contracts and protecting property. Governments will need to establish rules of the game that are appropriate to market economies as well as regulations in such areas as private pensions and competition while eliminating most discretionary regulations, often relics of the command economy. Such actions essentially amount to creating an environment conducive to the efficient functioning of market forces, and therefore are critical to fostering the growth of the private sector and shrinking the underground economy. They also reduce the perception of risk, thereby helping to attract foreign direct investment. The great difficulty of creating basic institutions should not be underestimated, however.
- *Second, the process of privatization has to be improved.* A strong institutional framework, and openness and transparency, are key to successful privatization. Numerous actions have to be taken to streamline privatization. Downsizing and restructuring can take place through a reallocation of ownership and control, which could be facilitated by involving foreign investors. But in reallocating ownership, officials must avoid transferring labor and social obligations of the old firms to the new owners. These steps

must be reinforced by reorienting the role of the state to promote market discipline and by putting in place effective bankruptcy procedures, while ensuring that financing is made dependent on a well-regulated and supervised financial sector and on good business practices. Such actions will effectively harden the budget constraints on enterprises.

- *Third, financial sector reform is fundamental to promoting growth because it improves the intermediation process and increases efficiency in the allocation of financial resources.* The progress made in giving greater autonomy to central banks represents a step in the right direction. However, a competitive system open to foreign financial institutions, and the enactment and effective implementation of strong prudential regulations, are key components that still need to be addressed in many transition economies.
- *Fourth, severe income inequalities must be tackled even if one accepts the fact that some increase in inequality is inevitable, and even desirable, when compared with that which existed in the socialist period.* Over time, institutional change and increased competition should help reduce economic rents and income inequalities. The process will take time, however, and governments will need to put in place a well-targeted social safety net for the most vulnerable segments of the population. Ensuring adequate support for the neediest is undoubtedly a role of the government, as is providing assistance to workers displaced by reallocation of production. A reform process that ignores the losers and fails to provide for the neediest may falter in the long run for lack of support.
- *Fifth, macroeconomic stabilization is essential for structural reform and the recovery of economic activity and sustained growth.* Empirical evidence shows that lower inflation rates, while not sufficient by themselves to ensure growth, are associated with faster economic growth in the long run. Further, transition countries with persistent moderate inflation, as well as other advanced transition countries, now enjoy favorable circumstances for continued disinflation. In transition countries, the inflation threshold above which output costs rise substantially is now comparable to the threshold in industrial countries; therefore, a commitment to slowing inflation to industrial country levels over the medium term is appropriate, especially in countries aspiring to join the European Union.

Opening Address　2

Michel Camdessus

It is a great pleasure for me to welcome you to this conference, A Decade of Transition: Achievements and Challenges. This gathering brings together leading experts—policymakers, academics, and staff of international financial institutions—who have been working closely on transition issues. Their experiences bring a wide range of perspectives on the accomplishments to date, as well as on the challenges that lie ahead, and the policies needed to address them.

The Berlin Wall fell in November 1989. The wrenching transformation that followed in countries east of that dividing line has brought liberty to those countries and, in many places, prosperity, but it has also strained their economic, social, and political makeup. Recognizing the historic importance and the unparalleled difficulty of the transition, the IMF became involved very early in helping about 20 of those countries to establish Fund membership. Since then, in collaboration with the World Bank, it has been working closely with the countries in transition in formulating stabilization programs and structural reforms to develop market institutions. The Fund has, along with others, provided a vast array of technical assistance to strengthen the institutional capacity of the emerging market economies. It has supported those efforts through a new instrument specifically created for transition economies—the Systemic Transformation Facility—as well as through stand-by arrangements, extended arrangements, and the Enhanced Structural Adjustment Facility.

At the outset of transition, little was clear, except that there was no turning back. There was no master plan and scarce relevant experience to guide action. In the economic sphere, a host of proposals quickly filled the vacuum, jostling with the force of events and circumstance to determine what happened. In Central and Eastern Europe, German reunification defined the options for the German Democratic Republic; Poland and countries of the former Yugoslav Republic confronted outright hyperinflation. In these and other countries, national consensus for change sometimes proved elusive, and, in some cases, hostilities broke out. All the countries had to grapple with the collapse of the trading arrangements under the Council for Mutual Economic Assistance (CMEA), of key export markets, and of economic activity. The breakup of the Soviet Union in 1991–92 brought further issues into play: planning mechanisms were more deeply entrenched there; hyperinflation was rife; and a raft of new countries and currencies were established.

The essential components of the transition reform agenda, however, rapidly crystallized: fiscal consolidation, monetary and financial reform, price and trade liberalization, and privatization. As a result of courageous decisions by many leaders, progress has been dramatic. By the end of 1997, inflation was close to or in single digits in many of these countries. Since 1993, output has been growing in Central and Eastern Europe and since 1995 in many of the Baltics and countries of the former Soviet Union. Although much remains to be done, a number of countries have all but completed the structural reforms that comprise the transition agenda. Indeed, some have already embarked on reforms aimed at accession to the European Union. So, undoubtedly, the foundations for prosperity have been laid. Even to those with no more than a passing acquaintance with the region prior to 1990, the transformation is obvious. In just one short decade, centrally planned systems already seem like defunct and discredited relics of a distant past. What an exhausting job! And since many of you, in one capacity or another, have been actors in the transition, let me express the Fund's admiration and pride in having been associated with those efforts. But, of course, not everything is rosy!

After the reversals in Albania, Bulgaria, and Romania in 1996 and 1997, and the events in Russia in 1998, surely no one still harbors the illusion that continued progress will be straightforward. These events remind us of important lessons: that the region is exposed to developments elsewhere in the world; that incomplete transition reform is hazardous; and that interlinkages in the region remain strong.

We are clearly far from the end of the road. But even where structural reforms have been incomplete, they have at least provided the preliminary foundations for private ownership, market pricing, and market discipline. Now, most of the countries can turn to the much more difficult and time-consuming task of implementing second generation reforms, even though some of those countries still have far to go in tackling the first generation of reforms.

I admit to taking an advance look at some of the conference papers. I was impressed that the paper on privatization, while admitting to problems and the need to rethink privatization, gives compelling reasons as to why the new thinking should be *better* privatization rather than *less* privatization. More generally, I will hazard a guess that a similar theme—that of sustaining and deepening reforms, rather than reversing the buildup of market institutions—will emerge in your discussions as key to the success of other essential elements of reform: creating a market-friendly environment, developing a sound financial sector, establishing effective government operations, and providing equitable social protection. These issues are surely the right ones to examine in this conference and should provide a basis for exploring the policy strategy—the road map—for the next stage of the transition journey.

Let me highlight one specific task of great importance for the future: enforcing the rule of law and fostering a culture that respects and, indeed, welcomes a framework of law, regulation, and codes of good practice. Within such a framework, governments, enterprises, financial institutions, and individuals should be able to deal with each other at arm's length and in a transparent manner. An important ingredient is that the discipline of the market should be allowed to work. This will reduce restraints on the activity of enterprises, whether old or new, encouraging the initiatives of entrepreneurs, who are the source of productivity growth, new output, and more value added—in short, growth of GDP. Ultimately, that is what stabilization, structural reform, and transition are all about.

In conclusion, I would venture that much has been learned in the past 10 years about what works in transition, but many questions remain. I hope that the discussions in this conference will shed light on three issues that seem particularly important to me:

- For countries that have completed the bulk of the structural reform agenda for transition and have achieved moderate inflation, what are the key next steps to stimulate growth and strengthen their resilience to external shocks?
- For countries that still have some distance to go to complete their reform agenda, what should their priorities be?
- In assisting these two groups of countries, what key areas of reform should be the focus of the Bretton Woods institutions in the period ahead?

You have much to discuss, and we all have much to learn. I wish you well in your endeavors in the coming three days.

Disinflation in Transition—1993–97 3

Carlo Cottarelli and Peter Doyle

Almost all transition countries experienced an initial spike in inflation at the outset of the reform process as price controls were removed.
The speed of the subsequent disinflations, however, varied markedly,
partly reflecting the different times when countries gained monetary
and political independence. Some Central and Eastern European
(CEE) countries had managed to reduce inflation to the two-digit
range already by the end of 1992, while inflation remained close to or
above 1,000 percent in the Baltics, Russia, and other countries of the
former Soviet Union (BRO). Subsequently, inflation continued to fall
gradually in the Central and Eastern European countries, albeit with
some notable exceptions. But it fell sharply in the Baltics, Russia, and
other countries of the former Soviet Union, where, by the end of 1997,
it exceeded 100 percent only in one country. As a result, median 12-
month inflation in the whole transition group fell from 950 percent at
the end of 1992 to 11 percent at the end of 1997.

This chapter focuses on the experience during 1993–97 of 10 Central
and Eastern European countries and the Baltics, Russia, and other
countries of the former Soviet Union. It reviews a range of policies
implemented in transition economies through the prism of their
contribution to disinflation, and factors that were particular to the
transition context.[1] The chapter first outlines the recent inflation and
output record. It notes that inflation peaked at higher rates, the output
collapse was more marked, and disinflation came later in the Baltics,
Russia, and other countries of the former Soviet Union than in the
Central and Eastern European countries. Nevertheless, output began
to recover within two years of successful disinflation in both areas. It
then discusses the econometric evidence concerning the links between
inflation and output. No general evidence is found that disinflation
compounded other factors depressing output, but evidence is found
that the moderate and low inflation environment brought about by

---

This chapter was first published in 1999 as Occasional Paper No. 179, International Monetary Fund, Washington, D.C.
    [1]The disinflations in Central and Eastern European countries during 1990–92 have been dis-
cussed in Bruno (1992).

disinflation stimulated growth. Next, the chapter identifies the factors that facilitated such apparently low-cost disinflation, including the transition context in which disinflation occurred and the role of fiscal policy. It then discusses the experience of countries that, having successfully reduced high inflation, remained in a moderate inflation range for several years. The conclusion summarizes the findings and draws out the implications for the inflation rates that transition countries should target in the years ahead.

Inflation Developments

By the end of 1992, major results in stabilizing inflation had been achieved only in the Central and Eastern European countries: inflation had dropped below 60 percent in the Czech Republic, Poland, and Slovak Republic (Table 1).[2] Hungary had always remained well below this threshold.[3] Inflation in the ruble zone was high and rising at this time. It surged dramatically in many countries that exited the ruble zone and established independent currencies and new central banks thereafter.

A new wave of stabilization efforts followed during 1993–94 and enjoyed considerable success: during 1993–97, 19 other transition economies managed to break the 60 percent inflation threshold (Table 2)—in most cases without reversals—and by the end of 1997, 16 countries had brought inflation below 15 percent (Table 1). Georgia is a particularly dramatic case, reducing 12-month inflation from 50,000 percent during 1994 to single digits in 1997.

While many countries delayed inflation stabilization for several years—with a relative cluster of stabilizations in late 1994–early 1995—inflation stabilization, once undertaken, was usually rapid. In many cases, less than six months elapsed between the initiation of a major stabilization effort and quarterly annualized inflation falling below 60 percent on a sustained basis (Table 2).[4] Only five countries (Estonia,

---

[2]The term "inflation stabilization" is used here to indicate a stable decline of inflation below the 60 percent threshold (see footnote 1 in Table 2 for a more precise definition). While this threshold is arbitrary, few countries that managed to break it experienced major inflation reversals. Moreover, the results discussed in this review are quite robust to the choice of the threshold. The term "disinflation" is instead used to indicate the overall process of reduction in inflation, including in the poststabilization period.

[3]This partly reflects its gradual price liberalization during the 1980s and, in comparison to some transition countries, its generally cautious monetary policy in that period and thereafter.

[4]The stabilization initiation dates adopted by Fischer, Sahay, and Végh (1996) have been used to construct Table 2. Most stabilization dates coincide with the starting date of an arrangement with the IMF. When multiple attempts were made (as occurred in six of these countries), "the most serious attempt" was taken. Fischer, Sahay, and Végh stress that the judgment about the seriousness of the stabilization program was not based on eventual inflation performance, but rather on an evaluation of the policy package associated with the stabilization effort.

Table 1. Twelve-Month Inflation Rates in Transition Economies
(End of period)

Country	1992	1993	1994	1995	1996	1997
Albania	236.6	30.9	15.8	6.0	17.4	42.1
Bulgaria	79.4	63.8	121.9	32.9	310.8	578.6
Croatia	937.3	1,149.7	-3.0	3.7	3.5	3.9
Czech Republic	12.6	18.8	9.7	7.9	8.6	10.1
Hungary	24.7	21.1	21.2	28.3	19.8	18.4
Macedonia, FYR	1,935.0	241.9	55.0	9.0	-0.6	2.7
Poland	44.5	37.7	29.5	21.6	18.5	13.2
Romania	199.2	295.5	61.7	27.8	56.9	151.6
Slovak Republic	9.1	25.0	11.7	7.2	5.4	6.4
Slovenia	. . .	22.9	18.3	8.6	8.8	9.4
CEE median	79.4	34.3	19.8	8.8	13.1	11.7
Armenia	1,241.2	10,896.1	1,884.6	32.1	5.7	21.8
Azerbaijan	. . .	1,291.6	1,788.1	84.5	6.7	0.4
Belarus	1,561.5	1,995.0	1,957.3	244.2	39.1	63.4
Estonia	942.2	35.7	41.6	28.8	15.0	12.3
Georgia	1,335.1	7,543.8	6,471.6	57.4	13.7	7.3
Kazakhstan	2,960.7	2,172.6	1,157.6	60.5	28.6	11.3
Kyrgyz Republic	1,257.0	766.9	95.7	32.3	34.9	14.7
Latvia	958.2	34.9	26.5	23.6	13.5	7.1
Lithuania	1,162.5	188.8	45.0	35.5	13.1	8.5
Moldova	2,198.4	836.8	115.9	23.8	15.1	11.1
Russia	2,321.6	841.6	202.7	131.4	21.9	11.0
Tajikistan	. . .	7,346.3	1.1	2,135.2	40.6	163.6
Turkmenistan	. . .	. . .	1,328.6	1,261.5	445.9	21.5
Ukraine	2,005.0	10,153.6	401.1	181.4	39.7	10.1
Uzbekistan	910.0	885.0	1,281.4	116.9	64.4	50.2
BRO median	1,296.1	1,088.3	401.1	60.5	21.9	11.3

Source: IMF staff estimates.

Kazakhstan, the Kyrgyz Republic, Lithuania, and Ukraine) took about 18–24 months from the beginning of the stabilization to get below 60 percent.[5]

But after the initial inflation stabilization phase, further disinflation was often slow. After breaking the 60 percent disinflation threshold, inflation persisted at moderately high levels (the 15–60 percent range) for more than two years in a number of countries. This slower disinflation group includes the same countries that reached 60 percent

---

[5]The marked volatility of inflation throughout the transition area is reflected in findings that lagged inflation has been relatively unimportant in explaining inflation in transition economies (Cottarelli, Griffiths, and Moghadam, 1998; and Coorey, Mecagni, and Offerdal, 1998).

slowly (except Ukraine), though Latvia and Albania, which had quickly reduced inflation to 60 percent, joined the group thereafter. However, the most often-quoted cases of persistently moderate inflation (see Cottarelli and Szapáry, 1998) are given by a number of advanced transition economies where inflation had dropped below the 60 percent threshold before the end of 1992. These include Poland (where it took more than four years to bring inflation down from 60 percent to below 15 percent), Hungary (where inflation was still over 18 percent at the end of 1997), and Slovenia (where inflation remained in the 15–30 percent range for over two years after the initial stabilization). Inflation in the Czech Republic and Slovakia has remained stuck to close to 10 percent for a number of years. The median inflation rate of those Central and Eastern European countries that began stabilization before 1993 fell from 27½ percent in 1993 to 15½ percent in 1997; the median inflation rate in the Baltics, Russia, and other countries of the former Soviet Union meeting the same criteria declined somewhat more rapidly, from 35½ percent to 12 percent over this period. Only Croatia and the former Yugoslav Republic of Macedonia have maintained inflation in low single digits for a number of years.[6]

Despite this persistent moderate inflation, the relapses into high inflation were relatively rare (Table 1). During 1993–97, there were three major reversals of inflation after initially successful stabilizations: Bulgaria and Romania in 1996, and Albania in 1997 (Table 1). And Albania and Bulgaria have since renewed their stabilization efforts. While outside the period covered by this chapter, the resurgence of inflation in Russia during the summer of 1998 is also notable: the 12-month inflation rate jumped from less than 6 percent in July to 59 percent in October (following a monthly inflation rate of almost 40 percent in September), reflecting the depreciation of the ruble during August 1998. As discussed below, this resurgence of inflation shares many of the features characterizing the relapses into inflation observed during 1993–97.

Disinflation, Output, and the Current Account Balance

Disinflation occurred while output was collapsing, and was often followed by large deteriorations in the external current account balance. This section discusses the links between these developments.

---

[6]The upward biases in inflation measurement identified by the Boskin report for the United States may be larger in transition economies, given the faster rate of introduction of new products and the proliferation of new retail outlets (Škreb, 1998). On the other hand, lagged adjustments of the weights for goods subject to administered pricing tend to cause inflation to be understated when administered prices rise relative to market prices.

Table 2. Disinflation Thresholds[1]

Country	Peak Inflation (1990–97)	Peak Inflation Date	Stabilization Program Date[2]
(Countries that stabilized before 1993)			
Czech Republic	67.6	1991, June	1991, Jan.
Hungary	31.0	1995, June	1990, Mar.
Poland	1,173.0	1990, Feb.	1990, Jan.
Slovak Republic	73.7	1991, June	1991, Jan.
Slovenia	88.2	1992, Dec.	1992, Feb.
(The 1993–97 stabilizations)			
Albania	336.8	1992, Oct.	1992, Aug.
Armenia	29,600.9	1994, May	1994, Dec.
Azerbaijan	1,899.0	1994, Nov.	1995, Jan.
Belarus	2,809.6	1994, Aug.	1994, Nov.
Bulgaria (1st stabilization)	304.5	1992, Jan.	1994, Dec.
Bulgaria (2nd stabilization)	2,040.4	1997, Mar.	1997, Apr.
Croatia	1,944.9	1993, June	1993, Oct.
Estonia	1,241.9	1992, Sep.	1992, June
Georgia	50,654.0	1994, Sep.	1994, Sep.
Kazakhstan	3,033.3	1994, June	1994, Jan.
Kyrgyz Republic	1,257.0	1992, Dec.	1993, May
Latvia	1,444.6	1992, Nov.	1992, June
Lithuania	1,412.6	1992, Nov.	1992, June
Macedonia, FYR	2,100.3	1992, Oct.	1994, Jan.
Moldova	2,198.4	1992, Dec.	1993, Sep.
Romania	317.0	1993, Nov.	1993, Oct.
Russia	2,321.6	1992, Dec.	1995, Apr.
Turkmenistan	2,669.1	1996, Oct.	N/A
Ukraine	10,155.0	1993, Dec.	1994, Nov.
Uzbekistan	1,936.0	1994, Sep.	1994, Nov.
(Countries that did not stabilize)			
Tajikistan	7,343.7	1993, Dec.	1995, Feb.

Sources: National authorities; IMF, International Financial Statistics; and IMF staff calculations.
[1]Periods between thresholds were defined using the annualized three-month inflation rates. When these first fell below a threshold, and remained there for a year, and if the 12-month inflation rate fell below that level during the following year without rising above it again in that year (except for countries in which inflation fell below the threshold during 1997), the country was deemed to have crossed the threshold.
[2]From Fischer, Sahay, and Végh (1996), except for Turkmenistan and Bulgaria.

Disinflation and Output Growth

The sharp output drop that accompanied some of the early disinflations led some commentators to voice concerns about the additional output costs that could be associated with fast disinflation

Months To	Inflation < 60	Months To	Inflation < 30	Months To	Inflation < 15	Months To	Inflation < 7.5
			(Countries that stabilized before 1993)				
3	1991, Apr.	1	1991, July	2	1991, Oct.	N/A	N/A
N/A	N/A	N/A	N/A	N/A	N/A	N/A	N/A
18	1991, June	33	1994, Dec.	21	1996, Oct.	N/A	N/A
3	1991, May	1	1991, June	2	1991, Oct.	46	1995, Sep.
N/A	N/A	3	1992, Oct.	27	1995, Feb.	N/A	N/A
			(The 1993–97 stabilizations)				
5	1993, Feb.	3	1993, May	23	1995, Apr.	2	1995, July
6	1995, June	10	1996, May	N/A	N/A	N/A	N/A
5	1995, June	1	1995, Aug.	7	1996, May	7	1996, Dec.
9	1995, Oct.	11	N/A	N/A	N/A	N/A	N/A
3	1995, Mar.	N/A	N/A	N/A	N/A	N/A	N/A
6	1997, Oct.	N/A	N/A	N/A	N/A	N/A	N/A
4	1994, Feb.	1	1994, Mar.	2	1994, May	0	1994, May
18	1993, Dec.	8	1994, Aug.	23	1996 July	N/A	N/A
3	1994, Dec.	17	1996, May	1	1996, July	N/A	N/A
17	1995, May	13	1996, June	11	1997, May	N/A	N/A
23	1995, Apr.	24	1997, May	N/A	N/A	N/A	N/A
9	1993, Mar.	27	1995, June	12	1997, June	N/A	N/A
21	1994, Mar.	26	1996, May	2	1996, July	11	1997, June
6	1994, June	8	1995, Feb.	5	1995, July	5	1995, Dec.
9	1994, June	9	1995, Mar.	14	1996, June	N/A	N/A
9	1994, July	N/A	N/A	N/A	N/A	N/A	N/A
9	1995, Dec.	5	1996, June	N/A	N/A	N/A	N/A
N/A	1997, Mar.	3	1997, June	N/A	N/A	N/A	N/A
18	1996, May	1	1996, June	11	1997, Apr.	N/A	N/A
N/A	N/A	N/A	N/A	N/A	N/A	N/A	N/A
			(Countries that did not stabilize)				
N/A	N/A	N/A	N/A	N/A	N/A	N/A	N/A

(Calvo and Coricelli, 1992; Portes, 1993; Amsden, Kochanowicz, and Taylor, 1994; and Fedorov, 1995). Other commentators, however, have subsequently noted that, as inflation stabilized, growth resumed, often within two years (Figures 1a and 1b), thus suggesting that disinflation was a condition for sustainable growth (Fischer, Sahay, and Végh, 1996; and de Melo, Denizer, and Gelb, 1997).[7] These

[7]The "transition index" referred to in Figures 1a and 1b and elsewhere is drawn from various European Bank for Reconstruction and Development (EBRD) transition reports and from

Figure 1a. The Baltics, Russia, and Other Countries of the Former Soviet Union and Central and Eastern Europe—GDP Growth, Inflation, and Transition Index
(In chronological and disinflation time)[1]

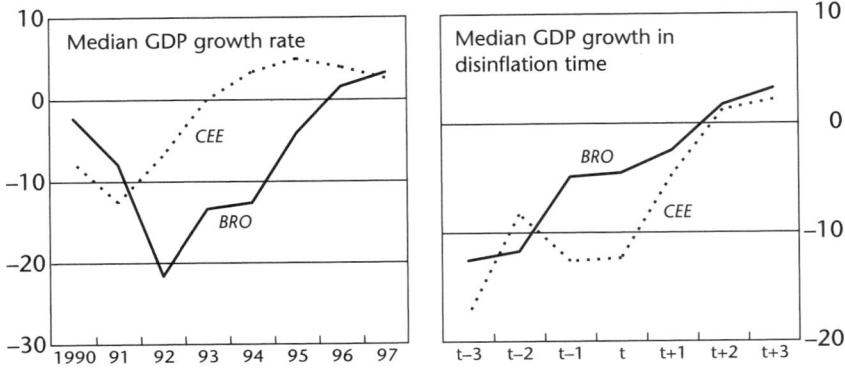

Sources: National authorities; IMF, *International Financial Statistics*; EBRD *Transition Report*, various issues; and IMF staff estimates.
[1]Stabilization dates are taken from Fischer and others (1996), and are reported in Table 2.

two views are not, of course, inconsistent—the former focusing on the transitory costs of disinflation, the latter on the long-term relationship between inflation and growth—and they underscore the complications in assessing the relationship between inflation and growth from simple indicators. These complications are particularly apparent in a period of deep structural changes affecting potential output: the drop in output may have been due to the collapse of central planning, rather than to disinflation, while the recovery may have been due to the effect of structural change, rather than to the stabilized inflation environment. Only a few studies conduct formal tests of the relationship between inflation and growth for transition economies and they draw somewhat divergent conclusions. Lougani and Sheets (1997) find that, controlling for progress with transition reform (as well as other variables), output growth is negatively af-

de Melo, Denizer, and Gelb (1997). It is a composite of scores for eight institutional characteristics, ranging from privatization to price liberalization to banking reform and interest rate liberalization. The eight scores are weighted together to yield the aggregate "transition index" for each country. The highest scores indicate institutional structures similar to those prevailing in fully fledged market economies.

Figure 1b. The Baltics, Russia, and Other Countries of the Former Soviet Union and Central and Eastern Europe—GDP Growth, Inflation, and Transition Index

(In chronological and disinflation time)[1]

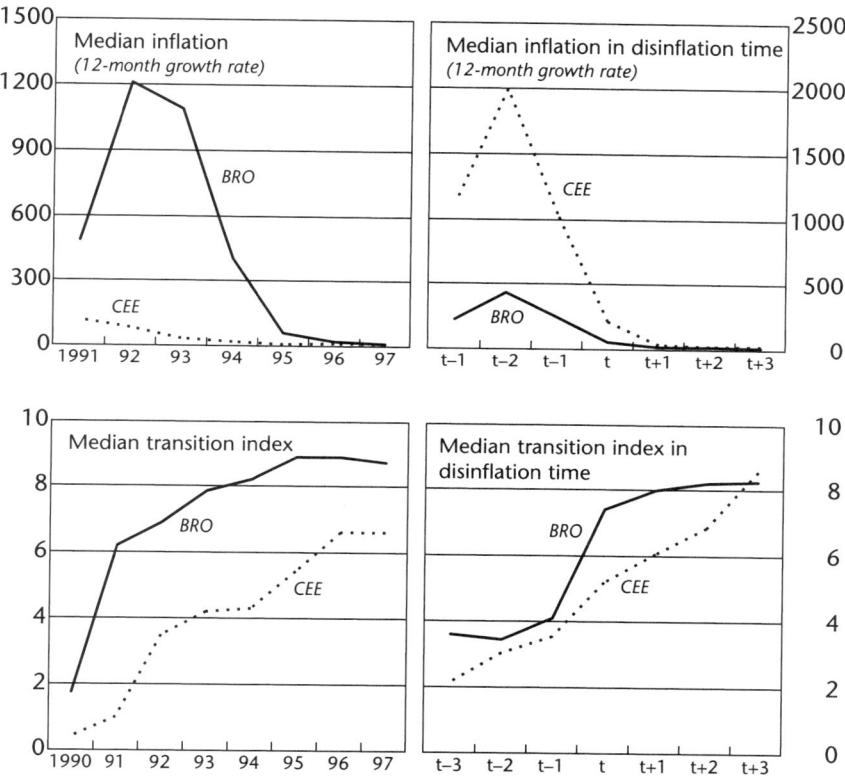

Sources: National authorities; IMF, *International Financial Statistics*; EBRD *Transition Report*, various issues; and IMF staff estimates.

[1]Stabilization dates are taken from Fischer and others (1996), and are reported in Table 2.

fected by inflation: a country with 500 percent inflation in one year loses about 2 percentage points of GDP the following year and 4 percentage points of GDP in the longer run. This finding is echoed by Berg and others (1998) who find different effects of inflation on the private and public sectors: whereas doubling inflation is associated with a decline of 5–15 percent in private sector output, it is associated with increased state sector output by about half that magnitude.

They suggest that the latter arises because subsidies to state-owned firms boost their output, but also stoke inflation by raising the fiscal deficit. Thus, they conclude that the impact of inflation on output depends on the relative shares of the private and public sectors. Åslund, Boone, and Johnson (1996) find no significant role for inflation in determining output once both war-torn and ruble-zone dummies are included.

These studies, however, share two main shortcomings. First, they do not investigate whether the relation between inflation and growth may vary at different inflation levels—though there is increasing evidence of this pattern for nontransition economies. Second, they shed no light on the output costs of disinflation, namely whether the change in inflation, rather than the level of inflation, has implications for output. In background work for this paper, Christoffersen and Doyle (1998) address these issues, using panel data on 22 of the 25 transition countries reviewed here (see Appendix I). They find evidence of an inflation threshold for transition economies at about 13 percent: inflation above that level reduces output growth, while no significant effect on growth is apparent if inflation is below that level. They also find no evidence of generalized output loss owing to disinflation.

It is notable that the inflation threshold appears to be higher than that found in market economies (see Appendix I). This suggests that the threshold may be falling in transition time, implying that the threshold is lower for the advanced reformers than for the panel as a whole. More specifically, Christoffersen and Doyle (Chapter IV, p. 29) note that inflation may have played a role in facilitating the large growth-enhancing relative price changes at the outset of transition, offsetting other negative effects of inflation on growth. But with structural reforms and the largest of the initial relative price adjustments completed, these initial benefits from inflation would decline, and the relationship between inflation and output in transition economies would come to resemble that of long-established market economies more closely. Thus, the net benefits from low inflation may increase as transition deepens.

In summary, there is evidence that low inflation boosts growth, even after controlling for structural reform and for an inflation threshold that may fall over time as structural reform proceeds. Such a decline in the threshold would be consistent with findings in Fischer, Sahay, and Végh (1996) and Cottarelli, Griffiths, and Moghadam (1998) that fast reformers have, ceteris paribus, lower inflation rates. No clear evidence of a high output cost of disinflation has been found.

Disinflation and the External Current Account

Cukierman (1992) notes that one of the motives for inflation is the perceived risk that disinflation may pose for the external current account. An exchange rate based disinflation may lead to a real appreciation and, thus, affect competitiveness; and competitiveness may also deteriorate in the context of a floating exchange regime if the nominal exchange rate overshoots (Dornbusch, 1976). Indeed, concerns about the possible impact of tighter monetary policies on the external current account have been mentioned by some country authorities (for example, in Hungary) as one of the reasons why accelerating disinflation through a tighter exchange rate policy or the shift to a float was regarded as excessively risky (Surányi and Vincze, 1998).

External current account deficits relative to GDP have increased significantly during the 1990s in both the Central and Eastern European countries and the Baltics, Russia, and other countries of the former Soviet Union. In the early 1990s, the median balance in both was close to zero, while in 1997, it was a deficit in excess of 5 percent of GDP.

Recasting the current account data in inflation stabilization time highlights possible links between these trends and disinflation. The top panel of Figure 2 shows that inflation stabilization was accompanied by a weakening of the external accounts: the external balance declined sharply after disinflation in the Central and Eastern European countries, recovering somewhat in the third year. The Baltics, Russia, and other countries of the former Soviet Union exhibit a smoother decline, of similar magnitude.

Evidence of a widening of the external accounts, however, should not necessarily be taken as a proof that stabilization was accompanied by a shift to an unsustainable external position. As noted above, stabilization is a precondition for growth and a recovery of investment. In transition economies, such an acceleration of investment should be expected to be financed partially from abroad, through FDI and other long-term capital inflows. In turn, these inflows are likely to increase in stabilized macroeconomic conditions. Thus, the observed weakening of the external account after the stabilization may, at least in part, reflect the recovery of growth and investment, rather than an unsustainable loss of competitiveness. In this respect, it is useful to note that the external current account net of FDI in stabilization time shows stronger trends (bottom panel of Figure 2): the debt-financed external balance weakens markedly in the Central and Eastern European countries in the first two years, while in the Baltics, Russia, and other countries of the former Soviet Union, the initial weakening is less marked. But by the third year, the balance has strengthened considerably due to the strong inflow of FDI.

Figure 2. The Baltics, Russia, and Other Countries of the Former Soviet Union and Central and Eastern Europe—Current Account Balance, in Percent of GDP, 1990–97
(In disinflation time)

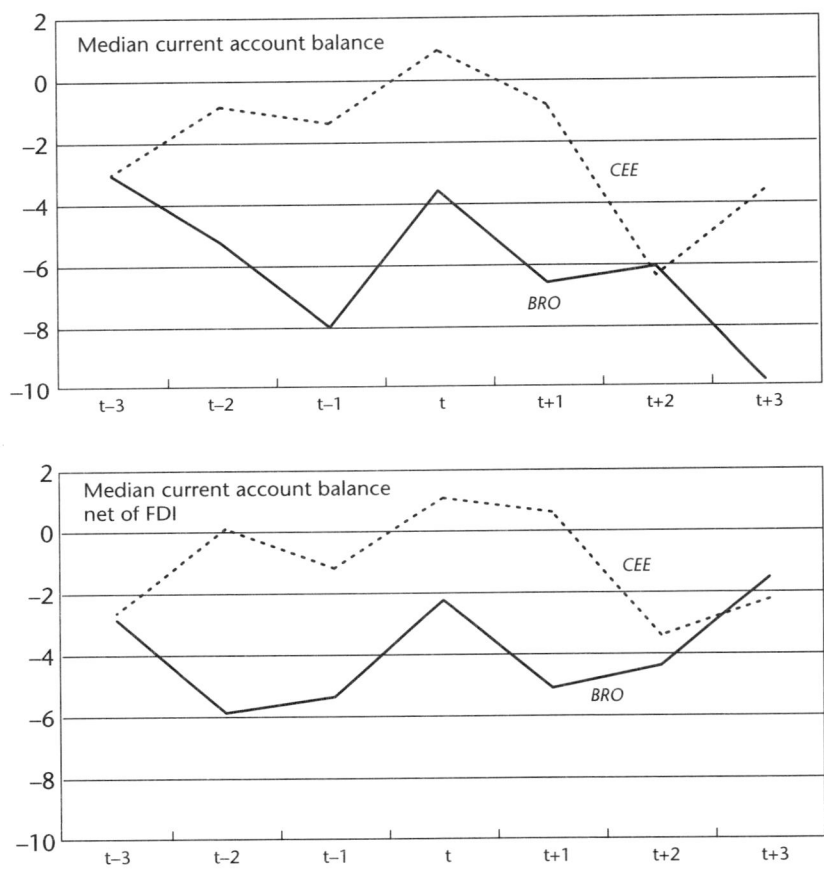

Sources: IMF, *World Economic Outlook*; and IMF staff calculations.

Inflation Inertia, Credibility, and Disinflation

The speed of disinflation and the apparent resilience of output in that context are remarkable features of transition economies' disinflation experience, and they are evident in the stabilizations of cases of extreme and more moderate inflation.

This section will suggest that disinflation reflected the implementation of decisive financial policies that curtailed excessive monetary growth, and that the absence of evidence of output costs in this context reflected various combinations of low inflation inertia and policy credibility.[8] In the highest inflation cases, inflation uncertainty was reflected in a shortening of the duration of nominal contracts, implying that aggregate price expectations were formed for relatively brief periods. This flexibility reduced output losses during decisive disinflation. In these cases, it was more important that financial policies were adjusted to eliminate the source of inflation than that they were adjusted credibly. But in the cases of less extreme inflation, where the duration of nominal contracts was largely unchanged, inflation inertia remained present. In these cases, policy credibility likely played a greater role in accounting for the low output costs associated with rapid disinflation.

The discussion attempts to identify the factors that facilitated the tightening of monetary policy needed to disinflate the economy, those that account for the evidence of limited output cost during inflation stabilization, and the extent to which these factors also explain the relatively slow disinflation in some countries, particularly during the poststabilization period. It addresses first the context in which disinflation occurred; second, the role played by fiscal policy; third, the role of credibility-enhancing devices; and last, the speed and sequencing of disinflation and structural reform. It concludes that fiscal consolidation and the decision of most authorities to disinflate rapidly were key to the success and the low output cost of these disinflations.

The Context for Disinflation

In many respects, the context for disinflation was more favorable than it might have appeared to be: inflation had not persisted for long; backward indexation was limited; the financial system, though fragile, turned out to be less susceptible to stress from disinflation than feared; and political economy factors favored disinflation in some countries. Furthermore, while price liberalization and relative price adjustment initially boosted the price level, they subsequently facilitated disinflation efforts.

---

[8]Policy credibility is a key factor in affecting the output cost of disinflation. If a disinflation package is credible, inflation expectations will decline rapidly, bringing down nominal interest rates and nominal wage growth. This will reduce the risk that disinflation is accompanied by an initial rise in real wages and real interest rates and the output losses associated with that. Of course, another factor at play is the duration of wage and lending contracts. If this duration is short, as it is likely when inflation is high, wage and interest rate dynamics can react more rapidly to changes in inflation.

Where these circumstances did not hold, disinflation was slower. For example, widespread indexation was a problem in Poland and Slovenia, two of the slow disinflation cases identified earlier. In Hungary—another slow disinflater—creeping inflation had persisted throughout the 1980s, possibly contributing to the stickiness of inflation expectations lamented by policymakers in that country (Surányi and Vincze, 1998). Unresolved financial sector problems contributed to the inflation reversal in Albania and Bulgaria. And gradual administered price adjustments slowed disinflation significantly in some countries (notably in Moldova and Ukraine).

Indexation

Backward indexation implies a lagged response of nominal wages to prices. This raises the output cost of disinflation, thereby reducing its credibility. Formal indexation, however, was exceptional in transition countries, possibly reflecting that while inflation had been violent, it had also been relatively brief, so that indexation had not had time to take root. As a result, even though wages and prices were frequently adjusted in the higher inflation cases, only six countries out of the sample of 25 transition economies ever used backward-looking indexation.[9] And one of these (Croatia) abolished indexation at the start of the disinflation program. Even when indexation was present, it did not always increase inflation inertia. Where goods and factor prices were de facto indexed to the exchange rate, such as in Bulgaria, exchange rate stabilization fed directly into the stabilization of domestic prices.

The only two countries where indexation was pervasive are Poland and Slovenia. Both countries are part of the slow disinflation group, and there is evidence that indexation contributed to keeping these countries in the moderate inflation range for an extensive period (Pujol and Griffiths, 1998; and Ross, 1998).

Financial fragility

The banking sector in all these economies was critically weak in the early stages of transition: two-tier systems and the associated legislative and accounting frameworks were generally in their infancy, and the banks were ill-prepared for a competitive environment, let alone

---

[9]Those from the Baltics, Russia, and other countries of the former Soviet Union that continued the Soviet era practice of linking social payments to the minimum wage did not thereby establish de facto backward-looking indexation, as adjustments of the minimum wage were ad hoc in scale and timing.

one in which output, relative prices, and the price level were subject to major shocks.

While restructuring to address these problems would have facilitated disinflation by improving the strength, efficiency, and competitiveness of the financial system, it also seemed probable that disinflation would exacerbate financial fragility. This appeared likely to complicate disinflation efforts: the additional call on fiscal resources directly would challenge the fiscal consolidation; the additional calls on central bank refinance could undermine the monetary framework; the commitment to sustain disinflation might be weakened by concerns that increased interest rates could have indiscriminate effects, given poor credit assessment; and higher real interest rates could further undermine credit quality if solvent borrowers who expected to repay disproportionately stopped borrowing. Another potential danger, underscored by Cukierman (1992) with reference to nontransition economies, was that the monetary tightening associated with disinflation might be accompanied by lower bank interest rate spreads—owing to the longer maturity of lending rates than deposit rates.

Despite these difficulties, disinflations were rarely accompanied by up-front bank restructuring. In only two cases—the former Yugoslav Republic of Macedonia and Slovenia—were operations to buttress the banking system initiated at the same time as disinflation, and even in these cases, the measures taken began, rather than completed, the task. Furthermore, despite the manifest weakness of many financial systems, rarely were these concerns uppermost in the authorities' minds when weighing the risks and modalities of disinflation.

There were several reasons why financial fragility did not undermine monetary control and the credibility of disinflation. In some of the high-inflation cases, the financial system had shrunk in real terms prior to disinflation due to negative real interest rates. For example, in Georgia and Moldova in 1994, M2 was 3 percent of GDP and 12 percent of GDP, respectively, and even now in the Baltics, Russia, and other countries of the former Soviet Union overall, banking system claims on nongovernment agencies are roughly half the level relative to GDP of Organization for Economic Cooperation and Development (OECD) countries. This contained the fiscal and refinancing contingent liabilities posed by financial fragility. Furthermore, while a number of banks had profited from transactions predicated on the high-inflation environment, this source of income was rarely critical to their overall profitability. So the demise of that environment rarely affected the overall health of individual banks, or of the banking system.

Fast disinflation and the maintenance of banking spreads also diminished the risk that financial fragility would deepen. The potential sluggishness of lending rates with respect to deposit rates when monetary policy is tightened turned out to be unimportant. At times, the contractual basis for bank loans was sufficiently unclear that lending rates were rapidly adjustable in practice, though more often, banks had shifted to variable rate or short-term lending prior to disinflation. Furthermore, nominal interest rates started falling rapidly along with inflation. So even to the limited extent that lending rates were stickier than deposit rates, rapidly falling inflation allowed spreads to widen during disinflation.

This is not to say that financial instability played no role, or that it may not become a problem in the future. Banking difficulties occurred during the Baltic and Czech disinflations. And most countries had to recapitalize banks at some point, though these operations were generally financed by issuing bonds, rather than by printing money, softening their impact on inflation. In addition, as illustrated by Estonia in 1993, firm decisions were taken to restructure or close banks, rather than to recapitalize them. But in addition to these direct links between financial fragility and inflation, indirect links also played a role. In the Czech Republic, a combination of banking inefficiencies, reflected in large interest rate spreads, accompanied by confidence in the currency, may have induced both domestic disintermediation and capital inflows in the mid-1990s. In this way, financial fragility may have indirectly stoked inflationary pressures.

While fragility remains, there are risks of further calls on the budget and for central bank refinance, and the financial sector's contribution to flexibility and performance of the whole economy is diminished. Albania and Bulgaria show that, even though much-abused financial systems can survive a remarkably long time, they eventually collapse with serious implications for macroeconomic stability. Recent difficulties in a medium-sized regional bank in Croatia underline that strong inflation performers are not immune from these difficulties. And the exchange rate crisis in Russia in August 1998 reflected to some extent increases in liquidity to sustain the banking sector. While progress has been made in strengthening financial structures and supervision in most transition countries, significant risks remain (see Appendix II).

Political economy

Social and political characteristics of the preinflation stabilization period may also account for the decisiveness of the disinflation effort and its credibility. In some Central and Eastern European countries and in the Baltic States, the perceived short-term costs of disinflation were seen as the price of national liberation. This muted the political backlash to "shock therapies," and partly explains why determined reformers were often politically successful (Åslund, Boone, and Johnson, 1996). Moreover, when the old economic interest groups were discredited and disorganized, an opening for "extraordinary politics"—in the words of Poland's Finance Minister Balcerowicz (Bruno, 1996)—appeared, which eased the introduction of tough disinflation and reform programs, albeit sometimes only temporarily.

Such openings were, however, rarely apparent in most BRO countries (outside the Baltics), which partly explains why disinflation was often delayed there. Even in some Central and Eastern European countries, such as Bulgaria and Romania, it proved impossible to gather sufficient political support to implement sustained disinflation. In some cases, coalitions of various political interests may have delayed disinflation. Bruno (1996) notes that a high-inflation equilibrium can be generated when interest groups disagree on who should bear the brunt of the adjustment. In other cases, interest groups may have had an indirect interest in inflation, having privileged access to fiscal subsidies or transfers that generate it. Clearly, political instability and war played a key role in delaying disinflation in Armenia, Croatia, Georgia, and Tajikistan. Disagreement between the central bank and the government on the appropriate policy course or insufficient understanding of the economics of inflation—the view that inflation was caused by "speculators" rather than by financial policies—were also factors in some countries (notably, Belarus, Bulgaria, Tajikistan, Turkmenistan, Uzbekistan, and, initially, Ukraine).

By the mid-1990s, however, even in cases where political impediments to disinflation had been most severe, it had become apparent to most policymakers that inflation was a monetary phenomenon fueled by large fiscal and quasi-fiscal deficits. At the same time, the costs of inflation for vulnerable social groups (such as pensioners) were becoming apparent.[10] These factors may have eventually strengthened the resolve to stabilize and the credibility of the disinflation programs subsequently implemented.

Relative price disequilibria

The environment for disinflation was complicated by the need for large relative price changes, given that relative prices were far from

---

[10]Bulir (1998) finds evidence from a large sample of developing countries that high inflation increases economic inequality. Evidence on the drop in real pensions and its relation with inflation in 11 transition economies can be found in Cangiano, Cottarelli, and Cubeddu (1998). Other aspects of inequality in transition are discussed in EBRD (1997).

competitive equilibrium, combined in some cases with monopolistic pricing that emerged after price liberalization (IMF, 1997, pp. 108–11). A shock in relative prices, from either source, risks inducing inflation if there is downward price stickiness. If this pressure is accommodated to avoid an output loss, inflation will rise, with legal or de facto indexation delaying the disinflation process.

In transition economies, the inflationary pressure arising from relative price changes was exacerbated by the type of price shocks that accompanied the transition. Prior to the transition, some goods were largely underpriced while most were marginally overpriced (Pujol and Griffiths, 1998; and Coorey, Mecagni, and Offerdal, 1998). This pattern imparted an inflationary impulse because, while the few largely underpriced goods were rapidly repriced, the many overpriced goods were not cut (possibly reflecting microeconomic adjustment costs) and so were adjusted in real terms through inflation (Ball and Mankiw, 1994).

The role of relative price adjustments in inflation was particularly strong in the early phases of the transition when most prices were liberalized, but seems to have declined over time (Pujol and Griffiths, 1998; Coorey, Mecagni, and Offerdal, 1998; Cottarelli, Griffiths, and Moghadam, 1998; Krajnyák and Klingen, 1998; and Woźniak, 1998). This is because the relative price adjustment process appears to have been fairly rapid, partly reflecting limited indexation in most countries (Koen and de Masi, 1997). A key remaining inflationary impulse from relative price changes concerns administrative price adjustments.[11] However, with price ceilings applied only to a limited number of products (energy, transportation, rents, and utilities), these have also declined in importance (Box 1).

Policy Response: Fiscal Policy

The early phase of the transition was accompanied by large fiscal imbalances in virtually all transition countries, as a result of falling revenues and rigid public expenditure. Government securities markets were virtually nonexistent and access to foreign finance was limited. So the emerging deficits had to be monetized when the potential for direct funding from the banking sector was exhausted. Of the Baltics, Russia, and other countries of the former Soviet Union, 7 of 15 countries recorded seignorage in excess of 10 percent of GDP in 1993, when inflation was at or near its peak (Ghosh, 1997).

---

[11]In Belarus and Ukraine, administered price adjustments spurred inflation, as did energy and other price increases in Romania alongside liberalization of the exchange rate in early 1997. Administrative price changes were most important in Hungary in the early 1990s, and again in 1995–96, when increased energy prices stimulated a renewed acceleration of inflation.

Box 1. Relative Prices and Inflation: A Look Ahead

Several years into the transition, goods price levels and structures remain distinct from industrial countries (Koen and de Masi, 1997). This does not necessarily mean, however, that a rapid convergence should be expected, as price levels and structures are generally correlated with GDP (Nuxoll, 1996). Market-determined prices are likely to converge to industrial country standards only in the long run. Thus, the main contribution of relative price changes to inflation in the near future is likely to come primarily from changes in administered prices.

The remaining inflationary potential from changes in administered prices depends on the share of administered prices in the CPI, how far they are below their market-determined level, and the response of other prices. In most cases, the share of administered prices in the baskets used to calculate the CPI is small, albeit possibly understated to the extent that the weights have not been fully adjusted as administered prices have been raised toward full cost coverage (Table 3). In only a few cases is removing all remaining price controls thought likely to add more than 10 percentage points to the CPI (Table 3).[1] But in some low-inflation countries (such as the Czech Republic and Croatia), as well as in some moderate high-inflation countries (Belarus), administered price increases could put significant pressure on inflation developments.

The reaction of nonadministered prices to changes in administered prices will depend, inter alia, on the degree of indexation, the overall credibility of the authorities, and, of course, the degree of monetary accommodation. In countries where the authorities' credibility is in doubt, an increase in administered prices may be regarded as signaling that inflation is accelerating, and lead to parallel increases in all prices. A case in point is Romania where in early 1997, the increase in some energy prices started a wave of general price increases. Conversely, the recent experience in Azerbaijan shows that even fairly large increases in administered prices can be absorbed with only a temporary rise in inflation.

Finally, there is evidence that after the initial impact of relative price changes on inflation, price liberalization is generally found to reduce inflation (Fischer, Sahay, and Végh, 1996; and Cottarelli, Griffiths, and Moghadam, 1998). This may be due to the fact that those countries that adjusted to administered prices more slowly through subsidies or price controls, such as Moldova, experienced larger fiscal or quasi-fiscal deficits, and due to the boost to supply-side flexibility that price liberalization engenders.

---

[1]These estimates neither take into account the reaction of other prices nor the degree of monetary accommodation. Moreover, the figures should be taken cum grano salis as, in many cases, it is difficult to evaluate what the market-determined price of certain products would be. Comparisons with industrial countries may be misleading for products (as services) that involve significant labor input. The case of rents is also complex: Zavoico (1995) argues that rents in transition countries may not need to incorporate amortization costs for a number of years, because currently there is an excess supply of houses.

Table 3. Administered Price Changes

Country	Weight of Administered Price Changes on CPI	Estimated Effect on the CPI of Removing Administered Price Controls		Inflation Rate End-1997
		Minimum	Maximum	
Albania	5	2	3	42.1
Bulgaria	15	6	12	578.6
Croatia	18	4	10	4.4
Czech Republic	15–20	5	6	10.0
Hungary	15	2	4	18.4
Macedonia, FYR	30	2	3	2.7
Poland	11	3	6	13.2
Romania	13	2	5	151.6
Slovak Republic	15–20	5	6	6.5
Slovenia	28	3	9	9.5
Armenia	. . .	. . .	. . .	22.0
Azerbaijan	30	1	2	0.4
Belarus	33	15	25	63.4
Estonia	22	. . .	. . .	12.5
Georgia	. . .	. . .	. . .	7.2
Kazakhstan	10	1	2	11.3
Kyrgyz Republic	10	5	10	14.7
Latvia	20	5	10	7.0
Lithuania	17	1	3	8.5
Moldova	15	2	5	11.1
Russia	7	4	7	11.0
Tajikistan	7–8	15	20	163.1
Turkmenistan	3	. . .	. . .	21.8
Ukraine	16	3	5	10.1
Uzbekistan	8[1]	. . .	. . .	50.0

Source: IMF staff estimates.

[1]Includes energy and utility prices only. If the prices of basic consumer goods—including flour, sugar, bread, and so on—are also included, the weight of administered prices is at least 40 percent.

The development of a broader range of financing options for government alongside fiscal consolidation were key elements underlying the subsequent disinflations. The former reduced the pressure for monetization, given public deficits,[12] and the latter reduced the risk of explosive paths for public debt-GDP ratios (Buiter, 1997). This reduced inflationary pressures arising from the expectation of future monetization (Sargent and Wallace, 1981).

---

[12]In some cases, however, the additional financing option provided by new securities may have facilitated increased fiscal deficits. Ukraine through 1997 may be one example of this.

Table 4. Development of Government Securities Markets

Country	Date of Introduction of Treasury Bills	Share of General Government Deficit Covered by Sales of Securities, Excluding Sales to Domestic Banks (1997)	Degree of Development of Interbank and Government Securities Markets (1997)
Albania	1994	—	—
Bulgaria	1993	26.4	—
Croatia	1996	21.7	—
Czech Republic	1991	75.0	Substantial
Hungary	Before 1990	30.1	Substantial
Macedonia, FYR	No treasury bill market	0.0	Substantial
Poland	1991	70.4	—
Romania	1997	9.6	Limited
Slovak Republic	1991	—	Substantial
Slovenia	1990	9.0	—
Armenia	1995	8.8	Limited
Azerbaijan	1996	—	Limited
Belarus	1994	21.5	Limited
Estonia	No treasury bill market	—	Moderate
Georgia	1997	0.1	Moderate
Kazakhstan	1994	2.3	Substantial
Kyrgyz Republic	1996	3.3	Moderate
Latvia	1993	25.9	Substantial
Lithuania	1994	−29.6	Moderate
Moldova	1995	11.0	Moderate
Russia	1993	39.5	Substantial
Tajikistan	No treasury bill market	—	Limited
Turkmenistan	1994	—	Limited
Ukraine	1996	50.6	Moderate
Uzbekistan	1996	8.9	Limited

Source: IMF staff estimates.

Government securities markets

By 1997, all transition economies (with the exception of Estonia, Tajikistan, and the former Yugoslav Republic of Macedonia) had introduced primary treasury bill markets—mostly based on auctions—with many of the Baltics, Russia, and other countries of the former Soviet Union joining the group in 1995–96 (Table 4). In the most advanced

Table 5. Overall and Primary General Government Balances, and Central
Bank Financing to the Government[1]

(In percent of GDP)

	Overall Balance						
	1991	1992	1993	1994	1995	1996	1997
Albania	...	−21.8	−15.4	−13.0	−10.4	−12.6	−13.1
Bulgaria	−14.6	−5.2	−10.9	−5.8	−6.3	−12.7	−2.5
Croatia	−5.1	−3.9	−0.8	1.6	−0.9	−0.4	−1.3
Czech Republic	...	−2.1	0.5	−1.2	−1.8	−1.2	−2.1
Hungary	−3.7	−6.9	−8.4	−8.2	−6.2	−3.1	−4.8
Macedonia, FYR	...	−9.8	−13.4	−2.9	−1.2	−0.5	−0.4
Poland	−6.7	−6.2	−3.4	−3.2	−3.3	−3.6	−3.3
Romania	3.3	−4.6	−0.4	−1.9	−2.6	−4.0	−3.6
Slovak Republic	...	−11.9	−7.0	−1.3	0.2	−1.3	−5.1
Slovenia	...	0.2	0.3	−0.2	0.0	0.3	−1.1
Armenia[3]	−1.9	...	−54.3	−10.1	−12.0	−9.3	−5.9
Azerbaijan	−5.0	−29.0	−15.4	−12.1	−4.9	−2.8	−1.7
Belarus	1.9	0.0	−1.9	−2.5	−1.9	−1.6	−0.7
Estonia	5.2	−0.3	−0.6	1.3	−1.2	−1.5	2.0
Georgia	−3.1	−62.3	−26.1	−16.5	−4.5	−4.4	−3.8
Kazakhstan	−8.8	−7.3	−4.1	−7.7	−3.2	−5.3	−7.0
Kyrgyz Republic	3.9	−14.8	−14.4	−11.6	−17.3	−9.5	−9.4
Latvia	6.3	0.5	−5.3	−4.8	−4.5	−4.5	−1.8
Lithuania[4]	0.0	−0.8	0.6	−4.1	−3.3	−1.4	1.3
Moldova	0.0	−23.9	−7.4	−9.1	−5.8	−6.6	−6.8
Russia	−14.9	−6.6	−8.6	−10.5	−7.9	−9.5	−7.9
Tajikistan	−15.9	−30.5	−23.4	−5.1	−11.2	−5.8	−3.7
Turkmenistan	2.4	13.3	−0.5	−1.4	−1.6	0.3	0.0
Ukraine	−13.6	−23.2	−9.7	−8.7	−4.9	−3.2	−5.6
Uzbekistan	...	−18.5	−10.4	−6.1	−4.1	−7.3	−2.8

Source: IMF staff estimates.

[1]For the countries that stabilized during 1993–97, shaded areas indicate periods in which inflation dropped below the stabilization threshold (see definition in Table 2).

[2]The primary balance is calculated as the general government balance minus net interest payments. Primary balance calculations exclude interest receipts for Armenia, Azerbaijan, Belarus, Estonia, Kazakhstan, Kyrgyz Republic, Romania, Slovakia, and Ukraine.

[3]The higher overall deficit in 1995, the first stabilization year, is due to the payment of arrears related to government-guaranteed domestic loans.

[4]About one-half of the deficit in Lithuania during 1993–96 was due to net lending.

transition economies (such as the Czech Republic, Hungary, and Poland), primary government securities markets are more fully developed, and secondary markets are also active, usually organized around a system of primary dealers. The Baltics, Russia, and other countries of the former Soviet Union are lagging behind. However, "moderate" or "substantial" progress had been achieved by 1997 in

Primary Balance[2]						
1991	1992	1993	1994	1995	1996	1997
...	−20.6	−13.0	−10.6	−8.2	−9.3	−7.4
−14.6	1.2	−1.6	7.7	7.9	6.3	6.0
−4.9	−4.6	2.1	1.9	−1.1	0.7	0.2
...	...	...	−0.1	−1.1	−0.4	−0.9
2.1	−1.7	−4.0	−2.8	2.7	4.0	3.5
...	...	−9.7	−0.2	0.5	1.8	1.0
...	−10.9	−1.3	1.2	1.0	0.1	1.2
3.3	−4.4	0.6	−0.5	−1.3	−2.6	−0.2
...	−10.9	−4.0	2.5	2.4	0.9	−3.0
...	0.2	0.5	0.5	0.2	−0.3	−2.6
...	...	...	−8.2	−8.0	−6.7	−4.1
...	...	...	−11.4	−4.1	−2.4	−1.2
...	0.7	−1.0	−2.1	−1.1	−0.9	−0.7
5.2	...	−0.4	1.3	−0.9	−1.3	2.3
...	−62.3	−26.0	−14.1	−3.1	−3.4	−2.4
−8.8	−7.3	−10.2	−10.7	−9.3	−12.7	−2.9
...	...	−13.8	−11.4	−16.9	−8.4	−7.7
...	−0.7	1.6	−1.4	−2.1	−0.2	2.2
...	...	−5.9	−5.9	−4.6	−4.2	−0.5
...	−23.9	−6.3	−6.2	−2.3	−4.0	−3.1
...	−17.1	−6.1	−8.4	−3.6	−2.5	−3.1
...	...	...	...	−8.4	−4.6	−2.1
2.4	...	...	−1.2	−1.0	−1.2	−0.2
...	−23.2	−9.5	−9.5	−3.5	−2.1	−3.2
...	−11.9	−18.3	−1.0	−3.5	−5.7	−2.3

most of the Baltics, Russia, and other countries of the former Soviet Union (IMF, 1997).[13] As a result, the share of fiscal deficits financed by issuing domestic government securities is now sizable in a number of transition economies (Table 4).

---

[13]Qualitative assessments provided by IMF desk economists, summarized in index form (see Cottarelli, Griffiths, and Moghadam, 1998) also indicate significant progress in developing financial markets: on a 1–10 scale (10 indicating the degree of development of government securities markets in industrial countries), the index for the Baltics, Russia, and other countries of the former Soviet Union improved from 2.1 in 1993 to 5.5 in 1996, while that for Central and Eastern European countries improved from 4.4 to 5.6. As this index reflects subjective assessments, it should be taken as indicative of the direction of change, rather than for cross-country comparisons.

Table 5 (*Concluded*)

	Central Bank Financing					
	1992	1993	1994	1995	1996	1997
Albania	20.0	9.1	6.6	2.0	1.0	6.0
Bulgaria	6.0	11.0	5.5	4.9	14.5	−0.1
Croatia	. . .	. . .	−0.7	0.5	−0.1	0.0
Czech Republic	. . .	−2.1	−2.4	−1.0	−0.8	0.7
Hungary	16.5	13.2	11.2	7.5	7.3	1.7
Macedonia, FYR	. . .	. . .	1.3	0.1	0.1	0.4
Poland	5.2	1.5	1.5	0.1	0.1	0.5
Romania	. . .	. . .	. . .	. . .	. . .	. . .
Slovak Republic	. . .	. . .	. . .	. . .	. . .	1.5
Slovenia	0.0	0.0	0.0	0.0	0.0	0.0
Armenia[3]	. . .	. . .	3.5	0.4	1.4	−1.4
Azerbaijan	0.0	11.4	8.2	−2.7	1.4	−0.6
Belarus	. . .	. . .	0.8	2.6	1.4	0.4
Estonia	. . .	0.0	0.0	0.0	0.0	0.0
Georgia	. . .	. . .	2.0	1.8	2.7	2.2
Kazakhstan	. . .	. . .	3.2	1.7	−0.1	−0.3
Kyrgyz Republic	. . .	0.7	1.3	7.8	1.9	0.4
Latvia	0.0	0.0	0.0	0.0	0.0	0.0
Lithuania[4]	0.0	0.0	0.0	0.0	0.0	0.0
Moldova	26.1	5.0	1.9	1.5	−0.7	1.4
Russia	9.2	5.9	8.1	1.6	2.1	. . .
Tajikistan	30.6	24.8	9.6	13.1	2.3	1.5
Turkmenistan	9.9	6.0	1.6	1.8	−0.2	0.4
Ukraine	23.8	14.1	8.9	5.6	2.1	1.4
Uzbekistan	. . .	. . .	4.8	1.4	6.8	1.3

Fiscal consolidation

Public finances strengthened significantly during 1993–97. The average fiscal deficit-GDP ratio fell from 13½ percent in 1992 to 3½ percent in 1997; the decline was faster in the Baltics, Russia, and other countries of the former Soviet Union, but it was sizable also in Central and Eastern European countries (Table 5). Quasi-fiscal deficits—whose importance for macroeconomic developments has been stressed several times (Mackenzie and Stella, 1996; and Buiter, 1997)—also abated (see below).

A simple plot of inflation against the overall and primary fiscal balances of transition economies suggests that fiscal consolidation was closely related to the decline in inflation during 1993–97 (Figure 3).[14] A

---

[14]Focusing on the relationship between inflation and primary balance is important as the latter is not affected by the fall in interest expenditure that accompanies disinflation. This fall makes it more difficult to interpret the causal link between decline in the overall deficit and decline in inflation (see footnote 1 in Box 2).

Figure 3. Transition Economies: Fiscal Performance Versus Inflation Performance, 1994–97
(In percent)

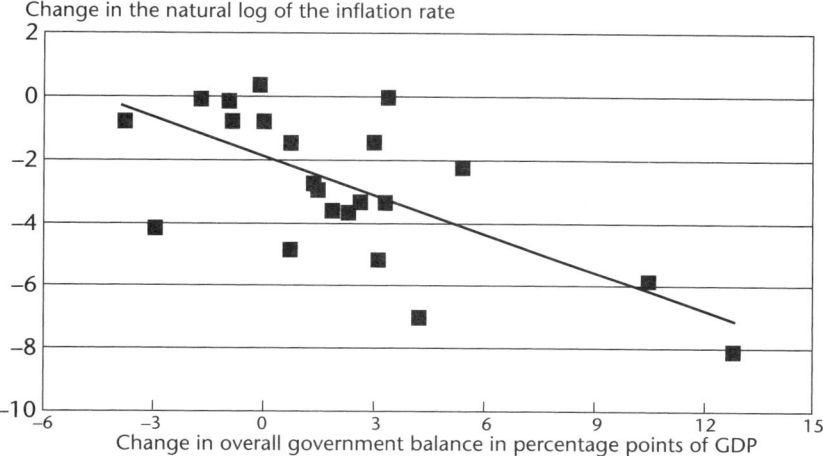

Change in the natural log of the inflation rate

Change in overall government balance in percentage points of GDP

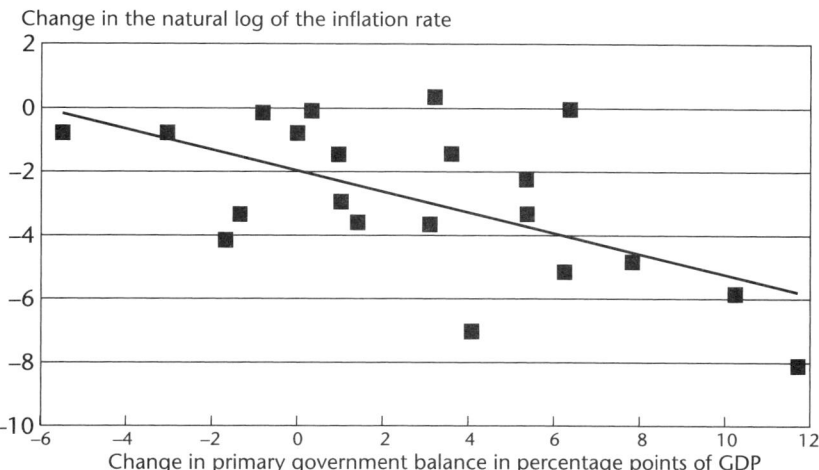

Change in the natural log of the inflation rate

Change in primary government balance in percentage points of GDP

Source: IMF staff estimates.

closer look at individual country data (Tables 6 and 7) reveals five key features: (1) a sizable fiscal tightening—with a corresponding tightening of money creation through credit to the government—characterized most inflation stabilization cases, a key finding of earlier reviews of the transition experience (Bruno, 1992); (2) fiscal adjustment focused on expenditure cuts; (3) when fiscal adjustment did not accompany the inflation stabilization, the fiscal position was already strong; (4) inflation stabilization did not require a fiscal position that was solvent according to standard formulas; and (5) the link between fiscal tightening and disinflation was weaker in moderate inflation cases.

Fiscal adjustment (typically up-front fiscal adjustment in the disinflation year or the year before) accompanied the drop in inflation in 13 of the 20 inflation stabilization cases observed during 1993–97 (Table 6). In two additional cases—Bulgaria (second disinflation) and Lithuania—the primary balance changed little, but quasi-fiscal losses were substantially reduced. In Lithuania, losses accruing as a result of arbitrage of interrepublican accounts after withdrawal from the ruble area were curtailed. In Bulgaria, quasi-fiscal losses accruing in both the financial and nonfinancial enterprise sectors as a result of widespread soft budget constraints were reduced under the first stabilization, albeit only to reemerge later, inducing a reversal of the associated disinflation gains. Quasi-fiscal deficits—particularly in the form of directed credit—were reduced also in countries that cut the general government deficits, especially in the Baltics, Russia, and other countries of the former Soviet Union (a case in point is Kazakhstan).

Fiscal consolidation allowed a sharp contraction in central bank credit to the government. In the 20 inflation stabilization cases, the average flow of central bank credit to the government fell from 10.6 percent of GDP in 1992 to 0.7 percent of GDP in 1997 (Table 5), contributing significantly to the decline in the growth rate of money (see below).

In almost all the above cases, the adjustment consisted primarily of expenditure cuts. Only in Croatia, Latvia, and Uzbekistan did the revenue-GDP ratio rise significantly, and only temporarily in the latter case. In the former Yugoslav Republic of Macedonia, after an initial increase in the revenue ratio, both expenditure and revenue ratios started declining. In six countries (Armenia, Azerbaijan, Belarus, the Kyrgyz Republic, Russia, and Ukraine), revenue ratios declined during disinflation. The predominance of expenditure rather than revenue adjustment to close fiscal imbalances may have helped the disinflation directly, given that tax increases often produce a one-off increase in the price level, particularly indirect taxes (Surányi and Vincze, 1998).

There are cases where fiscal strengthening did not accompany inflation stabilization. In Estonia, Latvia, and Turkmenistan, the fiscal position prior to stabilization was already fairly strong, and other factors underlay persistent inflation in that context. In Estonia, inflation was driven by price developments in Russia before June 1992, when an independent currency issued under a currency board was

Table 6. Fiscal and Inflation Developments

Country	Stabilization Quarter[1]	Fiscal Developments
		(Stabilization cases)
Albania	1993: Q1	Up-front adjustment based on expenditure cuts
Armenia	1995: Q2	Up-front adjustment, further progress later; cuts in expenditures and revenues
Azerbaijan	1995: Q2	Up-front adjustment, further progress later; cuts in expenditures and revenues
Belarus	1995: Q4	Up-front adjustment, cuts in expenditure and decline in revenue
Bulgaria (1st stabilization)	1995: Q1	Modest up-front adjustment, based on cuts in expenditures and revenues
Bulgaria (2nd stabilization)	1997: Q2	Strong primary surplus maintained; cuts in expenditures and revenues
Croatia	1994: Q1	Up-front adjustment based on revenue increases
Estonia	1993: Q4	Small primary surplus
Georgia	1994: Q4	Up-front adjustment, based on expenditure cuts
Kazakhstan	1995: Q2	Up-front adjustment based on expenditure cuts and reduction in quasi-fiscal deficits
Kyrgyz Republic	1995: Q2	Adjustment in 1994, with a temporary reversal in 1995; adjustment based on expenditure cuts
Latvia	1993: Q1	Small primary surplus
Lithuania	1994: Q1	Constant fairly sizable primary deficit, but strong reduction in quasi-fiscal deficit
Macedonia, FYR	1994: Q2	Up-front adjustment, with initial increases in revenues and expenditure cuts, followed by cuts in both revenues and expenditures
Moldova	1994: Q2	Up-front adjustment based on expenditure cuts
Romania	1994: Q3	Fiscal weakening and sizable quasi-fiscal deficits
Russia	1995: Q4	Up-front adjustment in the primary balance, followed by a partial relaxation; cuts in expenditure and revenues
Turkmenistan	1997: Q2	Small primary deficit maintained
Ukraine	1997: Q2	Up-front adjustment based on expenditure cuts, in cash terms. New arrears offset the expenditure reductions
Uzbekistan	1995: Q2	Up-front adjustment based on revenue increases
		(Countries that maintained inflation at moderate levels)
Hungary	—	Strong fiscal consolidation
Poland	—	Fiscal improvement
		(Low inflation countries)
Czech Republic	—	Declining primary surplus, with unchanged overall balance
Slovak Republic	—	Stable primary surplus
Slovenia	—	Stable primary surplus
		(Countries that failed to stabilize)
Tajikistan	—	Strong fiscal improvement

Source: IMF staff estimates.
[1]Quarter in which the 60 percent inflation threshold was broken (see Table 2).

Table 7. General Government Revenue and Primary Expenditures in Transition Economies[1]

(In percent of GDP)

Country	General Government Revenue						
	1991	1992	1993	1994	1995	1996	1997
Albania	. . .	22.5	24.9	23.3	23.9	19.0	17.2
Bulgaria	40.4	38.4	37.2	39.9	36.1	32.5	31.1
Croatia	216.9	32.2	34.2	42.2	44.1	45.4	45.0
Czech Republic	59.1	45.0	45.9	44.7	43.5	42.5	40.7
Hungary	53.5	53.1	53.7	51.2	47.6	46.5	45.7
Macedonia, FYR	8.2	39.3	40.2	46.4	42.0	41.0	38.9
Poland	42.3	43.3	47.1	46.0	44.8	44.0	44.5
Romania	41.9	37.4	33.9	32.1	31.9	29.8	27.7
Slovak Republic	50.7	46.0	44.2	46.4	46.9	47.4	40.9
Slovenia	0.6	45.8	47.0	45.9	45.7	45.2	43.8
Armenia	27.6	29.1	28.9	27.7	19.9	17.7	19.8
Azerbaijan	. . .	. . .	33.5	24.5	15.3	16.2	18.2
Belarus	. . .	46.0	54.3	47.5	42.7	40.9	46.1
Estonia	. . .	. . .	38.6	41.1	39.9	39.0	38.9
Georgia	34.1	13.1	12.4	7.7	7.1	9.4	10.2
Kazakhstan	27.6	24.5	21.1	18.5	16.9	13.2	13.3
Kyrgyz Republic	. . .	. . .	24.7	20.8	16.7	15.9	17.0
Latvia	37.4	28.1	36.4	36.5	35.5	36.7	39.4
Lithuania	. . .	. . .	30.2	31.7	32.3	29.6	32.7
Moldova	. . .	30.3	22.1	33.5	33.9	32.1	34.3
Russia	33.4	39.5	35.5	34.7	30.7	31.0	31.7
Tajikistan	. . .	. . .	. . .	. . .	15.2	12.1	11.7
Turkmenistan	38.2	42.2	22.6	10.4	12.5	15.4	29.2
Ukraine	. . .	34.2	42.8	41.9	37.8	36.7	38.4
Uzbekistan	. . .	31.5	35.3	32.3	34.6	34.2	30.2

Source: IMF staff estimates.

[1]For the countries that stabilized during 1993–97, shaded areas indicate years in which inflation was below the stabilization threshold (as defined in Table 2).

[2]The primary expenditure is calculated as the general government expenditure minus net interest payments. Primary balance calculations exclude interest receipts for Armenia, Azerbaijan, Belarus, Estonia, Kazakhstan, Kyrgyz Republic, Romania, Slovakia, and the Ukraine.

introduced. Thereafter, inflation fell sharply, but as Latvia also experienced later, the exchange rate peg was insufficient to eliminate inflation, despite the firm fiscal stance. In Turkmenistan, the reasons for the persistance of inflation are more difficult to assess, although they may have been related to the increasing scarcity of imported consumer goods until early 1997, when the central bank was allowed to sell foreign exchange on the market, relieving the shortage. In contrast to these cases, inflation in Tajikistan persisted in spite of the sig-

		Primary Expenditure[2]				
1991	1992	1993	1994	1995	1996	1997
. . .	43.1	37.9	34.0	32.1	28.3	24.7
54.9	37.1	38.8	32.3	28.1	26.2	25.4
39.9	36.8	32.1	40.3	45.2	44.7	44.2
. . .	. . .	. . .	44.8	44.6	42.8	41.7
51.4	54.8	57.7	54.0	44.9	42.5	41.3
. . .	. . .	49.9	46.6	41.5	39.2	36.9
49.3	54.2	48.4	44.8	43.8	43.9	43.6
38.6	41.7	33.3	32.6	33.2	32.4	29.7
. . .	57.0	48.2	44.0	44.5	46.5	44.0
. . .	45.6	46.6	45.4	45.5	45.5	47.3
. . .	. . .	. . .	35.9	27.9	24.4	22.6
. . .	. . .	. . .	35.9	19.4	18.6	19.4
. . .	45.3	55.3	49.6	43.8	41.9	46.8
. . .	. . .	39.0	39.8	40.8	40.3	36.7
. . .	75.5	38.4	21.8	10.1	12.8	12.5
36.5	31.7	31.3	29.2	26.2	25.9	26.3
. . .	. . .	38.4	32.2	33.6	24.3	24.6
31.1	28.8	34.8	37.9	37.6	36.9	37.6
. . .	. . .	36.1	37.6	36.9	33.7	34.4
. . .	54.2	28.4	39.7	36.2	36.1	37.4
. . .	56.5	41.6	43.1	34.3	33.5	36.0
. . .	. . .	. . .	. . .	23.6	16.7	15.8
. . .	. . .	. . .	11.6	13.5	16.6	28.9
. . .	57.4	52.3	51.3	41.3	38.8	40.2
. . .	43.4	53.6	33.3	38.1	39.9	33.0

nificant strengthening of the primary balance during 1996–98 because of political instability and civil war.

The only cases in which inflation stabilization succeeded while fiscal and quasi-fiscal deficits remained high were Romania and the Kyrgyz Republic. In the former case, the progress on inflation was ultimately reversed. In the latter case, there was a sharp temporary fiscal relaxation in 1995 associated with an election. But the inflationary impact of the fiscal position, both before and after this, was considerably less than is implied by the overall and primary fiscal balances. These reflect a large, import-intensive, and externally financed public investment program. Apart from 1995, domestic funding of the deficit remained about or below 2½ percent of GDP throughout the disinflation, and this shifted progressively from central bank to other sources of domestic finance. Thus, as with other cases, the Kyrgyz disinflation was underwritten by a firm fiscal position.

It is notable that inflation stabilization did not require fiscal solvency according to simple standard formulas. Such formulas identify the minimal primary balance necessary to avoid an explosive path for the debt-GDP ratio in terms of the initial debt level, the GDP growth rate, and the interest rate on debt (see formula in Table 8). By these standards, the fiscal position during most of the inflation stabilizations was insolvent, and still remained so in 1997.[15] The simple assumptions that underlie the formulas, however, may be particularly inappropriate in transition economies. Transition economies have strong potential productivity growth and this is likely to contribute to future strengthened primary balances. In addition, some of these countries also implemented structural reforms that bolstered long-term fiscal sustainability, even if they had little immediate fiscal impact.[16] This, and the fact that the Baltics and other countries of the former Soviet Union (excluding Russia) started the transition with negligible public debt and so could derive efficiency gains from added leverage, may explain why strict adherence to the standard formulas has not been necessary to support or sustain disinflation.[17]

The link between disinflation and fiscal adjustment is less clear at moderate inflation levels, however. In the Czech Republic, inflation remained moderate despite declining primary surpluses during 1993–96. Conversely, the drop in inflation in Slovenia during 1993–97, in the Slovak Republic during 1994–96, and in Poland during 1993–97 was not accompanied by a fiscal strengthening. Various factors may account for this. Moderate inflation countries are also relatively fast reformers with more developed government securities markets. This alleviates the monetary impact of fiscal deficits as illustrated by the case of Hungary, where large deficits in 1993–94 led to only a limited rise in inflation. In addition, once fiscal sustainability is achieved, disinflation may become a problem of expectation coordination (Blanchard, 1998). In this environment, a fiscal expansion that casts doubts on fiscal sustainability or that leads to overheating should be avoided, but a fiscal tightening may not be necessary. The results of more formal research into the relation-

---

[15]The table uses an interest rate-growth rate differential of 2 percentage points, as in the studies on transition economies by Budina and van Wijnbergen (1997) and Begg (1998).

[16]For example, the pension reforms approved in 1996 in Kazakhstan reduced future public liabilities without greatly affecting the current fiscal balance, and the reduction in arrears by the pension fund in the following year caused a deterioration in the measured fiscal balance.

[17]Furthermore, receipts from privatization can also ease the solvency condition, especially when privatization greatly increases the productivity of the privatized assets.

Table 8. Actual and Sustainable Primary Fiscal Balances
(In percent of GDP)

Country	1997 Actual	Sustainable[1]
Albania	–7.4	1.1
Bulgaria	6.0	2.1
Croatia	0.2	0.6
Czech Republic	–0.9	0.2
Hungary	3.5	1.3
Macedonia, FYR	1.0	0.8
Poland	1.2	0.9
Romania	–0.2	0.4
Slovak Republic	–3.0	0.5
Slovenia	–2.6	0.4
Armenia	–4.1	0.8
Azerbaijan	–1.2	0.3
Belarus	–0.7	0.2
Estonia	2.3	0.1
Georgia	–2.4	0.6
Kazakhstan	–2.9	0.3
Kyrgyz Republic	–7.7	0.8
Latvia	2.2	0.3
Lithuania	–0.5	0.2
Moldova	–3.1	0.8
Russia	–3.1	0.4
Tajikistan	–2.5	1.6
Turkmenistan	–0.2	0.6
Ukraine	–3.2	0.4
Uzbekistan	–2.3	0.3

Source: IMF staff calculations.

[1]The sustainable primary balance is the primary balance that would allow stabilizing of the public debt-GDP ratio; it can be computed as

$$p = [(i\text{-}g)/(1\text{+}g)]d$$

where p is the primary balance-GDP ratio, i is the nominal interest rate on government debt, g is the nominal GDP growth rate, and d is the initial debt-GDP ratio. The figures in Table 8 have been based on a nominal GDP growth rate of 8 percent, and an interest rate-growth differential of 2 percentage points. Actual figures for end-1996 have been used for the debt-GDP ratio. It should be stressed that for countries with high debt-GDP ratios, stabilizing the debt-GDP ratio is unlikely to be sufficient to ensure long-run sustainability. Reducing vulnerability would require lowering the debt ratio and, therefore, stronger fiscal positions than indicated above.

ship between fiscal balances, government securities markets, and inflation, at different inflation levels, are outlined in Box 2.

These findings have implications for fiscal policy in sustaining the progress toward low inflation. Fiscal consolidation, having been so central to laying the groundwork for inflation stabilization, will remain essential to sustain disinflation. Those countries that already

Box 2. Inflation and Fiscal Deficits: Summary of Econometric Results

The relationship between inflation and fiscal deficits in transition economies has been explored through regression analysis in several papers (Fischer, Sahay, and Végh, 1996; Lougani and Sheets, 1997; and Cottarelli, Griffiths, and Moghadam, 1998). All these papers find a significant statistical relationship between inflation and the fiscal deficit, which is robust to differences in the econometric specification and in the definition of the deficit.[1] Moreover, these studies show that fiscal factors remain important even after controlling for other factors (such as the exchange regime, measures of the overall progress in reforming the economy, central bank independence, indexation, and relative price changes).

The estimate of the direct quantitative effect of fiscal deficits on inflation is, however, relatively low. In most of the specifications, a decline in the deficit-GDP ratio of 1 percentage point when inflation is, say, 100 percent involves a decline in inflation of only 5–8 percentage points. The effect is larger at high inflation levels, but smaller when inflation is low.[2]

This result may be explained in two ways. First, in a number of countries, disinflation did not require a reduction in the deficit either because the fiscal position was already sufficiently strong or because the main problem was related to quasi-fiscal deficits. As the regression results "average out" the experience of all countries during the sample period, the effect of deficit cuts estimated from regressions using changes in the variables (rather than levels) appears to be lower than in reality for those countries that had a fiscal problem. Second, the results indicate that fiscal adjustment should not be seen in isolation but rather as a component of a comprehensive package that enhances the credibility of disinflation through appropriate exchange rate policies, and other institutional devices (such as central bank independence). One element of a comprehensive package may be the development of government securities markets. Cottarelli, Griffiths, and Moghadam (1998) report that the relation between inflation and fiscal deficits is stronger in those countries without a developed government securities market, presumably reflecting the greater reliance of such countries on central bank finance for the government deficit.

---

[1]In particular, Cottarelli, Griffiths, and Moghadam (1998) find that the relationship holds also after removing the effect of inflation on government interest payments, thus suggesting a line of causality that runs from fiscal deficits to inflation, and not vice versa.

[2]This is due to the semilogarithmic specification of the relation between inflation and fiscal deficits, adopted in all papers. This specification seems to fit the data better than alternative specifications.

have a strong underlying fiscal position, implying that inflation is an expectational problem, should maintain this strong fiscal stance. Whether a fiscal tightening will be necessary to disinflate further will depend on its contribution to reducing aggregate demand pressures. In many cases, however, the priority will be structural fiscal reform, including second-generation reforms aimed at fostering economic growth and medium-term fiscal credibility. Key issues will be the structure and level of taxation, social spending, and social transfers. Progress in these areas can benefit disinflation not only by strengthening the fiscal balances, but also by spurring productivity growth.

Policy Response: Credibility-Enhancing Devices

Various monetary frameworks, external agents, and incomes policies were adopted to bolster credibility. This section describes and discusses these devices and assesses their contribution to disinflation.

Monetary frameworks

A striking feature of the 1993–97 inflation stabilizations is the limited use of formal exchange rate or monetary targets. Though both monetary aggregates and exchange rates did stabilize during and after inflation stabilization (Table 9), the announcement of targets for these variables played a limited role: no country announced monetary targets (although several IMF-supported programs included indicative targets on base money) and, perhaps surprisingly, few announced exchange rate targets when initiating disinflation.

The absence of publicly announced monetary targets, other than rules directly implied by the exchange rate regime as in the case of currency boards, reflects structural change and uncertainty. Reform in the financial sector—particularly the advent of substitutes for bank deposits for household savings and innovations in payment systems—was substantial. This compounded the lack of knowledge of money demand and the prospect that disinflation itself would induce a strong, though unpredictable, recovery in real money demand. In this context, money targets appeared to be unworkable as signals for inflation expectation formation.[18]

---

[18]See Begg, Hesselman, and Smith (1996), and Begg (1998) for Central and Eastern European countries, and De Broeck, Krajnyák, and Lorie (1997) for the Baltics, Russia, and other countries of the former Soviet Union. Van Elkan (1998) discusses the case of Hungary. Anderson and Citrin (1995) discuss the response of money demand to inflation.

Table 9. Broad Money Growth and Depreciation Rates in Transition Economies[1]

(End of period, in percent)

Country	Broad Money					
	1992	1993	1994	1995	1996	1997
Albania	152.7	75.0	40.6	51.8	43.8	28.4
Bulgaria	. . .	53.5	77.9	39.6	117.9	359.3
Croatia	. . .	. . .	72.6	41.3	49.4	37.7
Czech Republic	. . .	. . .	19.9	19.8	9.2	10.1
Hungary	27.3	16.8	13.0	18.5	20.9	23.2
Macedonia, FYR	. . .	1,123.0	43.3	10.1	2.3	13.1
Poland	57.5	36.0	38.4	34.6	29.5	28.9
Romania	75.4	143.3	138.1	71.6	66.0	104.8
Slovak Republic	. . .	. . .	18.5	21.2	16.6	8.8
Slovenia	121.3	62.4	44.6	29.1	22.2	. . .
Armenia	41.5	1,444.1	726.9	129.7	34.2	8.6
Azerbaijan	265.6	685.8	486.1	122.2	25.8	29.8
Belarus[2]	482.0	572.6	1,321.5	325.7	66.7	102.8
Estonia	196.3	57.8	29.6	31.3	36.8	40.3
Georgia	416.4	1,225.4	2,055.8	319.4	38.2	35.4
Kazakhstan	482.1	581.0	540.2	113.7	20.9	. . .
Kyrgyz Republic	. . .	151.3	139.6	86.9	17.5	20.4
Latvia	. . .	109.3	45.8	−25.7	17.8	. . .
Lithuania	. . .	177.0	61.9	31.9	−1.5	. . .
Moldova	356.1	256.2	128.3	65.1	15.3	34.0
Russia	505.9	435.9	195.6	129.0	33.1	. . .
Tajikistan	513.8	1,587.4	156.3	. . .	142.8	110.7
Turkmenistan	960.0	871.7	985.4	448.0	428.8	78.4
Ukraine	776.4	1,556.7	467.3	147.1	42.8	42.2
Uzbekistan	. . .	987.0	585.6	163.4	113.3	37.0

Source: IMF staff estimates.

[1]The depreciation rates are computed vis-à-vis the U.S. dollar. For the countries that stabilized during 1993–97, shaded areas indicate years in which inflation was below the stabilization threshold (as defined in Table 2).

[2]The depreciation rates refer to the official exchange rate.

Exchange rate targets—the most obvious substitute for monetary targets—were initially adopted only by a handful of countries (Tables 10 and 11). They subsequently became more common: by 1997, the share of floaters had dropped to little more than one-half, and was thus close to the share of floaters in nontransition developing countries in the mid-1990s (Cottarelli and Giannini, 1997). Note that, in the most recent period (1995–97), the increase in the number of pegs reflects the increased popularity of broad band pegs. Former floaters, such as Russia and the Ukraine, as well as former narrow band pegs, such as

	Depreciation				
1992	1993	1994	1995	1996	1997
273.1	5.1	-5.7	-0.9	7.3	47.2
14.2	28.9	104.9	7.2	556.4	285.1
. . .	839.0	-11.0	-6.7	3.3	13.2
0.0	4.2	-5.1	-5.6	2.5	27.1
8.0	20.6	11.6	24.6	17.7	23.0
5,426.3	277.1	-2.8	-7.3	5.3	36.4
39.0	37.0	15.3	3.2	13.9	23.4
132.4	163.6	55.5	44.2	46.0	113.2
0.1	15.4	-4.7	-5.6	6.3	9.5
. . .	34.5	-1.0	-1.9	12.4	18.7
. . .	3,523.2	449.3	-2.1	9.9	11.9
. . .	427.4	1,589.4	2.5	-7.7	-5.1
7,767.9	1,835.3	1,262.8	214.5	15.3	97.1
. . .	7.0	-10.3	-7.4	8.5	15.3
218.8	24,580.3	1,151.2	-3.9	3.6	2.4
. . .	688.7	759.9	17.9	15.4	2.8
. . .	. . .	32.0	5.2	49.8	4.1
247.3	2.1	2.6	0.0	0.0	0.0
. . .	-28.7	-7.9	-2.0	3.5	6.1
143.8	778.2	17.3	5.4	3.4	0.2
. . .	200.8	184.7	30.7	19.8	7.2
. . .	200.5	184.7	644.1	11.8	127.7
. . .	. . .	. . .	166.7	1,935.0	2.3
43,446.5	3,237.8	316.8	72.2	5.3	0.5
. . .	201.2	1,904.8	42.0	54.9	45.7

Poland and the Slovak Republic, have shifted to this intermediate regime.[19] In contrast, only the Czech Republic has crossed the whole spectrum from a peg to a managed float.

Among the successful inflation stabilizations between 1993–97, only Bulgaria (in 1997), Lithuania, Estonia, and the former Yugoslav Republic of Macedonia formally pegged throughout, though Russia adopted a broad band a few months after the beginning of its disinflation program.[20] Croatia announced an exchange rate floor against the deutsche

---

[19]Russia floated in August 1998.

[20]In Table 11, the former Yugoslav Republic of Macedonia is classified as having a pegged exchange rate because the authorities announced their commitment to a certain exchange rate level. Croatia is similarly classified because it announced an exchange rate floor at the beginning of the disinflation.

Table 10. Number of Peggers and Floaters[1]

	1992	1993	1994	1995	1996	1997
Peggers						
Central and Eastern European countries	3	3	5	5	3	4
Baltics, Russia, and other countries of the former Soviet Union	1	1	3	3	3	3
Total	4	4	8	8	6	7
Broad band peggers						
Central and Eastern European countries	—	—	—	1	3	2
Baltics, Russia, and other countries of the former Soviet Union	—	—	—	1	1	2
Total	—	—	—	2	4	4
Floaters						
Central and Eastern European countries	7	7	5	4	4	4
Baltics, Russia, and other countries of the former Soviet Union	14	14	12	11	11	10
Total	21	21	17	15	15	14

Source: IMF staff reports.
[1]In this table, the exchange regime of the countries that had not yet introduced their own currency is the exchange regime of the preexisting currency.

mark and allowed the nominal exchange rate to appreciate initially, although most now consider that it is operating a de facto peg. Even in the four disinflations that occurred without a fiscal tightening, where weaknesses in the nominal anchor framework might have been thought to have been sustaining inflation, only Estonia used a formal exchange rate anchor to stabilize expectations. Latvia, Turkmenistan, and Ukraine formally floated (in the latter two cases, throughout).

The role of different exchange regimes in disinflation remains under dispute. Bruno (1992) concluded that exchange rate anchors had played a key role in the early disinflation cases, and is supported by econometric evidence for that period (Fischer, Sahay, and Végh, 1996; and Cottarelli, Griffiths, and Moghadam, 1998). However, others, focusing on more recent disinflations, have argued that formal exchange rate anchors were not critical for disinflation (Zettermeyer and Citrin, 1995; Budina and van Wijnbergen, 1997; Begg, 1998; and Gomulka,

1998). Indeed, in two-thirds of the inflation stabilization cases observed during 1993–97, the exchange rate was formally floating (Table 11).[21]

The popularity of exchange rate floats during the later inflation stabilization episodes is striking, particularly in light of the role pegs were thought capable of playing as "launching vehicles" for new fiat monies lacking initial credibility (Selgin, 1994), their high visibility and direct effect on prices through imported inflation, and the absence of sensible monetary anchors as alternatives. Most of these countries followed what in essence were discretionary monetary frameworks, or informal inflation targeting regimes.[22]

Not only has evidence of successful inflation stabilization with formally floating exchange rates mounted, but there is no clear evidence that these episodes have involved a higher sacrifice ratio. Indeed, if anything, the converse appears to be the case. The ratio between percentage change in output and percentage change in inflation during the disinflation year and in the following year is larger for countries with a pegged exchange rate than in the group of floaters, and this pattern is apparent even allowing for other determinants of growth (Christoffersen and Doyle, 1998).

There are various possible accounts of the declining frequency of formal pegs during disinflation in transition: that the disinflations after 1993 tended to confront more extreme inflations with less inflation inertia and so the credibility-enhancing role of formal pegs was less important; that informal pegging was both relatively frequent and proved to be a close substitute for formal pegs even in these higher disinflation cases; and that there were a number of practical "entry and exit" issues that qualified the general case for formal exchange rate pegs during disinflation.

Clearly, the inflation stabilizations after 1993 included a greater number of cases of extreme inflation than earlier (Table 1). Accordingly, the credibility-enhancing role of formal pegs may have been less important to effective disinflation than in earlier cases because inflation inertia was more limited. Thus, to the extent that sustained exchange rate stability signified the elimination of the excess monetary growth at the root of these later inflations, it may have been more important that the exchange rate was stabilized than that this was

---

[21]Latvia introduced a fixed exchange rate some 18 months after initiating stabilization.

[22]Transition economies have only recently begun to consider and to adopt formal inflation targeting frameworks. The Czech Republic adopted this framework informally in late 1997, and formalized it in early 1998. Poland introduced inflation targeting in late 1998.

Table 11. Exchange Rate Regime in Transition Countries

Country	1992	1993	1994
Albania	Floating	Floating	Floating
Bulgaria	Floating	Floating	Floating
Croatia[2]	Floating	Floating	Peg
Czech Republic	Peg	Peg	Peg
Hungary	Managed float	Managed float	Managed float
Macedonia, FYR	Managed float	Managed float	Peg
Poland	Crawling peg	Crawling peg	Crawling peg
Romania	Managed float	Managed float	Managed float
Slovak Republic	Peg	Peg	Peg
Slovenia	Managed float	Managed float	Managed float
Armenia	No national currency	No national currency	Managed float[7]
Azerbaijan	No national currency	No national currency	Floating[8]
Belarus	No national currency	No national currency	Managed float
Estonia	Currency board	Currency board	Currency board
Georgia	No national currency	Managed float[9]	Managed float
Kazakhstan	No national currency	No national currency	Managed float
Kyrgyz Republic	No national currency	Managed float	Managed float
Latvia	Floating	Floating	Peg[10]
Lithuania	Floating	Floating	Currency board[11]
Moldova	No national currency	No national currency	Floating[12]
Russia	Floating	Floating	Floating
Tajikistan	No national currency	No national currency	No national currency
Turkmenistan	No national currency	No national currency	Managed float[15]
Ukraine	No national currency	Managed float[16]	Managed float
Uzbekistan	No national currency	No national currency	Managed float

Source: IMF staff reports.

Notes: The exchange rate is regarded as floating in the absence of major exchange rate intervention; managed float means that some intervention takes place but the exchange rate is not regarded as the main monetary anchor; exchange regimes in which the exchange rate peg is frequently revised (as in Hungary before March 1995) are also classified as managed float; pegged exchange rates are formal pegs or regimes in which the authorities have, at least in some periods, announced their commitment to a certain exchange rate target and the exchange rate is regarded as pegged by most market participants. The term "crawling peg" refers to regimes in which the rate of exchange rate depreciation is preannounced. For the countries that stabilized during 1993–97, shaded areas indicate the years in which inflation was below the stabilization threshold (as defined in Table 2).

[1]As of July 1, 1997.

[2]In 1992–93, the exchange rate was repeatedly devalued (being formally floated between May and October 1993). In October 1993, an exchange rate floor (maximum depreciation) was announced; after a brief period of appreciation, the exchange rate stabilized.

[3]As of February 28, 1996.

achieved by means of a credibility-enhancing formal exchange rate commitment.

It is more difficult to assess the role of informal pegging—that is, exchange rate stabilization through intervention or adjustment in monetary instruments in the context of a formally floating regime. The sta-

1995	1996	1997
Floating	Floating	Floating
Floating	Floating	Currency board[1]
Peg	Peg	Peg
Peg	Broad band peg[3]	Managed float[4]
Crawling peg[5]	Crawling peg	Crawling peg
Peg	Peg	Peg
Broad band crawling peg[6]	Broad band crawling peg	Broad band crawling peg
Managed float	Managed float	Managed float
Peg	Broad band peg	Broad band peg
Managed float	Managed float	Managed float
Managed float	Managed float	Managed float
Floating	Floating	Floating
Peg	Managed float	Managed float
Currency board	Currency board	Currency board
Managed float	Managed float	Managed float
Managed float	Managed float	Managed float
Managed float	Managed float	Managed float
Peg	Peg	Peg
Currency board	Currency board	Currency board
Managed float	Managed float	Managed float
Broad band peg[13]	Broad band crawling peg	Broad band crawling peg
Floating[14]	Floating	Floating
Managed float	Managed float	Peg
Floating[17]	Floating	Broad band peg
Managed float	Managed float	Managed float

[4]As of May 27, 1997.
[5]As of March 15, 1995.
[6]As of May 1995.
[7]As of November 22, 1993.
[8]During the first quarter of 1994, the exchange rate was pegged to the U.S. dollar; in April and May 1994, it was pegged to the ruble.
[9]The Georgian coupon was introduced in April 1993, and the lari was introduced in September 1995.
[10]As of February 1994.
[11]As of April 1994.
[12]As of November 1993.
[13]As of July 1995.
[14]National currency introduced in May 1995.
[15]National currency introduced on November 1, 1993.
[16]National currency introduced in March 1993.
[17]As of October 1994.

bility of the nominal exchange rate in several transition economies with formally floating exchange rates after the inflation stabilization was notable, including for example, in Armenia and the Kyrgyz Republic in 1995 during their disinflations, and in Georgia from 1995 through 1997. However, while the exchange rate was closely monitored in all countries, it appears that only in relatively few cases, such as Moldova, Slovenia, and occasionally Kazakhstan, were intervention and monetary instruments focused on informal exchange rate targets as part of the policy framework underlying disinflation. And even acknowledging such cases, it remains remarkable that so few countries adopted formal exchange rate targets.

The declining incidence of formal pegs also reflects concerns about entry and exit issues (Gomulka, 1998; Begg, 1998; and IMF, 1997, pp. 114–15). On the entry side, many countries in the post-1993 period began their disinflations with low international reserves, and so may not have been able to operate pegs credibly at sensible exchange rates. The mirror image of this problem, on the exit side, was the risk for a country of entering the exchange rate peg at a substantially undervalued exchange rate. Pegging at such rates might have slowed inflation from its extremely high levels initially. But thereafter, it could have implied ongoing inflation above partner country levels to correct the real exchange rate, compounding similar pressures for this arising from relatively rapid productivity growth in the tradable sector (the Balassa-Samuelson effect).[23] And pegs, in the context of moderate inflation, might also induce large short-term capital inflows.

These difficulties with pegs as nominal anchors for disinflation took a particular form in a number of the BRO countries in the mid-1990s. Disinflation using pegs normally requires that the peg is set against a low inflation hard currency, such as the deutsche mark or the dollar, or a hard currency basket. However, the fact that Russia was a major trading partner for the Baltics and for the countries of the former Soviet Union created a dilemma for this approach to setting a peg in those countries. To eliminate shocks to competitiveness and inflation arising from changes in the real exchange rate of the ruble, the latter would need to be included among the currencies defining the peg. But this would have weakened the ex ante credibility of the peg as a nominal anchor because the ruble was so vulnerable. Hence, the uncertain prospects for the ruble in the mid-1990s qualified the merits of hard currency pegs as nominal anchors for the disinflation efforts elsewhere in the BRO countries.

The various difficulties with pegs are illustrated in the experience of transition countries that stabilized inflation both before and after 1993. After initial successes, advanced pegging reformers, notably the Czech Republic, Estonia, Hungary, Latvia, Lithuania, and Poland have made

---

[23]Transition factors have been found to add to the speed of real appreciation in oil-rich countries of the Baltics, Russia, and other countries of the former Soviet Union, such as Azerbaijan (Rosenberg and Saavalainen, 1998).

slow progress toward low inflation while they have retained their pegs. The inflationary pressures arising from an undervalued peg are illustrated by the kroon, the level of which at the outset of disinflation implied wages in Estonia of about one-seventh of those in Poland. Latvia is also thought to have pegged too low, despite its initial float (Hansson, 1997), and inflation above industrial country levels was slow to correct this undervaluation (Richards and Tersman, 1995). The recovery of the ruble between 1994–96 in real terms may have delayed the correction of the Latvian undervaluation further. In other cases (notably Hungary and Poland), rates of crawl in 1996–97 may have come to imply floors rather than ceilings on inflation because the authorities were unwilling to use the rate of crawl as an active disinflation tool, given the *uncertainty* about the real equilibrium exchange rate and their past exposure to external shocks. Difficulties in managing capital flows—most clear in the case of the Czech Republic up to 1997—may partly account for the recent trend toward broad band pegs.

The advantages of discretionary monetary frameworks are illustrated by Albania, Azerbaijan, and Georgia, and for some months after the start of their disinflations, Croatia and Russia. In these cases, rapid disinflation was accompanied by nominal appreciation of the exchange rate, correcting an initial undervaluation. In all these cases, appreciation boosted the disinflating effects of lower import prices compared to a peg, facilitating an even faster disinflation.[24] Moreover, in some countries, the nominal exchange rate appreciation, after years of continuous depreciation, signaled a clear break with the past, with a dramatic impact in inflation expectations (Škreb, 1998).

It should be recognized that a nominal appreciation of the exchange rate involves some risks. Unless prices and wages adjust rapidly to changes in the nominal exchange rate, a nominal appreciation will lead to a real appreciation. As noted, a real appreciation may be consistent with fundamentals in transition economies characterized by high productivity growth, or in case of an initial undervaluation. But whether this is the case or not in practice is a judgment call, involving a wide margin of uncertainty, particularly taking into account dynamic factors. In practice, it may be difficult for the authorities to assess whether a real appreciation following a nominal appreciation reflects

---

[24]This factor played a role in the Baltics and in the countries of the former Soviet Union closely integrated with Russia as its real exchange rate rebounded during 1994–96. In this context, such countries that did not respond to the ruble appreciation with offsetting appreciations against "hard" currencies experienced substantial overall real effective depreciations, and consequently high import price inflation. This delayed disinflation.

sluggishness in wage and price adjustment, with a negative impact at least in the short run on the external accounts, rather than an equilibrium appreciation. These considerations may be more important at moderate inflation levels, at which wage and price stickiness may be stronger. Indeed, as discussed earlier, the authorities of some moderate inflation countries have justified their reluctance to abandon exchange rate crawling pegs with the risks arising from such a move for external equilibrium.

The disinflations achieved under discretionary monetary regimes—similar to informal inflation targeting—are notable given the cautious assessment given to more fully fledged inflation targeting regimes in developing countries (Masson, Savastano, and Sharma, 1997). The low inertia in the initial inflation being stabilized—a key difference with respect to Latin American disinflation episodes—the drawbacks of monetary and exchange rate targets in the transition context, the focus on fiscal consolidation, and the credibility gained from increased central bank independence and the adoption of IMF-supported programs may account for these successes. In most cases, however, the performance of discretionary monetary frameworks has yet to stand the test of time.

Credibility through delegation

Central bank independence and IMF-supported programs featured in many of the inflation stabilizations and may have buttressed financial discipline and the credibility of the disinflation programs. During 1993–97, most transition economies enhanced the legal independence of their central banks (Knight, 1997; and Radzyner and Riesinger, 1997). Price stability is now the main mandated objective of central banks in most transition economies, and ceilings on central bank credit to the government have been tightened, with many countries having prohibited any credit to the government (Table 12). There has also been significant progress in extending the terms of central bank governors, the rules for their appointment and revocation, as well as in strengthening the financial independence of the central bank.

A survey of IMF desk economists used in Cottarelli, Griffiths, and Moghadam (1998) provides a summary indicator of this trend. Desk economists were asked to rate central bank independence in terms of control on monetary policy instruments, constraints on credit to the government, statutory mandate, and ability of the government to dismiss the central bank governor. On a 1–10 scale (10 being the maximum degree of central bank independence), the average rating of CEE transition economies moved from 4.7 in 1993 to 5.3 in 1996. The

Table 12. Developments in Central Bank Legislation

	Major Revision of Central Bank Legislation	Main Objective of the Central Bank	Credit to the Government Constraints on Central Bank
Albania	1998	Price stability	Percentage of revenues in the previous year[1]
Bulgaria	1997	Currency board	No credit
Croatia	1992[2]	Stability of national currency and payment liquidity	5 percent of budget , revenue repayable within the year
Czech Republic	1992	Stability of the national currency	5 percent of previous year's state budget revenue
Hungary	1996	Internal and external value of the currency	Small liquidity facility
Macedonia, FYR	1992	Safeguard the value of the currency	5 percent of budgeted revenues
Poland	1997	Price stability	No credit (constitutional law)
Romania	1998	Currency and price stability	7 percent of revenues in the previous year
Slovak Republic	1992[3]	Stability of the currency	5 percent of revenues in the previous year
Slovenia	. . .	Currency stability and general liquidity of payments	One-fifth of budgeted deficit
Armenia	1996	Price stability	
Azerbaijan	1996	Price stability (as one objective)	No constraint
Belarus	1995	. . .	. . .
Estonia	1992	Currency board	No credit
Georgia	1995	Price stability	. . .
Kazakhstan	1997	Internal and external stability of the currency	No credit
Kyrgyz Republic	1997	Price stability	No credit
Latvia	1992	Exchange rate peg	. . .
Lithuania	1994	Currency board	No credit
Moldova	1995	Stability of the national currency	Amount agreed in annual state budget
Russia	1995	Price stability (as one objective)	. . .
Tajikistan	1996	. . .	. . .
Turkmenistan	1993	Price stability (as one objective)	8 percent of normal budget revenue over past three years
Ukraine	1997	Monetary stability	. . .
Uzbekistan	1995	Stability of the national currency	No constraint

Source: IMF staff estimates.

[1]The percentage declined sharply starting in 1998.

[2]A new draft is in preparation.

[3]A new central bank law was submitted to Parliament in 1997, but was later withdrawn. The draft was regarded to weaken the independence of the central bank.

average in the Baltics, Russia, and other countries of the former Soviet Union (excluding those with currency boards) also improved from 4.7 to 8.4 in the same period.[25] Further progress was made in 1997 and in 1998 in several countries, including Albania, Hungary, Kazakhstan, the Kyrgyz Republic, and Poland. However, attempts—unsuccessful so far—have been made to weaken the central bank law in the Slovak Republic. Moreover, central bank credit to the government—possibly the most important indicator of central bank independence—remains unrestricted in a number of the Baltics, Russia, and other countries of the former Soviet Union (Table 12).

Some econometric studies shed light on the importance of central bank independence in transition (Cottarelli, Griffiths, and Moghadam, 1998; and Lougani and Sheets, 1997). Controlling for other factors, inflation is lower in countries with more independent central banks. Cukierman, Miller, and Neyapti (1998) find that central bank independence is unrelated to inflation during the early stages of liberalization, but it reduces inflation for sufficiently high levels of liberalization.

With only three exceptions—Croatia, Slovenia, and Turkmenistan—the inflation stabilizations of 1993–97 took place in the presence of IMF-supported programs; in seven cases, under the Systemic Transformation Facility, but more frequently under other IMF arrangements. And even in these three cases, the authorities maintained a dialogue with the IMF. The incidence of IMF-supported programs suggests that they were regarded as an important component of the disinflation effort throughout the transition area. However, with almost all countries following IMF-supported programs, it is virtually impossible to conduct statistical tests of the marginal impact of IMF-assistance on shaping appropriate policies or strengthening the credibility of those policies.

Incomes policies

Some countries also employed incomes policies, though their contribution to disinflation is disputed. Though they featured in various forms in many initial disinflations, it is difficult to identify their con-

---

[25]As indices reflect subjective views, they should be taken as indicative of direction of change, rather than of relative positions across countries. Following more rigorous methodology—which focuses only on legal independence—Cukierman, Miller, and Neyapti (1998) conclude that the level of legal independence of transition economies is even higher than in developed economies and is broadly the same on average for the Baltics, Russia, and other countries of the former Soviet Union and Central and Eastern European countries.

tribution to real or nominal wage adjustments or inflation, after controlling for other influences on these variables (Morsink, 1995).

The approaches ranged from excess wage taxes (Belarus, Estonia, Latvia, Poland, Romania, and Slovakia) through formal wage guidelines or controls for the public and private sectors (as in Croatia, Hungary, Lithuania, and the former Yugoslav Republic of Macedonia) to wage limits applied only in the public sector with the aim of influencing private wage setting by example (Albania and Moldova). Several countries, however, did not use any form of incomes policy, including many of the disinflations of 1994–95 in the Baltics, Russia, and other countries of the former Soviet Union (Azerbaijan, Georgia, Kazakhstan, the Kyrgyz Republic, and Russia). Even in countries where incomes policy was present, it is not regarded as one of the main factors behind disinflation, in some cases because of substantial noncompliance. Incomes policy is regarded to have played an important role only in a handful of Central and Eastern European countries (Albania, Bulgaria, Croatia, and the former Yugoslav Republic of Macedonia).

Blanchard (1998) suggests that incomes policies may not have affected inflation expectations in the transition context because they were often used to secure sizable shifts in income distribution that transition required. Wage growth was set at a level significantly below what inflation turned out to be, in this way leading to a sharp drop in real wages. While this adjustment was inevitable, it undermined the subsequent use of incomes policy as a tool of fast disinflation. A case in point is Hungary, in which a tight wage policy in 1995–96 resulted in a sharp contraction of real wages (inflation being sustained by the exchange rate depreciation in early 1995 and needed increases in administered prices). This undermined the credibility of incomes policy in 1997 and partly explains the lack of progress in inflation during that year. Finally, the resulting shifts in the distribution of income secured by the incomes policies weakened tax revenues in cases where the taxation of labor was more onerous than the taxation of nonlabor income. Concern with the consequent loss of revenue may at times have qualified the authorities' commitment to incomes policies. This was particularly apparent in Poland in 1990–91, where this incentive was compounded by tax receipts derived from the excess wage tax.

Policy Response: Sequencing and Speed

The final characteristic of the policies that appears to have contributed to the absence of evidence of output costs arising from disinflation concerns the sequencing of disinflation relative to structural reform and its intended speed.

Much theoretical reasoning about the relative sequencing of disinflation and structural reform was predicated on moderate inflation, and much of it advocated structural reform first, as a condition to enhance the credibility of disinflation. Blanchard (1998) suggests that disinflation is easier when it is purely a matter of inflation coordination, and is not accompanied by structural changes in relative prices and wages. Szapáry (1998) notes that inflation, in the presence of money illusion, may be needed to implement structural relative price changes, such as a redistribution from wages to profits. The findings of Berg and others (1998) on the differential impact of inflation on the public and private sector suggests that inflation should fall as the private sector expands. Kornai (1998) emphasizes that the behavior of unreformed economies is highly uncertain. So structural reform should precede disinflation, both to render macroeconomic developments during disinflation more predictable and to provide an offsetting underlying growth stimulus to any recessionary trend during disinflation.

Theoretical arguments favoring the reverse sequencing in a moderate inflation context are relatively few. They include that structural measures take so long that postponed disinflation risks entrenching inflation expectations (Cottarelli and Szapáry, 1998). Burton and Fischer (1998) add that the timing of disinflation should, in part, be opportunistic. It should exploit favorable supply shocks and political openings when they occur, rather than necessarily waiting for structural reforms or other desirable preconditions to be in place.

In practice, inflation stabilization in the Central and Eastern European countries was accompanied by a burst of structural reform, a pattern not evident in the Baltics, Russia, and other countries of the former Soviet Union (Figure 1). Nevertheless, by the third year of stabilization, both country groups had made similar structural progress. These patterns rarely reflected a sophisticated choice. Structural reforms inevitably take time, and particularly in the Baltics, Russia, and other countries of the former Soviet Union, inflation was so extreme that it clearly had to be addressed first. This may partly explain why political or technical trade-offs between disinflation and structural reform were apparent in only a few countries. For successful stabilizers such as Armenia, Croatia, and Ukraine, the precedence given to disinflation reflected its urgency, not that structural reform was sacrificed to disinflation or that disinflation was substituted for structural reform. In Hungary, however, the authorities argued that simultaneous disinflation and structural reform would have been politically impossible (Surányi and Vincze, 1998): as inflation was moderate, precedence was given to structural reform. The political difficulty of implementing structural reform and aggressive disinflation at the same time has also been stressed in the case of Romania.

While comprehensive structural reform was not a precondition for inflation stabilization in most cases, minimal progress may have been necessary, notably the establishment of a "hard-budget constraint" environment and the associated termination of interenterprise and tax arrears. The failure of some disinflation attempts, such as the first two attempts in Russia as well as other BRO countries, was in part due to the absence of such an environment.

Structural reform that is insufficiently comprehensive, for example, one that fails to develop effective corporate governance structures, is likely, however, to weaken the chances of maintaining price stability in the long run. As noted earlier, strong reformers have a lower incentive to inflate and have enjoyed lower inflation (see "Disinflation, Output, and the Current Account Balance" in this chapter). Moreover, it is significant that structural weaknesses—in public enterprises, in the financial system, and in governance structures—were behind the major episodes of inflation reversal during 1993–97 (Albania and Bulgaria after the first disinflation, and Romania; see Box 3). This suggests that those countries of the Baltics, Russia, and other countries of the former Soviet Union that stabilized inflation recently but that have not made more progress on structural reform than those countries that have experienced reversals may have difficulties in sustaining disinflation over time, unless wide-ranging reform is accelerated.

Having decided to stabilize first, most countries attempted to stabilize quickly. This likely helped credibility, given the high inflation context. As discussed above, when inflation has little inertia, as it generally has at high rates, the short-run output costs of rapid disinflation are usually lower. So a gradual approach risks signaling some lack of intent about disinflation, which undermines credibility. Bulgaria and Romania illustrate this difficulty, while the experience in Azerbaijan, Croatia, and the former Yugoslav Republic of Macedonia is suggestive of how successful such rapid disinflations could have been in these cases. But when inflation has some inertia, as more commonly occurs at less extreme rates, rapid disinflation may be more likely to incur short-run output losses. For this reason, a gradual approach is less likely to suggest a lack of commitment to disinflation because it may reflect appropriate concerns about output. This pattern does not mean that all rapid disinflations of high inflation and gradual disinflations of moderate inflation are credible, nor that the reverse pairings are always noncredible: the Czechoslovak experience in 1991 shows that rapid stabilization of moderately high inflation is possible. But the pattern suggests that

Box 3. Disinflation Reversals in 1993–97:
Albania, Bulgaria, and Romania

Albania, Bulgaria, and Romania stand out as cases where substantial disinflation was reversed.[1] By 1995, Albania had reduced 12-month inflation to 6 percent, and Bulgaria and Romania had reduced inflation to below 35 percent. But by the end of 1997, inflation had increased to 40 percent, 580 percent, and 150 percent, respectively.

Albania made substantial progress between 1993–95, with forceful privatization, large cuts in public employment, rapid disinflation, and strong output growth. Though electoral pressures were reflected in a deteriorating fiscal position in 1996, and some increase in inflation, the emergence and rapid growth of pyramid schemes operating on an unprecedented scale ultimately led to the financial crisis and public disorder of early 1997, and to the resurgence of inflation. Problems in Bulgaria were more long-standing. Structural reform had been intermittent and uneven since 1990. Combined with political instability, this bolstered the rent-seeking culture, undermined fiscal policy, and culminated in economic crises in 1994, 1996, and in hyperinflation in early 1997. Stop-go policy has been only slightly less marked in Romania. The political commitment to the agricultural and energy sectors has pervaded all aspects of policy, from privatization and price liberalization to the exchange rate, undermining all initiatives to implement sustained structural and fiscal reform.

Chronic financial fragility, revealed in the collapses of banks and pyramid schemes, is a common feature of all three cases. And, while all three cases illustrate how long even much abused financial sectors can survive, they also demonstrate how costly delayed financial sector reform can ultimately be. Financial fragility also reflected other underlying structural weaknesses. In Bulgaria, widespread soft-budget constraints in industry undermined disinflation. In Romania, inflation largely reflected support of energy and farming, with weaknesses in the banking sector being less directly important. However, central bank support to two banks at the end of 1997 led to a significant monetary relaxation. The immediate cause of the surge of inflation in Albania was civil disorder, but the root cause of this was inadequate control of unlicensed deposit takers.

Fiscal indiscipline also undermined disinflation. In 1997, large quasi-fiscal deficits persisted after the disinflation. The ratio of the overall fiscal deficit to GDP in Albania has remained in double digits since 1992. And while Bulgaria's primary fiscal balance recorded strong surpluses prior to the reemergence of inflation, heavy quasi-fiscal losses accruing in the financial sector persisted.

---

[1]Uzbekistan also experienced a resurgence of inflation in 1997, from a low point for 12-month inflation of 42 percent in October 1996, to a subsequent high of 82 percent in August 1997, as policies were relaxed following a poor agricultural harvest. However, thus far, this resurgence is not on the same scale as that of the Central and Eastern European countries discussed here.

gradual stabilization of high inflation and rapid stabilization of moderate inflation may have inherent credibility problems.

Persistent Moderate Inflation

Having stabilized inflation rapidly and credibly, a number of advanced transition countries appear to have got stuck with moderate inflation in the 10–30 percent range (see Table 1 and Figure 4). The Czech Republic and Slovenia have spent 3–4 years in the high single-digit range. The Baltic States have only recently come down to those levels from the 20 to 40 percent range in 1993–95. Hungary has hovered in the 20–30 percent range throughout transition, until 1998, when it began disinflating into the lower teens from there. And Poland, after its rapid disinflation in 1990–91, has taken six years to get to the low teens. This section considers the factors underlying the slow progress after the initial dramatic successes.

The characteristics of the transition countries that have sustained five or more years of disinflation are highlighted in Figure 4. The key features are as follows: growth resumed in the second year after disinflation was initiated; these are generally "big bang" structural reformers; after five years, the group has institutional characteristics closely resembling those of mature market economies; the group has achieved increasingly strong fiscal positions; and although large current account deficits have appeared, the debt financed component of the external current account deficit has generally been relatively contained, though latterly, with increased variance. Finally, a glance at Table 11 confirms that the group has overwhelmingly pegged their exchange rates or has applied crawling pegs, though the Czech Republic switched to a managed float in 1997, joining Slovenia.

This summary indicates that progress toward price stability halted despite a propitious environment for disinflation: output, the debt-financed external balance, and fiscal policies have been strong, and structural reforms are far advanced. Furthermore, the experience of two countries outside this group—Croatia and the former Yugoslav Republic of Macedonia—confirms that sustained low inflation is clearly possible in the transition context, although further policy adjustments, on both the structural and macroeconomic sides, may be necessary to sustain this performance.

Rather than reflecting a difficult environment for disinflation or an "inflation floor" in transition, the persistent inflation of advanced reformers appears to reflect their choices of exchange rate regime and their policy preferences about inflation. Some advanced moderate inflaters, including the Czech Republic and the Baltic States, were

Figure 4. Advanced Transition Reformers, 1990–97

(In disinflation time)[1,2]

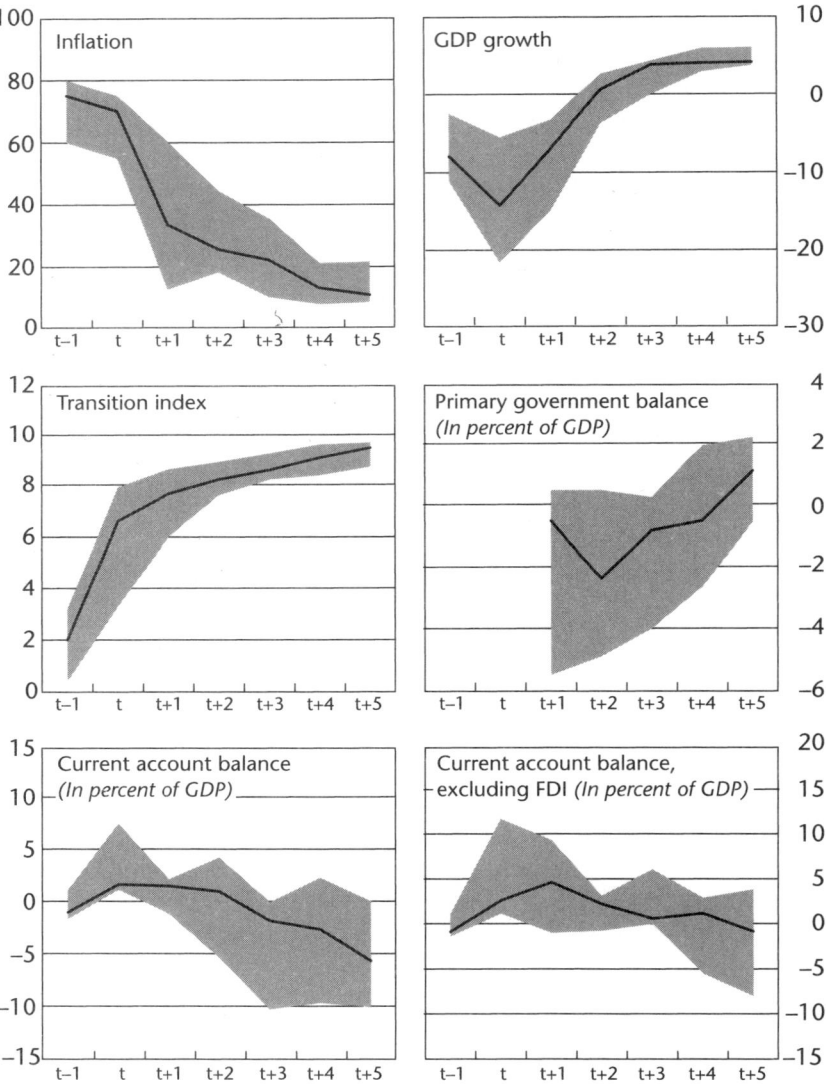

Sources: Country authorities; IMF, *World Economic Outlook*; EBRD *Transition Report*, various issues; and IMF staff estimates.

[1]The group consists of Estonia, Latvia, Lithuania, the Czech Republic, Hungary, Poland, the Slovak Republic, and Slovenia.

[2]The black line is the median. The shaded area represents the range containing all but the highest and lowest observations.

reluctant to abandon successful nominal exchange rate anchors. This commitment persisted even if initial undervaluation, reductions in underlying country risk premiums, and large relative price and relative productivity changes required real appreciations of their currencies. Clearly, in these circumstances, nominal appreciations would have been necessary to effect real exchange rate corrections with lower inflation. Persistent moderate inflation in the Baltic States appears to derive most clearly from this source (Richards and Tersman, 1995), compounded by the real effective appreciation of the ruble between 1994 and 1997. Paradoxically, after the initial stabilizations of inflation, further reductions toward industrial country rates may have been delayed by the commitment of these countries to nominal anchors that were intended to signal adherence to prudent policies. Mutatis mutandis, the same argument applies to countries with a crawling peg where the rate of crawl may have been lowered too gradually to avoid the risk of a real appreciation.

But the persistence of moderate inflation also reflected perceived trade-offs. Having reduced inflation to well below its recent peaks and to levels that international investors and the authorities perceived as "low by transition standards," some moderate inflaters saw no urgency to progress further. And some also feared that further progress would require output losses on top of those that had accompanied the initial stages of transition (Medgyessy, 1998). Thus, for example, Hungary prioritized structural reforms and reduced the external current account deficit and external debt after 1995 over further disinflation.

Finally, administered price adjustments often bulk large in relative price changes: typically, rents and utility prices have been held artificially low, and these sectors generally have limited scope for productivity gains to ease supply constraints. The consequent relative price adjustments have boosted headline CPI rates, with an impact that is particularly evident in moderate inflation contexts where relative price adjustments automatically loom larger. Accordingly, moderate inflaters that "backloaded" administrative price adjustments in their reform programs, including the Czech Republic, report higher headline CPI rates. Nevertheless, even underlying inflation rates have remained persistently above industrial country levels in these cases.

Persistent moderate inflation among advanced transition countries thus appears to reflect policy choices rather than structural features of transition. Those choices had various elements, including concerns about abandoning hitherto successful nominal anchors, the risks further disinflation might imply for output, and a perception that sufficient progress on inflation had already been made. These choices are changing, however. Many of the authorities in the group believe now that reducing inflation to industrial country levels is both feasible and desirable. These views are reflected in their accession programs to the European Union, and in recent reforms of exchange rate regimes, including the shift to formal inflation targeting in the Czech Republic and in Poland.

Conclusion

The reduction in inflation since the early 1990s right across the transition area is remarkable, particularly given the chaotic conditions at the outset. Inflationary pressures that had long been suppressed by price controls turned out to be one of the lesser challenges, as nascent policymaking institutions wrestled with collapsing output, employment, and fiscal revenues, as well as military conflicts and redrawn national boundaries. In such conditions, most currencies, new and old, collapsed, and inflation surged. But these difficulties notwithstanding, disinflation has been achieved throughout the region. Once undertaken, it was swift and there is no systematic evidence that it compounded output losses. Furthermore, major resurgences of inflation have been the exception. And in this lower inflation environment, growth has resumed, with formal evidence suggesting a direct link between reduced inflation and the resumption of growth.

The robustness of output during disinflation reflects three factors.

- The context for disinflation was better than it appeared: in the highest inflation cases, there was little inertia in prices and political support for disinflation was often strong; financial fragility rarely deepened during disinflation; and after the hurdle of initial relative price adjustment, price liberalization helped.
- Inflation stabilization was implemented first, without waiting for the completion of all-encompassing structural reforms, and it was intended to be rapid.
- Comprehensive fiscal consolidation underwrote disinflation, and funding sources were diversified through the development of financial markets.

Just as collapsing tax revenues, rigid expenditures, and limited financing options had forced heavy reliance on seigniorage—notably in the Baltics, Russia, and other countries of the former Soviet Union in the early 1990s—so fundamental fiscal adjustments, usually focused on expenditure cuts, underlay disinflation. However, inflation stabilization did not require "fiscal solvency," as defined by a primary surplus sufficiently high as to stabilize the public debt-GDP ratio. This is probably because dynamic solvency (the prospective evolution of the primary balance), rather than a snapshot of the primary balance, matters more in an environment characterized by deep structural changes. In addition, the relationship between fiscal adjustment and disinflation becomes more blurred at moderate inflation levels, when inflation is likely to be driven more by expectations than by fundamentals.

The role of monetary frameworks in strengthening disinflations is more controversial. Some, perhaps surprisingly few, countries adopted formal exchange rate pegs as their principal nominal anchors, especially in the disinflations after 1993. Most formally floated, though some of these pegged informally at times. Those that pegged throughout generally stabilized relatively rapidly but also experienced persistent moderate inflation, despite firm fiscal adjustment. The latter reflected Belassa-Samuelson effects and the correction of undervalued pegs through inflation above international levels, and was accommodated by capital inflows whenever domestic sources of monetary growth were restrictive. In some cases where fiscal adjustment accompanied an initial appreciation of the nominal exchange rate, such as Croatia and the former Yugoslav Republic of Macedonia, disinflation was more rapid and low inflation was sustained. Both formal floaters and countries that pegged their exchange rates attempted to boost the credibility of their chosen monetary frameworks by deepening the independence of their central banks and by disinflating in the context of IMF-supported programs.

The progress made in reducing inflation should not obscure the fact that the achievements are—with few notable exceptions—not longstanding. Even aside from the major inflation reversals (including Russia during the summer of 1998), a number of countries have experienced some resurgence of inflation (Armenia, Belarus, and Uzbekistan), and in some cases (Belarus and Uzbekistan), price controls on basic consumer goods have recently been intensified. It would be premature to presume that labor markets and financial markets in transition economies now generally discount a low inflation environment. For this reason alone, policymakers that are perceived to believe that inflation has fallen far enough are at risk of losing control of inflation once again. This risk is even evident in countries that experienced persistent moderate inflation, where inflation has repeatedly exceeded official targets, albeit within manageable margins thus far.

But even where a moderate inflation environment is reasonably assured, there is much to commend more ambitious goals—to lower inflation to industrial country levels soon. The estimated threshold above which inflation involves significant output costs appears to be close to industrial country inflation rates for fully fledged market economies, and this provides the relevant benchmark for the most advanced transition economies, including the Czech Republic, Estonia, Hungary, and Poland. With sizable relative price changes already achieved and substantial structural reform in place, those sequencing arguments that favor structural reform first may now be satisfied, setting the scene for further disinflation. And given that successful transition may entail currencies that appreciate in real terms and relatively large current account deficits—trends normally associated with weak policies—low and falling inflation may help to sustain investor confidence and the associated capital inflows.

Finally, there is no statistical evidence that the costs of disinflation are generally significant in transition economies, even at moderate inflation levels. This echoes findings for market economies (Ghosh and Phillips, 1998). And even if persistent moderate inflation has increased inflation inertia, rapid productivity growth should diminish the impact on profitability and employment of any inertia there may be in nominal wages during disinflation (Deppler, 1998).

Countries with persistent moderate inflation, as well as other advanced transition countries, now enjoy almost ideal circumstances for low-cost disinflation and would benefit from lowering inflation further. The commitment of many of them to achieving industrial country inflation rates in the near future in the context of entry to the European Union is appropriate, and others should be no less ambitious about their inflation goals.

Appendix I: Relation Between Inflation and Output in Transition Revisited

Christoffersen and Doyle (1998) recently published new panel data estimates of the relationship between GDP growth and inflation in 22 transition economies between 1990 and 1997. They aimed to address three key shortcomings of the existing research. First, the collapse of major export markets was clearly key for a number of BRO countries, but it had been ignored. Second, econometric studies had not attempted to identify if disinflation had compounded output declines, as many feared would happen at the time. Third, the earlier studies imposed the assumption that inflation impairs output at all rates, rather than only above a threshold. Empirical literature on market economies has found that this understates the output costs of high inflation and overstates those of low inflation. Sarel (1996), using a panel of industrial and developing countries, finds that inflation above 8 percent significantly impedes growth, while growth is unaffected by inflation below that; Ghosh and Phillips (1998) also find a significant threshold, which they estimate in the low single digits.[26] Using the same functional form to model the threshold, the authors sought to identify if similar results held in the transition context.

Econometric Estimates

Data and variable construction

The panel is unbalanced, and the longest series runs from 1990–97. Christoffersen and Doyle obtained annual real GDP data, population, and the share of exports in GDP from IMF desk officers (with their estimates for 1997), data on the transition reform index from de Melo and others (1997), and updated it using the data from EBRD transition reports, and information on the direction of trade to 1996 from the Direction of Trade Statistics of the IMF. A war dummy was kindly provided by Berg and others (1998), and is described in their paper. Following Sarel (1996), two negative 12-month inflation rates were converted into small positive numbers to allow logs to be taken.

The export market growth series for each country in the panel was constructed as follows. Three export markets were defined: the Central and Eastern European countries; the Baltics, Russia, and other countries of the former Soviet Union; and the rest of the world. The growth of each as an export market was represented by the growth of its GDP. These growth rates were weighted according to the share of each in the exports of goods for each country in the panel. That share was taken from the earliest annual direction of trade statistics data available for each country in the sample from 1990 onwards.[27] The resulting export market growth series were then multiplied by the average ratio of exports to GDP for each country in the panel to control for openness.

Several approaches to estimating the association between growth and disinflation were examined. Dummies were defined taking the value 1 when 12-month period end inflation fell by at least 20 percent (note, this is not percentage points) from the previous year. The exercise was repeated for inflation falling by at least 50 percent from the previous year. The former gave 84 disinflation episodes, while the latter gave 56 episodes. In a further exercise, disinflation dummies were

---

[26]Import volume growth was not used due to weak data on this for transition countries.

[27]Where data on the shares were available over several years, the weights were defined only on the basis of the share in the first year for which data were available.

defined according to the disinflation episodes identified by Fischer and others (1996).[28]

In all cases, these disinflation episodes were divided into episodes in the context of fixed exchange rates—defined as fixed, de facto fixed, or currency board arrangements—and other exchange rate regimes. The fixed exchange rate dummy is reported in Christoffersen and Doyle (1998). The definition of a pegged exchange rate is strict, and excludes a number of cases where some suggest that de facto pegs were operated.[29]

All observations for Tajikistan, Turkmenistan, and Uzbekistan were discarded, either because data on the direction of trade were unavailable or because the data seemed unreliable, even by the not very exacting standards of the rest of the data set. This left a panel of 22 CEE and BRO countries.

Methodology

The dependent variable, growth per capita, was selected in preference to GDP levels on the grounds that unrecorded activity may affect officially reported output levels more than growth rates. All regressions used 149 observations, and incorporated country fixed effects.

Sarel's (1996) approach to modeling a kinked relationship between inflation and output was adopted. Thus, two inflation terms are used: log inflation, and log inflation less a threshold. This second series is set to zero below the threshold. Ghosh and Phillips (1998) find that the log formulation of the twin inflation terms is accepted by their data, and it was adopted on that basis.

Following Sarel, the threshold in the second term was estimated using a grid search. The value of the threshold that maximizes the explanatory power (R-squared) of the overall equation determines the value of the threshold. If, after the grid search over R-squared, the second term in the regression that maximizes the explanatory power of the equation is insignificant, there is no nonlinearity apparent in the data. If, however, the second term is significant and negative, while the coefficient on log inflation is insignificant, then the threshold identifies

---

[28]In this case, when a stabilization program was reported to be implemented in the first five months of a year, one was assigned to that year. But it was assigned to the following year if the stabilization was introduced later than May. This rule was an attempt to capture possible delayed effects on disinflation on output.

[29]Fischer and others (1998) suggest that de facto pegs operated as of 1995 in Armenia, Azerbaijan, Georgia, Kazakhstan, and the Kyrgyz Republic during the sharp disinflations in that year. However, while nominal bilateral exchange rates with the U.S. dollar were relatively stable in these cases during 1995, they moved markedly in all cases except Georgia thereafter.

the point above which the output costs of inflation become apparent in the data.

The assessment of output costs associated with disinflation controls for structural and other factors affecting output. The decomposition of the disinflation dummies into pegged and other exchange rate regimes allows some insight into the association between the exchange regime and the sacrifice ratio (the percentage loss of output per each point of reduction in inflation).

The first step was to replicate the key findings of the earlier work, and, if possible, encompass it. The second step was to investigate how disinflation affected output, as described above. Robustness tests, checking how parameter estimates were effected by inflation outliers, and by the exclusion of countries one at a time from the panel are reported in Christoffersen and Doyle (1998).

Results (1): Replication and encompassing

GDP growth per capita was regressed on log inflation, the transition index, the change in the transition index, the war dummy, and country-specific fixed effects. The results are reported in Table 13 as regression 1. This replicates earlier findings associating low inflation and structural reform with growth (see "Disinflation, Output, and the Current Account Balance" in this chapter).

Then, export market growth was added to this regression, with results reported as regression 2. In this regression, inflation appears insignificant, while export market growth appears highly significant and powerful. This suggests that the earlier results concerning inflation may have been distorted by the omission of the export market growth variable.

To complete the encompassing exercise, we then added the term for log inflation less log threshold to regression 2. This is reported as regression 3.[30]

The key results are:

- Export market growth, adjusted for the share of exports in GDP, is significant at the 1 percent level, and is strongly associated with growth.
- The inflation-output threshold appears at 13 percent. The output losses associated with inflation above that level are significant at just above the 1 percent level and the term on log inflation is positive but insignificant.

---

[30]If the primary balance of general government is included in this regression, the parameter estimate is small and positive, but statistically significant. However, it was excluded on the grounds that it is misspecified and is therefore difficult to interpret economically.

Table 13. Regression Results

Regression	1	2	3

The dependent variable is the percentage growth rate of GDP per capita.
The p-values use White heteroskedasticity consistent standard errors and covariance.

	1	2	3
Independent variables			
I inflation	−0.93	−0.31	1.25
p-value	(0.077)	(0.537)	(0.100)
I inflation - I threshold			−2.00
p-value			(0.017)
ExMkGr		2.50	2.44
p-value		(0.000)	(0.000)
Transition	2.98	2.31	2.09
p-value	(0.000)	(0.000)	(0.001)
Change transition	−2.17	−1.47	−1.42
p-value	(0.000)	(0.007)	(0.008)
War	−14.1	−13.7	−14.3
p-value	(0.003)	(0.003)	(0.003)
Disinflation (>20 percent)			
p-value			
Disinflation (>50 percent)			
p-statistics			
Disinflation (Fischer)			
p-statistics			
Disinflation (>50 percent, peg)			
p-value			
Disinflation (>50 percent, other)			
p-value			
Inflation threshold			13.0
Number of inflation observations below the threshold			36
Adjusted R-squared	0.612	0.647	0.652
Standard error	6.746	6.435	6.395

Source: Christoffersen and Doyle (1998).

- The transition index is significant at the 1 percent level and is strongly associated with growth, though not as strongly as is implied in regression 1.
- The estimate on the change in the transition index is negative, is highly significant, and is large, though not as large as in regression 1.
- The war dummy is significant at 1 percent, and is large.
- The range of individual country error terms is large. For example, Georgia and Armenia have large negative errors in years of con-

4	5	6	7	8
1.74	1.24	1.26	0.84	0.87
(0.020)	(0.105)	(0.090)	(0.240)	(0.237)
−2.28	−2.04	−2.06	−1.56	−1.64
(0.006)	(0.016)	(0.013)	(0.076)	(0.047)
2.38	2.41	2.45	2.47	2.44
(0.000)	(0.000)	(0.000)	(0.000)	(0.000)
2.03	2.11	2.09	1.98	2.01
(0.001)	(0.001)	(0.001)	(0.002)	(0.002)
−1.42	−1.39	−1.19	−1.41	−1.38
(0.009)	(0.014)	(0.060)	(0.013)	(0.008)
−14.0	−14.4	−14.8	−14.9	−14.9
(0.003)	(0.002)	(0.002)	(0.002)	(0.002)
1.21				
(0.306)				
	−0.45			
	(0.729)			
		−1.76		
		(0.303)		
			−3.63	−3.70
			(0.040)	(0.037)
			0.48	
			(0.766)	
5.0	13.0	14.0	13.0	13.0
10	36	40	36	36
0.651	0.649	0.652	0.652	0.654
6.403	6.419	6.392	6.390	6.366

flict, as do Albania, Bulgaria, and Romania in 1996-97 during the financial crises in those years.

Hence, regression 3 encompasses the earlier findings in regard to the effect of inflation on output. It also suggests lower output costs from the change in the transition index and a weaker relationship between the level of the transition index and growth than is implied by the approach adopted by earlier researchers. Hence, the short-run output costs and long-run benefits of structural reform, while substantial, appear to be lower than earlier reported.

Results (2): Impact of disinflation on output

The various disinflation dummies were added in turn to regression 3.

First, the disinflation dummy for a decline of more than a fifth in the 12-month rate of inflation, along with its one-year lag, were added to regression 3. The latter was insignificant and was dropped. The regression was then rerun, and is reported as regression 4. This suggests no evidence of output loss arising from disinflation, either in the year that disinflation occurs or the following year. When the dummy was split into episodes with fixed exchange rates and other regimes, and the regressions rerun, both dummies had insignificant coefficients.

This exercise was repeated for disinflations where inflation more than halved in one year. The results are reported as regression 5. Again, the estimate is insignificant, though eliminating the slower disinflations (of between 20 percent and 50 percent) has changed the sign on the parameter to negative. The results using the Fischer and others (1996) disinflation dummy are reported as equation 6. Again, there is no significant evidence of output loss associated with these disinflations.

When we split the dummy for disinflations of more than half into pegged and other exchange rate regimes, however, significant and large output losses were found in the presence of exchange rate pegs. This result is reported as regression 7. This regression was rerun eliminating the "nonpeg" dummy. The results are reported as regression 8.

As a final exercise, the dummies for disinflations of more than one-half were decomposed by the inflation rate being stabilized. Thus, the disinflation dummies were decomposed by prior year inflation: the first dummy included all disinflations of prior year inflation of more than 10 percent, the second included all disinflations of prior year inflation of more than 25 percent, and dummies for prior year inflation of more than 50 percent, more than 100 percent, and more than 500 percent were also formed. Regression 8 was rerun with each of these dummies included one at a time, with each dummy decomposed into pegged and other exchange rate regimes. In all cases, the nonpegged dummy was insignificant and was eliminated. The results from all the regressions indicated that as the prior year inflation cutoff increases, the negative output effects associated with pegged exchange rates decline sharply, becoming insignificant for stabilizations of inflation above 500 percent. This implies that the output losses during disinflations with pegged exchange rates tended to occur most with disinflations of more moderate inflation.

On this evidence, rapid stabilization in the presence of pegs has been associated with a large loss of output that is not accounted for by other regressors, except where high inflation was stabilized. Equally rapid stabilization of similar inflation rates under other monetary regimes has not been associated with a similar loss of output.

Discussion and Assessment

Export-market growth

The association of export-market growth weighted with output is marked and robust. Given the dominant role of Russia as an export market for many of the BRO countries, these findings reflect the importance of developments there for many countries in transition. Earlier studies failed to reflect this feature of transition, and as a result, misspecified the relationship between inflation and output. This omission also causes the short-run output costs of structural reform and its long-run benefits to be overstated.

Structural reform

Notwithstanding the importance of external developments, there is evidence of a strong positive association between progress in transition and output growth, though structural reform is associated with immediate output losses.

Inflation

Evidence is found of loss of output at inflation rates above the threshold that is estimated in the low teens for the full sample, but at somewhat higher rates when the inflation outliers are excluded. As reported in Table 13, one-fourth of the inflation observations occur below the estimated threshold. Accordingly, the estimate is not simply the artifact of a small number of low-inflation observations. However, the procedure does not define the confidence intervals around the identified threshold, and this counsels against overemphasis on the particular number identified as the threshold.

For the full panel, the output losses associated with inflation above the threshold are lower than has been found in other studies of transition as well as for market economies. For the latter, Sarel (1996) finds that doubling inflation, above the threshold, reduces GDP growth by 1.7 percentage points; and Ghosh and Phillips (1998) find it reduces growth by 0.5 percentage points. In contrast, these results for the full panel imply that doubling inflation above the threshold is associated with reduced growth of 0.2 percentage points. While inflation outliers and measurement problems with stockbuilding may be downwardly biasing this estimate, it is not economically negligible. Recall that Russia halved inflation seven times, and Armenia nine times between the peak and end-1997 inflation rates. Disinflation on this scale is associated with a boost to annual GDP growth rates of 1.4 percentage points and 1.8 percentage points, respectively, according to this estimate.

These findings—on the output costs of inflation above the inflation-output threshold and on the level of the threshold—should be interpreted with considerable care, however. First, correlation is not causation. While there are output costs of inflation, output can also affect inflation through the output gap and political economy factors. Second, even if the correlation does reflect causation from inflation to output, these estimates could understate the output costs of inflation now. These estimates reflect the average behavior of transition economies since 1990, and the output costs of inflation may have been rising over time. Planning mechanisms, still in place early in the panel, made poor use of information on relative prices. This suggests that when inflation obscured this information, the associated output losses were relatively low. Any losses that occurred may also have been offset if inflation eased growth-boosting relative price changes in the presence of downward nominal rigidities. But with planning mechanisms now absent and the largest of the one-off relative price changes completed, the output cost of inflation may be higher than it was on average in the period covered by the panel. For these reasons, as transition takes root, these economies could be expected to behave more like other market economies, including exhibiting greater output costs from inflation and having lower thresholds above which output costs of inflation begin to appear.

Disinflation

No systematic evidence that disinflation was associated with declines in output was found. The low inertia of inflation and the determination of the country authorities to stabilize extremely high inflation contributed to making the stabilizations highly credible, when undertaken. Even disinflations of moderate inflation do not generally appear to have incurred output costs, possibly because labor productivity and real wages are often rising rapidly, providing an ideal context for further stabilization (Deppler, 1998). There is no general evidence here to suggest that the output costs of further disinflation now would outweigh the case for further reductions in inflation.

The only evidence found of output costs from disinflation arose when moderate inflation was more than halved in the presence of pegged exchange rates. Interpreting this result is not straightforward. Output losses would occur during disinflation from moderate inflation with overdepreciated pegs. In such circumstances, stabilization would normally be expected to fail (and hence would not be picked up by the disinflation dummies) because the domestic price level would rise to eliminate the undervaluation. Only if policy directly counteracted this response, by inducing a recession, would pegs be associated both with disinflation and with output losses. This combination of outcomes seems less likely for stabilizations of high inflation with pegged exchange rates. In these cases, inflation could still fall sharply (by more than one-half), while remaining sufficiently above partner country levels to correct the undervaluation in the peg, without the need for a fall in output to render disinflation consistent with this.

On this interpretation, output losses are not due to pegs per se, but reflect the rate of inflation being stabilized, the rate at which pegs are set, and the supporting policies. Perhaps significant output losses are found because a number of stabilizations with formally pegged exchange rates were undervalued. However, it proved impossible to test this interpretation of the results directly for lack of a tractable data set on the extent of undervaluation of exchange rates.

War

There is evidence that the simple dummy for war is insufficient. Restricting conflicts to have the same impact on output is a strong assumption, and it is not even always clear when conflicts are affecting activity. For example, on the one hand, Bulgaria suffered heavily from the blockade of the former Yugoslav Republic of Macedonia during that country's conflict, without itself being drawn into the conflict.[31] On the other hand, Albania may have accrued substantial rents by violating that blockade. The individual country error terms and the robustness tests suggest that the data reject the assumptions underlying the war dummy, even though they find that overall, war is highly costly. While the war dummy may be less innocent than it appears, the robustness tests suggest that its problems do not appear to be distorting the estimates of other parameters greatly.

---

[31]We are indebted to Luc Everaert for pointing this case out to us.

Appendix II: Financial Stability

Summary

Staff studies indicate that financial soundness is improving in most transition countries, though in only a few cases is the situation now comfortable. A staff study of overall Baltics, Russia, and other countries of the former Soviet Union country rankings for bank supervision places Belarus, Tajikistan, and Ukraine in the countries that have made least progress. These countries have also made least progress on bank restructuring, along with Turkmenistan and Uzbekistan. The report places all other countries into "moderate progress" and "substantial progress" groups. In the Central and Eastern European countries, the financial systems are generally most robust in moderate inflation countries, and weakest in countries with high or low inflation. This could be coincidental—moderate inflaters, such as the Czech Republic, Hungary, and Poland, have implemented more vigorous banking reforms.

Despite this progress, the soundness of the banking system remains a cause for concern for the medium-term inflation outlook. Most transition countries occupy the broad middle ground between achieving international standards of financial soundness and outright financial collapse. Further progress is needed. Moreover, assessments of financial fragility based on summary statistics are inevitably subject to major qualifications. Summary statistics, including risk-weighted capital and nonperforming credits, can mislead when accounting practices, supervision, and legislation are lacking; it is difficult to assess interest, exchange rate, or market risks at an aggregate level, though these risks may be particularly high in a transition environment where many financial institutions may be unfamiliar with them.

The Baltics, Russia, and Other Countries of the Former Soviet Union

A study prepared by IMF staff for the group of central banks providing technical assistance to transition countries concludes that since commencing transition, all the Baltics, Russia, and other countries of the former Soviet Union, except Tajikistan, have developed at least "adequate" prudential regulations, though some countries, such as Estonia, surpass this minimal standard. However, in important areas, including corrective action and market exit, implementation is still generally lacking.

There has been good progress in building bank supervisory capacity in Armenia, the Baltics, Kazakhstan, the Kyrgyz Republic, Moldova, and Russia, including the increase in numbers of supervisory staff in all Baltics, Russia, and other countries of the former Soviet Union, except Belarus. The key remaining supervisory weakness identified is the absence of clear accounting rules—on consolidation of balance sheets, rules for loan classification, loan-loss provisioning, and income recognition—the consequences of which include compromised off-site supervision.[32]

Bank restructuring, however, remains urgent. Of the Baltics, Russia, and other countries of the former Soviet Union with international accounting standards, the median ratio of nonperforming loans to total loans is estimated at 18 percent, and the largest share of bad debts is concentrated in large—often former state-owned—banks that dominate their banking systems. Many new private banks are also in difficulty due to poor management. Nonetheless, progress has been made. While the number of banks remained broadly unchanged in the Kyrgyz Republic, Latvia, Lithuania, Moldova, Turkmenistan, and Ukraine, 13 percent of banks in the Baltics, Russia, and other countries of the former Soviet Union were closed during 1996; the number increased only in Tajikistan. Formal restructuring strategies have been developed in Azerbaijan, Georgia, Kazakhstan, the Kyrgyz Republic, and Moldova. Others, including Armenia, Tajikistan, and Russia, are proceeding on a more ad hoc basis. Russia is focusing on strengthening its capacity to monitor its largest banks, which, unusually, are mostly new commercial banks.

Central and Eastern European Countries

The Macedonian and Slovenian authorities are alone in initiating efforts to address financial fragility as part of their disinflation programs, though the problems in the former case were also particularly severe. The Macedonian authorities recapitalized Stopanska Banka, which accounted for a little under half of deposits in the banking system; they assumed all Paris and London Club debt; and they assumed all households' foreign currency deposits. But M2 was only just over 10 percent of GDP, which limited the threat to disinflation posed by

---

[32]Other deficiencies noted include the following: seven countries had not introduced internationally acceptable accounting standards for commercial banks by 1997; Belarus, Moldova, and Russia had not yet introduced consolidated supervision; there were no limits on equity participation of banks in Moldova, Tajikistan, and Turkmenistan; and licensing procedures needed close surveillance, especially in Belarus and Tajikistan.

financial fragility. Following disinflation, Stopanska Banka continues to absorb public resources, but its bad debts, like those elsewhere in the banking system, are fully provisioned. Financial sector policy is now focused on stimulating growth and competition, and strengthening the financial sector. In Slovenia, bank rehabilitation dates from late 1991, in respect of the three most troubled banks, which held 65 percent of banking sector assets, but the procedure was not completed until 1997. Upgrading financial sector legislation has been similarly protracted, with the focus now on meeting EU norms. Banks report capital of over 20 percent of risk-weighted assets, with bad debts well below 10 percent of credit, but the authorities consider these data to be somewhat over optimistic.

In the Central and Eastern European countries, major restructuring of the banking systems in Hungary and Poland during the mid-1990s led to sharp reductions in the share of nonperforming loans in bank portfolios to 14 percent in Poland, and 11½ percent in Hungary at the end of 1996. In Poland, some progress has been made to privatize the banking system, while in Hungary, this progress has been even more marked. Hungary maintains capital and reserves well over double the Basle minimum risk-weighted capital adequacy guideline and nearly double the minimum guideline of 12 percent for developing countries.

While nonperforming loans in the Czech and Slovak Republics have also declined relative to credit, they remained at just below 30 percent in 1997, and at about one-third in the largest banks that dominate both financial systems. In the Czech Republic, this reflects both the slow growth of overall credit and the deliberately limited adoption of bad debts by the state. As a result, bank capital is only marginally above the Basle minimum guideline and is below the guideline for developing countries, and bank profitability is low and falling. In Slovakia, the three largest banks have capital of below 5 percent of risk-weighted assets, though smaller banks are usually well above the 8 percent minimum. Efforts to strengthen the regulatory framework and to privatize the main banks have recently been accelerated in the Czech Republic.

Several regional banks in Croatia suffered badly during the hostilities, and restructuring did not start in earnest until late 1995, well after disinflation. Several banks have been recapitalized, and the restructuring of the major troubled bank, Privredna Banka, which held about 20 percent of deposits in 1996, has thus far included recapitalization and bad debt write-offs. As a result, banks report capital in 1996 of just below 20 percent of risk-weighted assets, but there are considerable doubts about the accounting practices underlying these data. Efforts to strengthen banking supervision and accounting regulations continue.

In the three cases where disinflation has been reversed—Albania, Bulgaria after the first stabilization, and Romania—financial fragility has been severe. In Romania, while the banking legislative infrastructure is generally appropriate and most banks report capital in excess of the Basle minimum guideline, implementation and enforcement have been weak. By the end of 1995, nonperforming loans had risen to 35 percent of credit, underprovisioning was substantial, and pyramid schemes have flourished and (inevitably) collapsed. Two bank failures in 1996 highlighted these weaknesses and led to a relaxation of monetary policy.

In Bulgaria, a pervasive "soft-budget" constraint culture culminated in banking crisis in 1996, and in hyperinflation in early 1997. Poor lending throughout the 1990s led to negative net worth of the banking system estimated by the IMF at 10 percent of GDP in 1995, with 75 percent of loans nonperforming at that time. Attempts to avert a loss of confidence in banks from late 1995, including management changes, a new deposit insurance scheme, and bank closures, failed. Widespread runs on banks ensued, and subsequent bank closures accounted for just below 30 percent of bank deposits. However, only relatively healthy banks have survived, so the system is now considerably stronger. In Albania, 27 percent of loans made in the 18 months to the end of 1994 (posttransition) were nonperforming, in addition to the much larger nonperforming portfolio that commercial banks inherited. Initiatives to privatize the state-owned banks have made little headway in practice, and, in this environment, an informal market, including pyramid schemes, flourished. The latter collapsed spectacularly from the end of 1996 amid riots, causing a sharp depreciation in the currency. By September 1997, 39 percent of loans by state-owned banks were nonperforming.

Bibliography

Amsden, Alice H., Jacek Kochanowicz, and Lance Taylor, 1994, *The Market Meets Its Match: Restructuring the Economies of Eastern Europe* (Cambridge, Massachusetts: Harvard University Press).

Anderson, Jonathan, and Daniel A. Citrin, 1995, "The Behavior of Inflation and Velocity," in *Policy Experiences and Issues in the Baltics, Russia, and Other Countries of the Former Soviet Union*, edited by Daniel A. Citrin and Ashok K. Lahiri, IMF Occasional Paper No. 133 (Washington: International Monetary Fund).

Åslund, Anders, Peter Boone, and Simon Johnson, 1996, "How to Stabilize: Lessons from Post-Communist Countries," *Brookings Papers on Economic Activity*, No. 1, pp. 217–313.

Ball, Lawrence, and N. Gregory Mankiw, 1994, "Asymmetric Price Adjustment and Economic Fluctuations," *The Economic Journal*, Vol. 104, pp. 247–61.

Begg, David, 1998, "Disinflation in Central and Eastern Europe: The Experience to Date," in *Moderate Inflation: The Experience of Transition Economies*, edited by Carlo Cottarelli and György Szapáry (Washington: International Monetary Fund and National Bank of Hungary).

———, L. Hesselman, and R. Smith, 1996, "Money in Transition: How Much Do We Know?" (photocopy; International Monetary Fund).

Berg, Andrew, Eduardo Borensztein, Ratna Sahay, and Jeromin Zettlemeyer, 1998, "The Evolution of Output in Transition Economies: Explaining the Differences," IMF Working Paper 99/73 (Washington: International Monetary Fund).

Blanchard, Olivier, 1998, "The Optimal Speed of Disinflation: The Case of Hungary," in *Moderate Inflation: The Experience of Transition Economies*, edited by Carlo Cottarelli and György Szapáry (Washington: International Monetary Fund and National Bank of Hungary).

Bruno, Michael, 1992, "Stabilization and Reform in Eastern Europe—A Preliminary Evaluation," *Staff Papers*, International Monetary Fund, Vol. 39 (December), pp. 741–77.

———, 1996, *Deep Crises and Reform: What Have We Learned?* (Washington: World Bank).

———, and William Easterly, 1995, "Inflation Crises and Long-Run Growth," NBER Working Paper 5209 (Cambridge, Massachusetts: National Bureau of Economic Research).

Budina, Nina, and Sweder van Wijnbergen, 1997, "Fiscal Policies in Eastern Europe," *Oxford Review of Economic Policy*, Vol. 13, No. 2, pp. 47–64.

Buiter, Willem H., 1997, "Aspects of Fiscal Performance in Some Transition Economies Under Fund-Supported Programs," IMF Working Paper 97/31 (Washington: International Monetary Fund).

Bulir, Ales, 1998, "Income Inequality: Does Inflation Matter?" IMF Working Paper 98/7 (Washington: International Monetary Fund).

Burton, David, and Stanley Fischer, 1998, "Ending Moderate Inflations," in *Moderate Inflation: The Experience of Transition Economies*, edited by Carlo Cottarelli and György Szapáry (Washington: International Monetary Fund and National Bank of Hungary).

Calvo, Guillermo A., and Fabrizio Coricelli, 1992, "Stabilizing a Previously Centrally Planned Economy: Poland 1990," *Economic Policy: A European Forum*, No. 14, pp. 175–208 and 213–26.

Cangiano, Marco, Carlo Cottarelli, and Luis Cubeddu, 1998, *Pension*

Developments and Reform in Transition Economies, paper presented at the conference on Social Security Reforms: International Comparisons, held in Rome, March 16–17, 1998.

Christoffersen, Peter, and Peter Doyle, 1998, "From Inflation to Growth: Eight Years of Transition," IMF Working Paper 98/99 (Washington: International Monetary Fund).

Coorey, Sharmini, Mauro Mecagni, and Erik Offerdal, 1998, "Disinflation in Transition Economies: The Role of Relative Price Adjustment," in *Moderate Inflation: The Experience of Transition Economies,* edited by Carlo Cottarelli and György Szapáry (Washington: International Monetary Fund and National Bank of Hungary).

Cottarelli, Carlo, and Curzio Giannini, 1997, *Credibility Without Rules? Monetary Frameworks in the Post-Bretton Woods Era,* IMF Occasional Paper No. 154 (Washington: International Monetary Fund).

Cottarelli, Carlo, Mark Griffiths, and Reza Moghadam, 1998, "The Nonmonetary Determinants of Inflation," IMF Working Paper 98/23 (Washington: International Monetary Fund).

Cottarelli, Carlo, and György Szapáry, eds., 1998, *Moderate Inflation: The Experience of Transition Economies* (Washington: International Monetary Fund and National Bank of Hungary).

Cukierman, Alex, 1992, *Central Bank Strategy, Credibility, and Independence: Theory and Evidence* (Cambridge, Massachusetts: MIT Press).

———, Geoffrey P. Miller, and Bilin Neyapti, 1998, *Central Bank Reform, Liberalization and Inflation in Transition Economies—An International Perspective* (mimeo; Tel Aviv University, Israel).

De Broeck, Mark, Kornélia Krajnyák, and Henri Lorie, 1997, "Explaining and Forecasting the Velocity of Money in Transition Economies, with Special Reference to the Baltics, Russia, and Other Countries of the Former Soviet Union," IMF Working Paper 97/108 (Washington: International Monetary Fund).

de Melo, Martha, Cevdet Denizer, and Alan Gelb, 1997, "From Plan to Market: Patterns of Transition," in *Macroeconomic Stabilization in Transition Economies,* edited by Mario J. Blejer and Marko Škreb (Cambridge, United Kingdom: Cambridge University Press).

Deppler, Michael, 1998, "Is Reducing Moderate Inflation Costly?" in *Moderate Inflation: The Experience of Transition Economies,* edited by Carlo Cottarelli and György Szapáry (Washington: International Monetary Fund and National Bank of Hungary).

Dornbusch, Rudiger, 1976, "Expectations and Exchange Rate Dynamics," *Journal of Political Economy,* Vol. 84, pp. 1161–76.

European Bank for Reconstruction and Development, 1997, *Transition Report* (London: EBRD).

Fedorov, Boris, 1995, "Macroeconomic Policy and Stabilization in Russia," in *Russian Economic Reform at Risk*, edited by Anders Åslund (New York: Pinter).

Fischer, Stanley, Ratna Sahay, and Carlos A. Végh, 1996, "Stabilization and Growth in Transition Economies: The Early Experience," *Journal of Economic Perspectives*, Vol. 10, No. 2, pp. 45–66.

———, 1998, "From Transition to Market: Evidence and Growth Prospects," IMF Working Paper 98/52 (Washington: International Monetary Fund).

Ghosh, Atish, R., 1997, "Inflation in Transition Economies: How Much? And Why?" IMF Working Paper 97/80 (Washington: International Monetary Fund).

———, and Steven Phillips, 1998, "Inflation, Disinflation, and Growth," IMF Working Paper 98/68 (Washington: International Monetary Fund).

Gomulka, Stanislaw, 1998, "A Comment on David Begg," in *Moderate Inflation: The Experience of Transition Economies*, edited by Carlo Cottarelli and György Szapáry (Washington: International Monetary Fund and National Bank of Hungary).

Hansson, Ardo, H., 1997, "Macroeconomic Stabilization in the Baltic States," in *Macroeconomic Stabilization in Transition Economies*, edited by Mario J. Blejer and Marko Škreb (Cambridge, United Kingdom: Cambridge University Press).

Hendry, David, 1995, *Dynamic Econometrics* (New York: Oxford University Press).

Hernandez-Catá, Ernesto, 1999, "Price Liberalization, Money Growth, and Inflation During the Transition to a Market Economy," IMF Working Paper 99/76 (Washington: International Monetary Fund).

International Monetary Fund, 1997, *World Economic Outlook*, Chapter V (Washington), pp. 98–118.

———, 1998, *Status of Market-Based Central Banking Reforms in the Baltics, Russia, and Other Countries of the Former Soviet Union*, report prepared for the Eleventh Coordination Meeting of Cooperating Central Banks and International Institutions (Washington: International Monetary Fund).

Knight, Malcolm, 1997, *Central Bank Reforms in the Baltics, Russia, and the Other Countries of the Former Soviet Union*, IMF Occasional Paper No. 157 (Washington: International Monetary Fund).

Koen, Vincent, and Paula R. de Masi, 1997, "Prices in the Transition: Ten Stylized Facts," in *Staff Studies for the World Economic Outlook* (Washington: International Monetary Fund).

Kornai, János, 1998, "Comments on the Appropriate Speed of Disinflation," in *Moderate Inflation: The Experience of Transition Economies*, edited by Carlo Cottarelli and György Szapáry (Washington: International Monetary Fund and National Bank of Hungary).

Krajnyák, Kornélia, and Christoph Klingen, 1998, *Price Adjustment and Inflation in the Baltics, 1993–96* (photocopy; International Monetary Fund).

Lougani, Prakash, and Nathan Sheets, 1997, "Central Bank Independence, Inflation, and Growth in Transition Economies," *Journal of Money, Credit, and Banking*, Vol. 29, No. 3 (August), pp. 381–99.

Mackenzie, George A., and Peter Stella, 1996, *Quasi-Fiscal Operations and Public Financial Institutions*, IMF Occasional Paper No. 142 (Washington: International Monetary Fund).

Masson, Paul, Miguel A. Savastano, and Sunil Sharma, 1997, "The Scope for Inflation Targeting in Developing Countries," IMF Working Paper 97/130 (Washington: International Monetary Fund).

Medgyessy, Peter, 1998, "Introductory Remarks," in *Moderate Inflation: The Experience of Transition Economies*, edited by Carlo Cottarelli and György Szapáry (Washington: International Monetary Fund and National Bank of Hungary).

Morsink, James H.J., 1995, "Wage Controls during IMF Arrangements in Central Europe," in *IMF Conditionality: Experience Under Stand-By and Extended Arrangements*, by Susan Schadler and others, IMF Occasional Paper No. 129 (Washington: International Monetary Fund).

Nuxoll, Daniel, 1996, *The Convergence of Price Structures and Economic Growth*, paper presented at the NBER Conference on Research in Income and Wealth, Arlington, Virginia, March 15–16.

Portes, Richard, editor, 1993, *Economic Transformation in Central Europe: A Progress Report* (London: Centre for Economic Policy Research).

Pujol, Thierry, and Mark Griffiths, 1998, "Moderate Inflation in Poland: A Real Story," in *Moderate Inflation: The Experience of Transition Economies*, edited by Carlo Cottarelli and György Szapáry (Washington: International Monetary Fund and National Bank of Hungary).

Radzyner, Olga, and Sandra Riesinger, 1997, "Central Bank Independence in Transition: Legislation and Reality in Central and Eastern Europe," *Focus on Transition*, Vol. 2, No. 2, pp. 57–90.

Richards, Anthony, and Gunnar Tersman, 1995, "Growth, Nontradeables, and Price Convergence in the Baltics," IMF Working Paper 95/45 (Washington: International Monetary Fund).

Rosenberg, Christoph, B., and Tapio O. Saavalainen, 1998, "How to Deal with Azerbaijan's Oil Boom? Policy Strategies in a Resource-Rich Transition Economy," IMF Working Paper 98/6 (Washington: International Monetary Fund).

Ross, Kevin, 1998, "Post Stabilization Inflation Dynamics in Slovenia," IMF Working Paper 98/27 (Washington: International Monetary Fund).

Sarel, Michael, 1996, "Nonlinear Effects of Inflation on Economic Growth," *Staff Papers*, International Monetary Fund, Vol. 43 (March), pp. 199–215.

Sargent, Thomas J., and Neil Wallace, 1981, "Some Unpleasant Monetary Arithmetic," *Federal Reserve Bank of Minneapolis Quarterly Review* (Fall), pp. 1–17.

Selgin, George, 1994, "On Ensuring the Acceptability of a New Fiat Money," *Journal of Money, Credit, and Banking*, Vol. 26 (November), pp. 808–26.

Škreb, Marko, 1998, "A Note on Inflation," in *Moderate Inflation: The Experience of Transition Economies*, edited by Carlo Cottarelli and György Szapáry (Washington: International Monetary Fund and National Bank of Hungary).

Surányi, György, and János Vincze, 1998, "Inflation in Hungary (1990–97)," in *Moderate Inflation: The Experience of Transition Economies*, edited by Carlo Cottarelli and György Szapáry (Washington: International Monetary Fund and National Bank of Hungary).

Szapáry, György, 1998, "Disinflation Policies: Issues of Sequencing," in *Moderate Inflation: The Experience of Transition Economies*, edited by Carlo Cottarelli and György Szapáry (Washington: International Monetary Fund and National Bank of Hungary).

Van Elkan, Rachel, 1998, "How Stable Is Money Demand?" in *Hungary: Economic Policies for Sustainable Growth*, by Carlo Cottarelli and others, IMF Occasional Paper No. 159 (Washington: International Monetary Fund).

Woźniak, Przemystaw, 1998, "Relative Price Adjustment in Poland, Hungary and the Czech Republic. Comparison of the Size and Impact on Inflation," CASE-CEV, Working Paper Series, Budapest.

Zavoico, Basil, 1995, *A Brief Note on the Inflationary Process in Transition Economies* (photocopy; International Monetary Fund).

Zettermeyer, Jeromin, and Daniel A. Citrin, 1995, "Stabilization: Fixed Versus Flexible Exchange Rates," in *Policy Experiences and Issues in the Baltics, Russia, and Other Countries of the Former Soviet Union*, edited by Daniel A. Citrin and Ashok K. Lahiri, IMF Occasional Paper No. 133 (Washington: International Monetary Fund).

Growth in Transition Countries, 1990–98: The Main Lessons

4

Oleh Havrylyshyn and Thomas Wolf

Transition is a complex process involving changes in the political, economic, institutional, legal, and social domains. The focus of this chapter is on the record of economic recovery and growth and its relation to progress in transition. The study covers 25 countries in Central and Eastern Europe (CEE), the Baltics, and the Commonwealth of Independent States (CIS). Although, as of this writing, complete data are available only through 1997, and the bulk of the study was prepared in mid-1998, one cannot ignore the dramatic reality of the financial crisis in Russia in August 1998. That crisis resulted in a reversal of growth and had spillover effects on neighboring countries. Thus the discussion of growth performance includes preliminary estimates for 1998, and the conclusions reflect different interpretations of the Russian crisis and how it informs the lessons drawn by the study on the determinants of recovery in transition.

This chapter first summarizes the emerging consensus on the conceptual meaning of transition and, in particular, how recovery and growth are expected to come about as the transition proceeds. It then reviews the record of decline and recovery in these 25 non-Asian transition countries. The chapter then goes on to explore the possible explanations for the variations in growth performance among countries. The results of the empirical analysis do not provide any great surprises, but rather give an updated confirmation of findings from earlier as well as contemporaneous studies, namely, that controlling inflation is essential and that substantial structural reform is the key policy factor driving growth. The analysis also contributes several new perspectives on growth in transition. First, it provides more of a theoretical rationale for econometric specification than have other studies on growth in transition countries. Second, it shows the importance of distinguishing among three groups of countries: CEE, the Baltics, and the CIS. Third, it distinguishes the period of decline in output (about 1991–93) from the period of recovery (about 1994–98). Fourth, it demonstrates that privatization, despite the many shortcomings in its implementation, is clearly a positive factor in growth performance. Fifth, it shows that initial conditions may matter, but they matter much less than other factors. Sixth, it demonstrates that government size (perhaps by serving as a proxy for intervention) is very important. Finally, the study confirms that there is something to the view that early reforms cause pain, but it also shows that delaying reforms comes at the cost of delayed and slower recovery.

Theoretical Concepts of Growth and Transition

This section summarizes the emerging consensus on what, conceptually, transition means and, in particular, how recovery and growth are expected to come about as the transition proceeds. A comparison with traditional growth analysis for market economies highlights the common points and those unique to the transition.

New Growth Theory and Empirical Evidence

In the mid-1980s a revival of interest in the long-term determinants of economic growth led to the development of a new wave of models, which established a synthesis now known as *endogenous growth theory*. This theory has produced a large volume of empirical studies of growth. The first element in this synthesis is the earlier prevailing doctrine on economic growth, namely, the neoclassical model of Solow and Swan and of Cass and Koopmans, developed in the 1950s and 1960s, which attributed growth to the expansion of capital and labor, augmented by exogenous technological progress. Simple factor input and factor productivity calculations of the sources of growth are based on this paradigm and continue to be used widely.

The second element is the set of models developed in the mid-1980s and synthesized first in Romer (1990), then in Barro and Sala-i-Martin (1994). Although they retained the role of factor inputs, these models added an explanation of technical progress based on increasing returns, research and development, imperfect competition, human capital, and—an important addition—government policies. Examination of the role of policies was initially focused on narrow economic measures such as macroeconomic stability, openness of the economy, and the degree of distortion in key price signals.

A third element has been added from what might be called political economy growth models. Olson (1997), in particular, summarizes well the conceptual basis for the role of broader policy variables such as property rights, the rule of law, institutions, and corruption. Olson argued that both of the preceding theories incorrectly assume that countries (and policymakers) make the most efficient use of resource inputs and available technology; instead, he posited that many countries are poor simply because they waste a lot of resources. On the basis of earlier work on the political economy of interest groups, he added that the waste was greatest where the institutional basis of property rights and the rule of law is least well developed or observed; an association with a high degree of corruption readily follows from this.

A synthesis of these three elements characterizes growth theory today. In the long run, initial conditions and the expansion of factor inputs still play a role, but the magnitude of such expansion, the efficiency with which factors are employed, and the long-term technological improvements that also increase efficiency depend very much on policy. Good policy includes effective legal support of property rights. The past decade has seen numerous empirical studies based on this model seeking to explain the observed wide differences in growth patterns across countries. These studies have included as determinants various factor inputs (investment, human capital), government policies (monetary and fiscal policy distortions), and institutional indicators of the security of property rights (tax burden and tax fairness, extent of corruption, transparency, political stability, and others).

Some general conclusions can be drawn from this literature.[1] First, initial conditions are important in explaining cross-country differences in growth. In particular, most studies have found that growth per capita is inversely related to the initial level of output and that, once other factors are accounted for, poor countries tend to grow faster than rich ones. Further, greater availability of resources does not necessarily ensure growth, and unfavorable geographic circumstances (tropical climate, a landlocked position) can hinder it.

Second, there is a solid consensus that good economic policy (maintenance of macroeconomic stability and nondistortionary interventions) has a strongly positive effect on growth. Thus, reducing inflation not only to levels of 30 to 40 percent but probably even lower seems to be a necessary condition for achieving sustained growth.[2] Removing market distortions through price liberalization, more open trade, lower and more uniform taxes, and privatization also contribute to growth.

Third, the underlying legal, political, and institutional basis also matters a great deal. Most recent empirical studies make some attempt to capture these considerations and usually find that growth is higher in

---

[1]All of these results, however plausible, need to be interpreted with caution given the measurement and methodological problems involved, not least because many of the variables used are likely to be highly correlated. The pitfalls are well described in a paper by Sala-i-Martin (1997).

[2]Bruno and Easterly (1998) suggest the higher range; others, such as Fischer (1993), Sarel (1996), the *ESAF Review* (IMF, 1997), and Cottarelli and Doyle (in this volume) find the threshold to be much lower.

countries with better institutional quality, political stability, government credibility, and similar indicators of a market-friendly environment.

Application to Transition Economies

A decade ago it was popular to say that there is no theory to guide the practical process of transition; all we have are theories of capitalism and socialism. This may still be true in the sense that a new consensus paradigm is at best only beginning to emerge from the vast literature on transition. But it is not at all clear how much a unified, cohesive theory is needed. To the extent it is useful to have a compact rather than a complex analytical framework, it is not that difficult to cobble together from a few of the key writings a workable "model" of transition or transformation.

Kornai (1994), in describing the special circumstances of the "transformational" recession compared with a typical recession in a market economy, highlights two key changes that are needed. The first is to force a move from a sellers' to a buyers' market (through price liberalization), and the second is to enforce a hard budget constraint (through privatization and the elimination of various government support mechanisms). These provide the two principal incentives for profit-maximizing market behavior by all economic agents. Blanchard (1997) defines the core process of change as comprising two elements: reallocation of resources from old activities to new ones (through closures and bankruptcies, combined with the establishment of new enterprises), and restructuring within surviving firms (through labor rationalization, changes in product lines, and new investment). These can be thought of as the dynamic movements resulting from the establishment of the new incentives and are reminiscent of the Schumpeterian concept of "creative destruction" by entrepreneurial activity, only with a much greater impact than what Schumpeter's model envisioned.

The policy actions needed to put Kornai's new incentives structure in place—which also promote Blanchard's Schumpeterian changes in economic activity—are outlined in many works (including those by Kornai and Blanchard themselves) and are well exemplified in an early study by Fischer and Gelb (1991). The key measures of reform are macroeconomic stabilization and price and market liberalization; liberalization of the foreign exchange and trade systems; privatization; establishment of a competitive environment with few obstacles to market entry and exit; and redefining the role of the state as the provider of macrostability, a stable legal framework, and enforceable property rights, and occasionally as a corrector of market imperfections, for example, in providing income security for those with low incomes.

From these core concepts there follow some implications for growth, which differentiate the transition economies from market economies. First, output will most likely decline initially in the new, buyers' market and under hard budget constraints, as unsalable goods accumulate and signal the need for cutbacks in production. Further elimination of wastage under the old scheme (perhaps through "destruction" or closure) necessarily precedes creation of the new, and this adds to the production cuts. A second implication is that growth of the new economy will not occur until the new incentives are in place and made credible. That is, the sooner reforms achieve a hard budget constraint and a liberal price environment, the sooner reallocation and the restructuring of the old and the creation of new production can begin. Third, one can infer from this that the proximate sources of growth in the early recovery period are not likely to be the conventional factor inputs that explain medium-term growth (investment and new technology). Rather it may be expected that the initial output recovery will come primarily from a variety of efficiency improvements.

The emphasis on efficiency improvements, at least in the early years of recovery, is perhaps what differentiates the empirical models of growth in transition from the conventional growth literature. The econometric studies summarized below, and our own regression analysis described in the appendix, typically exclude all factor input variables and focus instead on policy variables (inflation, privatization, liberalization) plus initial conditions. The following stylized schema of how recovery and then sustained growth may occur in the process of transition provides a plausible and consistent ex post theoretical framework for such an approach (Box 1 and Figure 1 elaborate on the framework). Five types of mechanisms conducive to increased output may be postulated, some of which may be simultaneous or overlapping: recovery of underutilized capacity; elimination of egregious waste of labor, capital, and materials (X-efficiency, in theoretical terms); efficiency gains from a more appropriate combination of capital and labor (factor efficiency); efficiency gains from reallocation of resources toward goods in which the country has comparative advantage or for which there is unsatisfied consumer demand; and output expansion through new net investment and employment growth.[3]

---

[3]It is an oversimplification to say that all of the first four efficiency improvements can come about without new *net* investment; what is meant here is that often the investment required is small. Also, such efficiency improvements can take place at the sector or the firm level, even if aggregate net investment in the economy is zero, as new gross investment is directed not to replacing depreciated stocks in "old" industries but to expanding it in the "new" ones.

**Box 1. Efficiency Improvements, Reallocation, and Investment
as Proximate Sources of Growth in the Transition:
A Conceptual Framework**

The proximate sources of growth in the recovery phase of transition
are illustrated in Figure 1. In panel A, CP^* represents the point of potential production of goods A and B on the production possibilities frontier
under central planning where full capacity is utilized, factors are not
wasted (unlike at XI_1 in panel B, at which more capital K and labor L are
being used to produce one unit of good B than at the efficiency frontier),
and shadow prices of K and L are reflected in the central plan's factor allocation. In this case, the only error under CP^* is to ignore world prices.

CPI in panel A is a point where the factor and technical inefficiencies
of central planning exist, but capacity is fully utilized; historically this is
roughly equivalent to pre-1990 production in the transition economies.
CPU reflects a decline in production levels (like that after 1990 in the
transition economies) and lower utilization of existing capacity as well
as factor and technical inefficiencies.

XI_1 in panel B is inside the efficiency frontier of the unit isoquant for
good B; K and L are used wastefully relative to the theoretical best practice point for central planning, XI_1^*.

M_1 in panel A is a point on the production possibilities frontier "inherited" from resource accumulation during the period of central planning. No *aggregate net* investment is necessary in moving to M_1, but there
could be gross new investment in the expanding sector, so that allocation among goods can change, reflecting adjustment of production (allocation) to world prices. M_2 is an efficient goods allocation point with
new net investment.

Using this figure, five types of changes (structural shifts) can be defined that provide growth in the sense of more output for a given level
of factor availability, and more factor inputs:

1. Recovery from capacity underutilization (from CPU to CPI)
2. Technical or X-efficiency gains, or movement to the efficiency frontier by eliminating wasteful usage of production factors (from CPI
   to CP^*, and from XI_1 to XI_1^*)
3. Efficiency gains from achieving optimal factor proportions (from
   XI_1^* to BCP^*, and from CPI to CP^*)
4. Resource reallocation gains (from CP^* to M_1; that is, production of
   more B and less A, hence also from BCP^* to BM_1)
5. Net factor expansion gains (from M_1 to M_2, and from BM_1 to BM_2,
   plus an analogous shift to a higher-level isoquant for good A).

These shifts are identified by the numbered arrows in panels A and B
of Figure 1.

Figure 1. Sources of Growth in the Recovery Phase of Transition

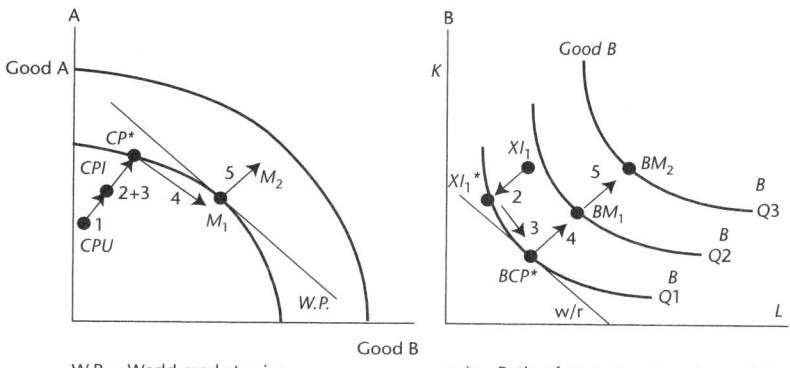

W.P. = World market price.   w/r = Ratio of wage to return to capital.

Growth Performance in Transition Economies, 1990–98

This section presents the basic facts on growth in the transition economies with an elaboration of the main patterns to be observed. The 25 CEE, Baltic, and CIS countries (Mongolia is not included in this study) have been undergoing a process of transition from a centrally planned to a market-oriented economy for the better part of a decade. Although this transition has depended in all cases on major changes in the political system, particularly during 1989–91, there have been considerable differences across countries in the speed with which the old system of planning has been dismantled and market-oriented reforms have been introduced. In a few countries, such as Hungary and Poland, a number of market-oriented reforms were well under way long before 1989, and the former Socialist Federal Republic of Yugoslavia had achieved a relatively high degree of market liberalization some time earlier. On the other hand, in some countries, such as Belarus, Turkmenistan, and Uzbekistan, comprehensive market-oriented reforms have barely begun.

The year 1989 was probably the last "normal" year for nearly the entire region under the old system. This was the year in which officially measured output peaked in the Soviet Union as well as in most other countries in the region. By 1990 significant economic reforms were under way in such key countries as Hungary and Poland; by the end of 1990 the German Democratic Republic, one of the linchpins of the former Council for Mutual Economic Assistance (CMEA), had merged with the Federal Republic of Germany.[4] In part because of these

---

[4]The CMEA consisted of Bulgaria, Cuba, Czechoslovakia, the German Democratic Republic, Hungary, Mongolia, Poland, Romania, the Soviet Union, and Vietnam.

developments, by 1990 the CMEA trading system had already been subjected to major shocks, even before its formal breakup at the beginning of 1991. Of course, partial economic reforms, formal or informal, were already under way by 1990–91 in the Soviet Union as well, before its formal dissolution in late 1991. Thus it is not a simple matter to pinpoint the exact year in which the transition began. However, for purposes of this discussion it is assumed that, for each country, the last pretransition year is the year in which it experienced the significant social and political changes that made possible the beginning of comprehensive market-oriented reform.

Although official data on output in the region are subject to many problems, available alternative estimates are not necessarily better. Estimates of the size of the unofficial economy exist, but different studies use different methodologies, and coverage is incomplete. Consensus is also lacking on the size of GDP. Therefore, despite the probable measurement error, we rely necessarily on official data, which are believed to underestimate the size of the unofficial economy.[5]

Given the highly distorted production structures and the sheer wastage of resources that characterized central planning, together with the long time lags involved in reallocating resources to more efficient uses in a new, market context,[6] it is not surprising that virtually every transition economy experienced a substantial decline in recorded output with the onset of transition. From Table 1 and Figure 2 (upper left panel), however, it is clear that the depth of the decline associated with the beginning of the transition was, in most cases, much greater in the Baltics, Russia, and other countries of the former Soviet Union (BRO) than in CEE. This difference can be attributed to differences in both initial conditions and policies.

First, the BRO countries shared a generally more highly integrated and specialized production structure prior to independence, and this, combined in most instances with greater insulation from the world market, probably meant a greater degree of initial price distortion. Many of the BRO countries were hit by a severe terms-of-trade shock with the transition, as the relative price of imported energy and raw

---

[5]The official data may include breaks in series due to revisions of GDP, and there may be reason to believe that the underestimates are less serious for growth rates than for absolute levels. There is also an offsetting bias: initial GDP was overstated under the old regime by distorted pricing and the unaccounted-for cost of queuing in a shortage economy. The elimination of queues has doubtlessly raised welfare, but this is not reflected in the new official GDP figures.
[6]The time lag in factor reallocation was particularly pronounced because labor markets were underdeveloped, labor mobility was severely impeded by housing shortages, and capital markets were similarly underdeveloped.

Table 1. GDP Growth in Transition Economies

Country	Index (1991 = 100)										Percent Change from Previous Year								
	1989	1990	1991	1992	1993	1994	1995	1996	1997	1998	1990	1991	1992	1993	1994	1995	1996	1997	1998
Central and Eastern Europe																			
Albania	154.3	138.9	100.0	92.8	101.7	111.2	121.2	132.2	122.9	132.8	-10.0	-28.0	-7.2	9.6	9.4	8.9	9.1	-7.0	8.0
Bulgaria	124.6	113.3	100.0	92.7	91.3	92.9	94.9	84.6	78.6	81.4	-9.1	-11.7	-7.3	-1.5	1.7	2.2	-10.9	-7.0	3.5
Croatia	136.4	126.7	100.0	88.3	81.2	86.0	91.9	97.4	103.7	106.5	-7.1	-21.1	-11.7	-8.0	5.9	6.8	6.0	6.5	2.7
Czech Rep.	118.1	116.6	100.0	96.7	97.3	99.9	106.3	110.3	110.7	108.1	-1.2	-14.3	-3.3	0.6	2.7	6.4	3.8	0.3	-2.3
Macedonia, FYR	126.7	113.8	100.0	92.0	83.6	82.1	81.1	81.8	83.0	85.4	-10.2	-12.1	-8.0	-9.1	-1.8	-1.2	0.8	1.5	2.9
Hungary	117.6	113.5	100.0	96.9	96.4	99.2	100.7	102.1	106.7	112.2	-3.5	-11.9	-3.1	-0.6	2.9	1.5	1.3	4.6	5.1
Poland	121.6	107.5	100.0	102.6	106.5	112.1	119.9	127.1	135.7	142.2	-11.6	-7.0	2.6	3.8	5.2	7.0	6.0	6.8	4.8
Romania	121.6	114.8	100.0	91.2	92.6	96.2	103.0	107.0	99.6	92.4	-5.6	-12.9	-8.8	1.5	3.9	7.1	3.9	-6.9	-7.3
Slovak Rep.	120.0	117.0	100.0	93.5	90.0	94.5	101.0	107.6	114.6	119.7	-2.5	-14.6	-6.5	-3.7	4.9	6.9	6.6	6.5	4.4
Slovenia	119.4	109.8	100.0	94.5	97.2	102.4	106.6	110.3	115.4	119.9	-8.1	-8.9	-5.5	2.8	5.3	4.1	3.5	4.6	3.9
Average	126.0	117.2	100.0	94.1	93.8	97.6	102.7	106.0	107.1	110.1	-7.0	-14.7	-5.9	-0.4	4.1	5.1	3.3	1.0	2.8
Baltics																			
Estonia	...	...	100.0	78.4	72.0	70.7	73.7	76.7	84.8	88.2	...	...	-21.6	-8.2	-1.8	4.3	4.0	10.6	4.0
Latvia	...	...	100.0	64.8	54.4	55.5	55.7	57.5	61.3	63.6	...	...	-35.2	-16.1	2.1	0.3	3.3	6.5	3.8
Lithuania	...	...	100.0	78.7	66.0	59.5	61.5	64.3	69.0	72.6	...	...	-21.3	-16.2	-9.8	3.3	4.7	7.3	5.1
Average			100.0	74.0	64.1	61.9	63.6	66.2	71.7	74.8			-26.0	-13.3	-3.4	2.8	4.0	4.7	8.3	4.3

Table 1 (*Concluded*)

Country	Index (1991 = 100)										Percent Change from Previous Year								
	1989	1990	1991	1992	1993	1994	1995	1996	1997	1998	1990	1991	1992	1993	1994	1995	1996	1997	1998
Commonwealth of Independent States																			
Armenia	...	...	100.0	47.7	40.6	42.8	45.8	48.4	49.9	53.5	...	...	-52.3	-14.8	5.4	6.9	5.8	3.1	7.2
Azerbaijan	...	...	100.0	77.9	59.9	49.1	43.7	44.2	46.8	51.5	...	...	-22.1	-23.1	-18.1	-11.0	1.3	5.8	10.0
Belarus	...	...	100.0	90.4	83.5	73.0	65.4	67.3	75.0	81.2	...	...	-9.6	-7.6	-12.6	-10.4	2.9	11.4	8.3
Georgia	...	...	100.0	55.2	41.2	36.5	37.4	41.3	45.8	47.2	...	...	-44.8	-25.4	-11.4	2.4	10.5	11.0	2.9
Kazakhstan	...	...	100.0	94.7	86.0	75.2	69.0	69.3	70.7	69.0	...	...	-5.3	-9.2	-12.6	-8.2	0.5	2.0	-2.5
Kyrgyz Rep.	...	...	100.0	86.1	72.8	58.1	55.0	58.9	64.7	66.0	...	...	-13.9	-15.5	-20.1	-5.4	7.1	9.9	2.0
Moldova	...	...	100.0	70.3	69.5	47.8	47.1	43.4	44.0	40.2	...	...	-29.7	-1.2	-31.2	-1.4	-7.8	1.3	-8.6
Russia	...	...	100.0	85.5	78.1	68.2	65.4	63.1	63.7	60.8	...	...	-14.5	-8.7	-12.6	-4.2	-3.4	0.9	-4.6
Tajikistan	...	...	100.0	71.0	63.2	51.2	44.8	42.9	43.6	45.9	...	...	-29.0	-11.0	-18.9	-12.5	-4.4	1.7	5.3
Turkmenistan	...	...	100.0	94.7	85.0	68.9	63.2	58.4	43.2	45.2	...	...	-5.3	-10.2	-19.0	-8.2	-7.7	-25.9	4.5
Ukraine	...	...	100.0	83.0	71.2	54.9	48.2	43.4	42.1	41.4	...	...	-17.0	-14.2	-22.9	-12.2	-10.0	-3.0	-1.7
Uzbekistan	...	...	100.0	89.0	86.9	83.3	82.5	83.8	85.8	88.7	...	...	-11.0	-2.3	-4.2	-0.9	1.6	2.4	3.3
Average	...	...	100.0	78.8	69.8	59.1	55.6	55.4	56.3	57.5	...	...	-21.2	-11.4	-15.4	-5.9	-0.4	1.6	2.2

Sources: National authorities; and IMF staff estimates.

Figure 2. Growth in 25 Transition Economies by Region and Growth Performance[1]

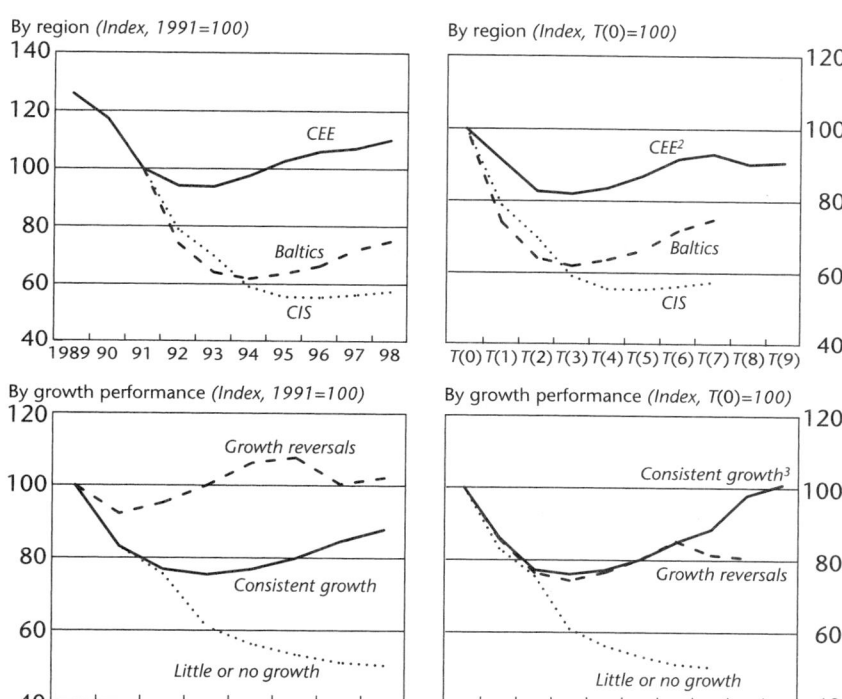

By region *(Index, 1991=100)*

By region *(Index, T(0)=100)*

By growth performance *(Index, 1991=100)*

By growth performance *(Index, T(0)=100)*

Sources: National authorities; and IMF staff estimates.

Note: T(0) is the full year immediately preceding the beginning of transition; CEE is Central and Eastern Europe; CIS is Commonwealth of Independant States.

[1]The country groupings are defined in Table 2, except that there the CEE countries are divided into two groups: central Europe and southeastern Europe. Data for the Baltics and the CIS are available only from 1991.

[2]The CEE group comprises 10 countries for the first seven years, but only 7 countries in T(8) and 6 countries in T(9).

[3]The consistent growth group comprises 16 countries for the first seven years, but only 4 countries in T(8) and T(9).

materials rose sharply when the implicit trade subsidies received from Russia were phased out and only partially and temporarily offset by financial transfers.[7] Second, the military-industrial complex

---

[7]See IMF (1994). See also Tarr (1994), who shows that the BRO countries on average were subjected to greater terms-of-trade shocks than most of the CEE countries. Koen and de Masi (1997) also provide evidence on price distortions.

was proportionately larger in many of these countries, and this led to a greater collapse in output when the transition to a more market-driven, civilian-oriented production structure got under way. Third, in the BRO countries there was a serious lack, at the outset of transition, of independent national institutions and infrastructures within which a framework for comprehensive reform and stabilization programs could be effectively implemented. Fourth, in the CIS countries at least, the inertia of 70 years of Soviet political and administrative structures may explain the early lack of political will and consensus necessary to push ahead boldly with reform and stabilization.[8] Finally, in some cases, output declines associated with the transition were exacerbated by civil conflicts, blockades, or sanctions, notably in Armenia, Azerbaijan, Georgia, and Tajikistan among the BRO countries, and in Croatia and the former Yugoslav republic (FYR) of Macedonia in CEE. This affected output directly and delayed reform. For the CEE countries as a group (in terms of the unweighted average of these countries' growth rates), positive growth had begun by 1994 (Figure 2, upper left panel). For the Baltic countries as a group, output began to recover in 1995. For the CIS group, recovery was evident only by 1997–98, and even then by no means for all countries.

A more appropriate comparison takes into account the differences among countries with respect to the onset of the transition and considers each country's performance in "transition time."[9] Keeping in mind the earlier caution that the beginning of the transition is hard to pinpoint, it is assumed here that, for Bulgaria, the Czech Republic, Hungary, Poland, Romania, and the Slovak Republic, the first transition year was 1990. Albania, where political developments moved a bit more slowly, is assumed to have begun the transition in 1991. Three of the successor states of the former Socialist Federal Republic of Yugoslavia—Croatia, FYR Macedonia, and Slovenia—are assumed to have begun their transition in 1992, their first full year of independence, and therefore the first year in which more or less independent economic policies became possible. For the BRO, for which the first full year of independence was 1992, this is also considered (again, somewhat arbitrarily) as their first transition year.

When growth performance is viewed from this perspective, three broad categories of transition economies can be identified (Tables 2

---

[8]Wolf (1997) attempts a statistical explanation of the political will to reform.
[9]The concept of transition time is developed in Berg and others (1999).

Table 2. Country Groupings by Economic Performance and Region

	Central Europe	Baltics	Southeastern Europe	CIS	Total
Consistent growth	Croatia Czech Rep. Hungary Poland Slovak Rep. Slovenia	Estonia Latvia Lithuania	Macedonia, FYR	Armenia Azerbaijan Belarus Georgia Kyrgyz Rep. Uzbekistan	16
Growth reversals			Albania Bulgaria Romania		3
Little or no growth				Kazakhstan Moldova Russia Tajikistan Turkmenistan Ukraine	6
Total	6	3	4	12	25

Sources: National authorities; and IMF staff estimates.

and 3).[10] First, 16 countries, after an average of 3.1 years of output decline, have been growing now for several years, although, as will be explained below, growth in two and possibly three of these countries may well not be sustainable on the basis of unchanged policies. The three Baltic states have grown at an (unweighted) average annual growth rate during the recovery of 4.7 percent, and the six countries of Central Europe (Croatia, the Czech Republic, Hungary, Poland, the Slovak Republic, and Slovenia) have averaged 4.3 percent growth during their recovery periods (Table 4). Poland stands out by virtue of its relatively early output recovery and clear rising trend in output growth, which has exceeded 4.5 percent for each of the last five years. Growth in each of the Baltic countries has exceeded 3 percent a year for each of the past three years. Although growth slowed significantly in the Czech Republic in 1997 and output actually declined in 1998, most observers view this as a temporary phenomenon associated with exchange rate and corporate governance issues, and this country is

---

[10]It is noteworthy that these geographical categories, which are based on a consideration of growth performance, to some degree reflect the initial conditions noted earlier, with Central Europe and the Baltics showing better growth performance than southeastern Europe and most of the CIS.

Table 3. GDP Growth in 25 Transition Economies by Country Group

Group[1]	First Year of Transition T(1)	Index (T(0) = 100)								
		T(0)	T(1)	T(2)	T(3)	T(4)	T(5)	T(6)	T(7)	T(8)
Consistent growth										
Central Europe	1990–92	100.0	94.0	85.6	85.8	87.6	91.2	96.2	100.1	...
Baltics	1992	100.0	74.0	64.1	61.9	63.6	66.2	71.7	74.8	...
CIS	1992	100.0	74.4	64.2	57.1	55.0	57.3	61.4	64.7	...
CIS excl. Belarus and Uzbekistan	1992	100.0	66.7	53.6	46.6	45.5	48.2	51.8	54.5	...
Southeastern Europe	1992	100.0	92.0	83.6	82.1	81.1	81.8	83.0	85.4	...
Growth reversals										
Southeastern Europe	1990–91	100.0	85.8	76.4	74.2	76.5	80.3	85.3	81.5	80.2
Little or no growth										
CIS	1992	100.0	83.2	75.5	61.0	56.3	53.4	51.2	50.4	...

Sources: National authorities; and IMF staff estimates.
[1]Countries in each group are listed in Table 2.

placed in the "consistent growth" category despite this small, temporary reversal.[11]

Six CIS countries have been consistently growing now for three to four years, and indeed their average annual rate of growth during these recovery years has been quite high, at 5.7 percent (Table 4). This is a fairly heterogeneous group, however, since rapid growth in Armenia, Azerbaijan, and Georgia has proceeded from a very low base, in large part reflecting civil conflict in those countries in the early 1990s. But this growth has also been strongly correlated with macroeconomic stabilization and reform (see below) and is likely to be sustainable. Although growth in the Kyrgyz Republic has also been associated with strong financial and structural policies, it appears to be more narrowly based (with the gold mining sector playing a dominant role), and its sustainability is somewhat more open to question. The recent growth of Belarus and Uzbekistan has taken place despite continued high inflation and a fundamental lack of structural reform, and its sustain-

---

[11]The period of time before the initial level of GDP is regained is in most cases probably exaggerated for two reasons. One is that, as already noted, official statistics probably underestimate the size of the unofficial economy during the transition. The other is the likelihood that, again as already noted, initial GDP was in most cases overstated, since it did not reflect the welfare losses due to disequilibrium pricing and associated shortages and queues.

								Cumulative Growth Since $T(0)$ (%)	No. of Years of Decline Before Initial Recovery	Cumulative Decline from $T(0)$ to Initial Recovery (%)	Average Growth Since Initial Recovery (% a year)
$T(1)$	$T(2)$	$T(3)$	$T(4)$	$T(5)$	$T(6)$	$T(7)$	$T(8)$				
-6.0	-8.9	0.3	2.0	4.2	5.5	4.0	...	5.0	2.7	-14.4	4.3
-26.0	-13.3	-3.4	2.8	4.0	8.3	4.3	...	-25.2	2.7	-38.1	4.7
-25.6	-13.8	-10.9	-3.8	4.3	7.0	5.4	...	-35.3	3.5	-45.0	5.7
-33.3	-19.6	-13.0	-2.5	6.1	7.5	5.3	...	-45.5	3.3	-54.5	6.1
-8.0	-9.1	-1.8	-1.2	0.8	1.5	2.9	...	-14.6	4.0	-18.9	1.7
-14.2	-10.9	-2.9	3.1	4.9	6.3	-4.6	-1.5	-21.0	3.3	-25.8	1.4
-16.8	-9.3	-19.2	-7.8	-5.1	-4.1	-1.6	...	-49.6	5.3	-49.6	0.5

The column group heading "Percent Change from Previous Period" spans columns $T(1)$ through $T(8)$.

ability is very much open to question in the absence of significant progress toward both bringing down inflation and liberalizing the economy.

Finally, FYR Macedonia, alone among the countries of southeastern Europe, has been growing now for three years, and at an accelerating rate. This country would now appear to belong in the category of "consistently growing" countries as well.

A second broad grouping consists of three countries, all in southeastern Europe (Albania, Bulgaria, and Romania), which began growing three to five years into the transition period but then encountered major output declines in 1996 and/or 1997. The initial output decline for this "growth reversals" group was not as great as for the average of the other two groups (bottom right panel of Figure 2).[12] At the same time, and as will be discussed below, these countries had failed to address some important structural reform issues along the way and were consequently unable to sustain the recovery that eventually took place. Only when important structural reforms were initiated and programs of macroeconomic stabilization were renewed did two of these

---

[12]In the case of Bulgaria, this can in part be attributed to a break in the GDP time series, whereas in the case of Romania the output decline had already started during the 1980s.

Table 4. Average Growth Rates Since Initial Recovery, by Region
(In percent a year)

	Central Europe	Baltics	Southeastern Europe	CIS
Consistent growth	4.3	4.7	1.7	5.7
Growth reversals			1.4	
Little or no growth				0.5

Sources: National authorities; and IMF staff estimates.

countries (Albania and Bulgaria) recover again in 1998, whereas output in Romania continued to decline. The average annual rate of growth of these three countries since their initial recovery has been only 1.4 percent (Table 4).

A third broad grouping is composed of six CIS countries, which thus far, after eight years of transition, have shown little or no growth. As a group, since their initial recovery, these countries have grown at an average annual rate of only 0.5 percent (Table 4). Tajikistan, following the second-largest cumulative output decline among the 25 transition economies—due largely to civil conflict—actually grew in both 1997 and 1998, and at an accelerated rate. Kazakhstan, which began to recover in 1996–97, experienced a fall in output in 1998, although this was at least partly due to the decline in the world price for oil and the crisis in neighboring Russia. Both Moldova and Russia showed signs of recovery in 1997, only to see output decline sharply in 1998, also, in large part, because of the crisis in Russia itself. After years of decline, Turkmenistan managed to grow in 1998, but output in Ukraine continued to fall, although at the lowest rate during the transition to date.

As of 1998, only three countries had reattained or surpassed their measured output levels in the first year preceding their transition.[13] All three were in Central Europe: real GDP in 1998 in both Poland and Slovenia exceeded that in the year immediately prior to the beginning of transition by 17 and 20 percent, respectively, and output in Croatia surpassed the immediate pretransition level by 6.5 percent. At the other extreme, with measured output still less than half the immediate pretransition level, were five CIS countries. One of these, Georgia (at 47 percent of 1991 output), has actually been growing for four straight years. The other four are all in the third grouping (little or no growth): Tajikistan and Turkmenistan (with output around 45 percent of the 1991 level), Moldova (40 percent), and Ukraine (41 percent).

---

[13]Initial output was likely overstated, however, as discussed above.

Finally, it should be emphasized that the growth rates in most transition economies in 1998 were adversely affected by factors well beyond their control or by the process of transformation itself. For CEE, the general slowdown in the world economy and the region's diminished export prospects, together with contagion effects for most emerging economies, undoubtedly had a negative influence on growth. For the BRO countries, not only these factors but, more important—for those countries deeply dependent on Russia (either directly or indirectly through their trade ties with other BRO countries)—the Russian crisis had a profound impact on economic growth in 1998.

Main Factors Associated with Growth in the Transition

This section assesses the key factors that may explain the differences in growth performance among these transition economies. We start with a brief summary of earlier empirical studies. The first and probably least controversial conclusion is that stabilization is a necessary condition for recovery of output (Fischer, Sahay, and Végh, 1996 and 1998).[14] Two apparent exceptions, Bulgaria and Romania, fell into line when their growth and stabilization reversed. Two other exceptions exist at present—Belarus and Uzbekistan—and their similarity to the reversal cases is discussed below.

A second and somewhat more controversial conclusion relates to the additional, necessary conditions to promote growth, namely, liberalization and structural reforms. Whether the framework was a simple one relating only to growth and some index of structural reforms (Sachs, 1996; Selowsky and Martin, 1996; Åslund, Boone, and Johnson, 1996) or a more sophisticated one reflecting the effects of stabilization, initial conditions, conflicts, and the like (Fischer, Sahay, and Végh, 1996 and 1998; Hernández-Catá, 1997; de Melo and others, 1997; Berg and others, 1999), the conclusion was firm: more comprehensive reform is associated with better growth performance. These results, too, are not without exceptions, Belarus and Uzbekistan today being the key ones, and Bulgaria and Romania earlier. Åslund, Boone, and Johnson (1996) point to a dichotomy here: whereas empirical studies concluded that fast and early reforms result in early and strong recovery, theoretical work on transition has often shown that a gradual pace might lead to a smaller initial decline of output (Aghion and Blanchard, 1993).

---

[14]These papers also analyzed the factors behind countries' success at disinflation, such as budget deficits and exchange rates. These issues are addressed more fully in IMF (1998b).

A third set of conclusions relates to other factors such as war and initial conditions; these do have an effect that is country-specific. Some studies have tried to determine the relative importance of adverse initial conditions and of policies (de Melo and others, 1997; Berg and others, 1999). However, they have not been specific about the trade-offs, such as how *much* a high share of industrial output impedes growth or how much compensation is needed from faster reforms.[15]

A fourth set of conclusions relates to such institutions and conditions as the rule of law, the climate for corruption, and the fairness of the tax burden. These factors are even less easily measured than the degree of liberalization; hence, not surprisingly, the statistic used varies a great deal from study to study. Nevertheless, studies such as Brunetti, Kisunko, and Weder (1997a–c); Johnson, Kaufmann, and Shleifer (1997); and Olson, Sarna, and Swarmy (1997) concur that growth is higher where these elements show higher levels of institutional achievement.

Fifth and finally, the conventional factor input explanations of growth theory (which focus on investment, labor, human capital, and the like) are not considered in any of the empirical studies, reflecting the view, noted earlier, that the initial recovery from transitional recession is of a special nature. Only Wolf (1997) actually tests for the statistical importance of investment-GDP ratios, and he finds a *negative* correlation.

This chapter provides some new facts that illustrate, confirm, and elaborate on these conclusions; it also reports the results of new econometric analysis using data through 1998.[16] The new data make it easier to distinguish the factors influencing the decline from those inducing recovery and permit a considerable updating of previous empirical studies. The very fact that recovery began much earlier in some countries and still has not started in others, and that recent rates of growth vary considerably among countries, speaks to the view that recovery and sustained growth are not automatic, nor do they represent merely a cyclical rebound. Six main issues concerning the transition and growth are elaborated here. The first is the applicability of conventional explanations of growth in market economies. The second is the effect of special initial conditions in the transition. The third is the contribution of government policies, in particular financial stabilization and structural reform. The fourth is the sustainability of growth. The fifth is the time pattern of reform, whether gradual or more rapid,

---

[15]We report below the results of a background econometric study on the magnitudes of these trade-offs.

[16]Detailed results with data through 1997 are given in Havrylyshyn, Izvorski, and van Rooden (1998). Using preliminary estimates for 1998, regressions reported in the appendix give virtually the same results.

early or delayed. The sixth is the political economy determinants of the nature and speed of reform. We summarize the findings by considering which of these explanatory factors deserve greatest policy priority. The assessment made in this section draws on the following evidence: the conclusions of earlier studies; new statistical evidence summarized in comparative group averages; and new regression analysis covering the period 1991–98 (summarized in the appendix).

Conventional Factor Input Explanations

It appears that the conventional determinants of investment, labor, and human capital expansion played only a limited role in the recovery. Although there does appear to be a correlation between investment and growth once the recovery is under way (see below), movements in labor productivity have been a somewhat better predictor of the onset of recovery or output reversals (Figures 3 and 4). There is little disagreement in the general growth literature that investment is a major engine of growth in the medium to long term.

As de Broeck and Koen (2000) have shown for Central Europe the most common pattern for the investment-GDP ratio is a decline from levels of the central plan period near 30 percent to levels near 20 percent or even lower, and then a strong recovery simultaneous with a rebound in output (this latter phenomenon is captured in Figure 4). In the short run, however, and especially in transition economies with a history of excessive capital accumulation and its inefficient use, the role of new investment in the initial recovery phase may be relatively less important. Unfortunately, investment data for most transition economies are generally not very reliable, and this hypothesis is difficult to test. Available data present a suggestive but incomplete picture, described in Havrylyshyn and others (1999). Of the 16 countries that have shown consistent growth, 13 have adequate data on investment.

A substantial upturn in the ratio of investment to output preceded recovery in only one case, but coincided with the beginning of recovery in three countries and actually lagged the upturn in output in nine. For nine of these same countries for which real investment growth data were available, there was virtually an even three-way split among the number of countries for which the substantial recovery of real investment led, coincided with, or lagged the recovery of real output.

Econometric analysis of growth determinants does not show the usual positive effect of investment on GDP (Wolf, 1997; see also the appendix). At the same time, however, there does not appear to be a correlation between relatively rapid investment growth and recovery in general (Figure 4).

Figure 3. Labor Productivity and Output in 25 Transition Economies
(Index, 1992=100)

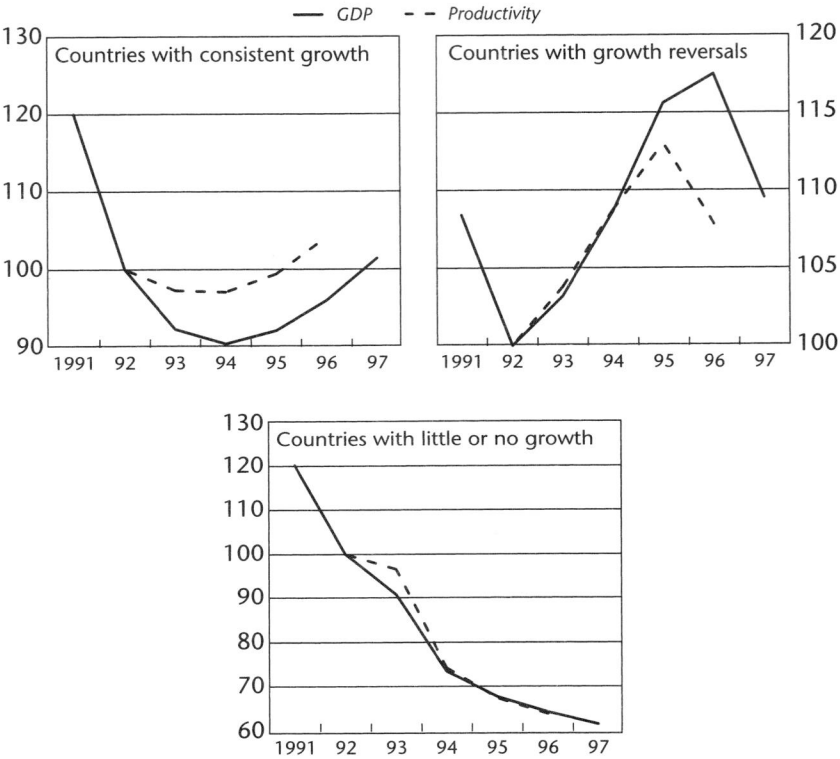

Sources: National authorities; and IMF staff estimates.

A plausible way to reconcile all this evidence would be to conclude that although aggregate net new investment may not be that important in the initial recovery phase, it becomes increasingly so as the recovery continues.[17] For overindustrialized, distorted, and inefficient transition economies, recovery only comes after some elimination of the wasteful old production (see Hernández-Catá, 1997) and usually cannot be based on a large investment effort to build new productive capacity before the proper incentives for efficient resource use are in place.

---

[17]The econometric analysis summarized in the appendix does not find a systematic contribution of aggregate investment to the output recovery in transition economies. This in no way denies, however, that individual investment projects are key in spurring growth in certain sectors, or that the level of aggregate investment does become more central in sustaining growth as the recovery proceeds.

Figure 4. GDP and Investment in 25 Transition Economies

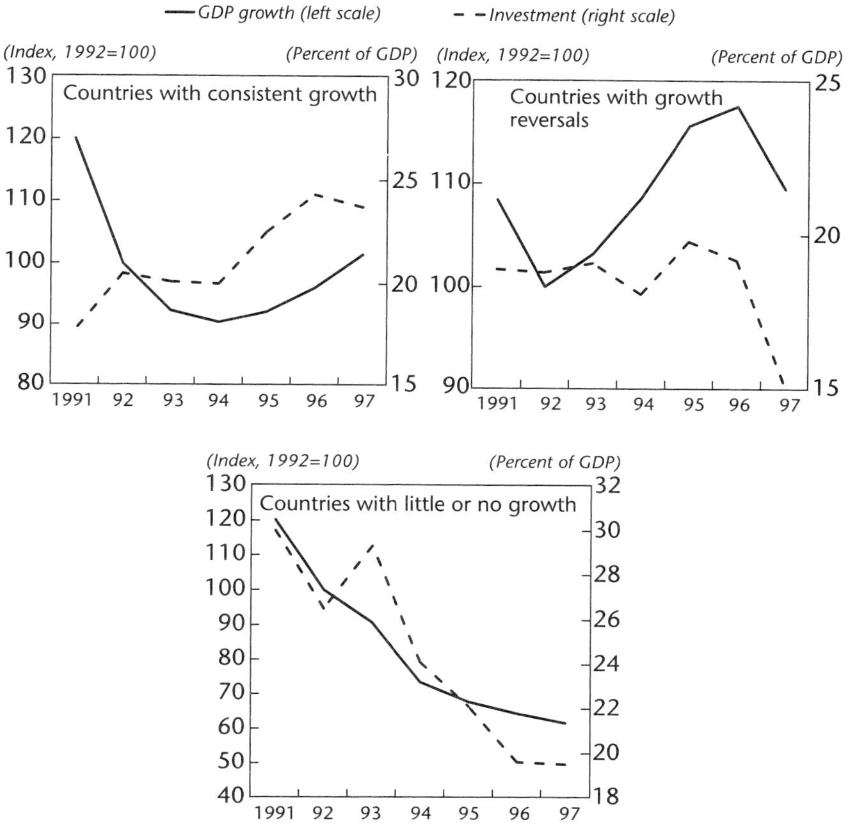

GDP growth (left scale)   – – Investment (right scale)

Sources: National authorities; and IMF staff estimates.

The impact of export growth is less clear. The group averages for export growth (Table 5) show a broad statistical association with economic growth, although the empirical studies generally do not test for openness to exports. (Exceptions are Wolf, 1997, who finds no correlation, and Christoffersen and Doyle, 1998, who find indirect evidence of a correlation between growth and expansion of market opportunities.) The explanation may be simply that almost all transition economies became relatively open very quickly, and those that achieved restructuring earlier were able to reorient their trade quickly to new markets. That is, exports did not simply become the engine of growth, but rather restructuring—which is necessary for growth—also tended to promote exports.

Table 5. Average Growth Rate of Exports, by Region, 1994–97

(In percent a year)

	Central Europe	Baltics	Southeastern Europe	CIS
Consistent growth	15.4	24.4	2.9	14.3
Growth reversals			11.2	
Little or no growth				8.4

Sources: National authorities; and IMF staff estimates.

A similar conclusion applies to foreign direct investment (FDI). Although there is a clear association between economic growth and cumulative FDI per capita (Table 6), at least for CEE and the Baltics, the relationship between growth and FDI may be mutually reinforcing. In other words, although there is little doubt that FDI promotes growth, those factors that promote greater stabilization and reforms, and therefore growth, also attract FDI. Because of this simultaneity, econometric analysis of growth has been unable to isolate FDI as an explanatory factor, although it has been attempted in several of the studies mentioned.

Effect of Initial Conditions

This study finds that initial conditions are not without importance, but that their impact becomes smaller over time and can be offset by better policies, in particular by slightly faster progress on structural reform. It is not a straightforward matter to observe statistically the effect of initial conditions, such as historical experience and attitudes, differences in the degree of economic distortion under central planning, or levels of development. One reason is the difficulty in measuring these conditions; thus, although there is a broad consensus that before 1990 the Central European countries had relatively less distorted economies than the Soviet Union, this does not provide a quantifiable measure of how much they differed. Another reason is that the impact of initial conditions may be indirect; that is, they may affect growth through policies: the degree of commitment to reforms and their effective implementation may be partially explained by such differences in initial conditions. Three recent studies address this: de Melo and others (1997), Hérnandez-Catá (1997), and Wolf (1997). They find generally that the Central European countries and the Baltics, because of their history of less economic distortion, shorter history of communism, and closer proximity to market economies, were more likely to implement market-based policies early and quickly.

Although such difficulties will qualify any statistical analysis, it is still useful to undertake such analysis, using measures of initial conditions

Table 6. Cumulative Foreign Direct Investment per Capita, by Region, 1990–96
(In dollars)

	Central Europe	Baltics	Southeastern Europe	CIS
Consistent growth	74.1	68.7	5.6	7.5
Growth reversals			9.8	
Little or no growth				15.9

Sources: National authorities; and IMF staff estimates.

compiled by de Melo and others (1997). The appendix details the results, which illustrate the relative impact of initial conditions on growth. Initial overindustrialization is found to lower the rate of output growth by about 0.4 percentage point for each additional 5 percentage points of the share of industry in total output. But this effect is offset by improvements in the growth rate arising from even modest progress on structural reform. A move from a low level of reform of 0.2 (as measured by the reform index compiled by the European Bank for Reconstruction and Development, or EBRD; Table 7) to one of 0.3 yields 1 to 2 percentage points of additional growth. Thus, moving from an intermediate stage of reform, as indicated by an index value of 0.4, to a more advanced level of 0.7, would add 3 to 6 percentage points of economic growth.

Another method frequently used to capture initial conditions is the use of dummy variables to identify groups of countries: countries of the former Soviet Union from other countries, countries beset by civil conflict from countries at peace, and so on. Earlier growth studies, as noted above, found these differences to be significant. The regression reported in the appendix, using data through 1998, shows no statistically significant results, suggesting that the impact of such effects diminishes over time. This reaffirms the conclusion of Berg and others (1999); however, when regression analysis is done separately for the CIS and other countries, an interesting result emerges: the impact on growth of a given amount of reform, as measured by an EBRD-type index, is less for the CIS countries.

Other initial conditions matter as well, such as very low income (including after civil strife) and resource availability. Thus in Albania, Armenia, Georgia, and the Kyrgyz Republic, substantial progress toward reform saw growth rates surge, reflecting a catch-up phenomenon as well as the availability of natural resources to be exploited (such as gold in the case of the Kyrgyz Republic). But resource wealth can also be an impediment to reform, providing only temporary, unsustainable (or at least weak) growth; Uzbekistan, with its exportable cotton production, may be such a case (Zettelmeyer, 1999). Civil strife is found by many

Table 7. Structural Reform Indices for 25 Transition Economies

Economy	1990	1991	1992	1993	1994	1995	1996	1997
Albania	0.00	0.24	0.66	0.70	0.63	0.61	0.64	0.63
Armenia	0.04	0.13	0.39	0.42	0.46	0.54	0.61	0.61
Azerbaijan	0.04	0.04	0.25	0.31	0.33	0.40	0.44	0.51
Belarus	0.04	0.10	0.20	0.33	0.42	0.50	0.44	0.37
Bulgaria	0.19	0.62	0.86	0.66	0.63	0.61	0.57	0.67
Croatia	0.62	0.62	0.72	0.79	0.79	0.71	0.75	0.74
Czech Republic	0.16	0.79	0.86	0.90	0.88	0.82	0.82	0.82
Estonia	0.20	0.32	0.64	0.81	0.83	0.77	0.78	0.82
Georgia	0.04	0.22	0.32	0.35	0.33	0.50	0.61	0.66
Hungary	0.57	0.74	0.78	0.82	0.83	0.82	0.82	0.87
Kazakhstan	0.04	0.14	0.35	0.35	0.42	0.50	0.64	0.66
Kyrgyz Republic	0.04	0.04	0.33	0.60	0.71	0.71	0.67	0.70
Latvia	0.13	0.29	0.51	0.67	0.71	0.67	0.74	0.74
Lithuania	0.13	0.33	0.55	0.78	0.79	0.71	0.74	0.74
Macedonia, FYR	0.62	0.65	0.68	0.78	0.71	0.64	0.67	0.67
Moldova	0.04	0.10	0.38	0.51	0.54	0.64	0.64	0.64
Poland	0.68	0.72	0.82	0.82	0.83	0.79	0.79	0.81
Romania	0.22	0.36	0.45	0.58	0.67	0.65	0.64	0.66
Russia	0.04	0.10	0.49	0.59	0.67	0.64	0.71	0.72
Slovak Republic	0.16	0.79	0.86	0.83	0.83	0.79	0.79	0.77
Slovenia	0.62	0.71	0.78	0.82	0.79	0.79	0.79	0.79
Tajikistan	0.04	0.11	0.20	0.26	0.42	0.40	0.40	0.39
Turkmenistan	0.04	0.04	0.13	0.16	0.29	0.27	0.27	0.36
Ukraine	0.04	0.10	0.23	0.13	0.33	0.54	0.57	0.59
Uzbekistan	0.04	0.04	0.26	0.30	0.50	0.57	0.57	0.54

Sources: de Melo, Denizer, and Gelb (1996); and EBRD, *Transition Report*, various issues.

analysts to affect growth adversely, but the effects seem to disappear quickly (see especially de Melo and others, 1997); the quick recoveries in Armenia, Georgia, and now Tajikistan are examples. Thus, on balance, the evidence suggests that initial conditions have had an effect, but the effect should not be exaggerated, because it declines over time and can be offset by stronger progress toward reform. Furthermore, the effect is possibly more on the political will and capacity to implement reforms than directly on growth; hence the conclusion remains that where more reforms are implemented, more growth will occur.

Economic Reform and Macroeconomic Policies

This study also finds that macroeconomic stabilization and general progress on market-oriented reform are dominant determinants of recovery in the transition period. Both Table 8 and the appendix show this clearly: inflation control is a sine qua non for growth, and greater progress in reform is associated with more rapid growth. The role of

Table 8. Average Inflation During Years of Positive Growth, by Region
(In percent a year)

	Central Europe	Baltics	Southeastern Europe	CIS
Consistent growth	14	18	1	27
Growth reversals			67	
Little or no growth				37

Sources: National authorities; and IMF staff estimates.

stabilization is well established in the growth literature as perhaps the first, virtually necessary condition for recovery, and the hyperinflations in some transition economies in the early to mid-1990s were without question inimical to growth. A recent paper on disinflation in transition economies (Cottarelli and Doyle, in this volume) confirms this relationship and demonstrates further that although recovery may begin once inflation has declined to double-digit levels, sustained growth requires sustained disinflation. But although stabilization appears, with few exceptions,[18] to be a necessary condition for achieving growth, it is not a sufficient condition: several of the "little or no growth" cases— Kazakhstan, Turkmenistan, and Ukraine, and until recently, Russia— also have had relatively low inflation rates in recent years. However one may view the "necessary but not sufficient" issue, it is clear that high inflation has generally been detrimental to growth, and that stabilization, along with structural reform, has helped growth to resume.

Indeed, accompanying structural reforms, as reflected in the EBRD index, were equally necessary for growth. It is surely not pure coincidence that Poland, which was among the earliest to begin and sustain recovery, was also among the earliest to put in place structural reforms. This was reflected in an increase in its rescaled EBRD index from 0.68 in 1990 to 0.83 in 1994 (Table 7); growth in the Baltics, beginning in 1994–95, was associated with improvements in their reform indices from around 0.30 in 1991 to between 0.70 and 0.85 in 1994; and six CIS countries that have thus far achieved only little or no growth have had an average index well below most others (Table 9).

It is also noteworthy that, in 1997, the share of the private sector in (officially recorded) GDP tended to be higher in countries with sustained growth than in countries with growth reversals or little or no growth (Table 10). In early discussions of transition, privatization was seen as the key mechanism for achieving efficiency and new growth by

---

[18]There are several instances of countries beginning recovery with inflation still above 50 percent. These include the three reversal cases as well as Belarus and Uzbekistan, whose recent recovery is questioned by some analysts, and Armenia and Croatia.

Table 9. Average Index of Liberalization, by Region, 1995[1]

(In percent a year)

	Central Europe	Baltics	Southeastern Europe	CIS
Consistent growth[2]	0.79	0.72	0.64	0.54
Belarus and Uzbekistan				0.54
Growth reversals			0.62	
Little or no growth				0.50

Sources: EBRD *Transition Report, 1996.*
[1]Average of selected EBRD transition indicators normalized between values of 0 and 1.
[2]Excluding Belarus and Uzbekistan.

enforcing a hard budget discipline and providing profit incentives. This would lead first to restructuring, enabling enterprises to reach commercial viability through a variety of measures: labor shedding, increases in sales, closure or sale of unprofitable units, creation of a retail network and marketing, development of new products, seeking contracts with new partners, renovations to improve productivity, a quality control process, and a reduction in barter transactions. Viable firms would increase their productivity and market share, attract more resources, and increase production—hence new growth would occur. Nonviable firms would shrink or close down, and their assets (both human and physical capital) would be reallocated to alternative production. John Nellis (in this volume) summarizes the initial evidence showing that privatization in general does help growth, but only if done right.

The structural reform index is, of course, a composite of several dimensions. Although some effort has been made to isolate the subcomponents, it has generally not been possible to isolate one element as more important than others. Such a decomposition is, however, found in Fischer, Sahay, and Végh (1996 and 1998) and de Melo and others (1997), as well as in Havrylyshyn, Izvorski, and van Rooden (1998). From the statistical analysis in the appendix, it can be seen that the subcomponents—price liberalization, privatization and enterprise reform, trade and exchange liberalization, and legal reforms—are all closely correlated with general reform. In a statistical test, none is important separately from the general index, although each of them alone "substitutes" for the general index as an explanatory factor of growth. Only price liberalization stands out as unique in its effects over time, as described in the discussion of the timing and pace of reforms below.[19]

---

[19]One factor that might also play a role but has not generally been analyzed in the growth studies, perhaps because of the difficulty of measuring it, is the fragility of banking systems and the low degree of financial intermediation.

Table 10. Share of Private Sector in GDP, by Region, Mid-1997
(In percent a year)

	Central Europe	Baltics	Southeastern Europe	CIS
Consistent growth[1]	66	67	50	53
Belarus and Uzbekistan				33
Growth reversals			48	
Little or no growth				44

Sources: EBRD *Transition Report, 1998.*
[1]Excluding Belarus and Uzbekistan.

The role of an effective legal framework in promoting growth in transition economies has taken on increased importance, as many analysts of the process have begun to point to the practical barriers in exercising de jure freedom of economic action (see World Bank, 1996a; EBRD, 1997). The finding by some empirical growth studies that the institutional climate of property rights matters is illustrated by the statistical results described in the appendix: the legal framework index (estimated by the EBRD since 1995) is strongly associated with better growth performance.

Sustainability of Growth

There appear to be two groups of counterexamples to the conclusion that growth requires significant progress toward reform. Belarus and Uzbekistan are two "puzzle cases": they have shown strong positive growth despite limited reforms (rescaled EBRD index figures in 1997 of 0.37 and 0.54, respectively; Table 7); Albania, Bulgaria, and Romania achieved early recoveries only to see them reversed. The two groups are similar in several respects and provide an object lesson in the sustainability of growth. The three cases of reversal had achieved greater reform progress than the two "puzzle" cases, but financial stabilization was incomplete, and the elimination of soft enterprise budget constraints was generally not achieved. Albania, as a result of social upheaval triggered by its pyramid financial schemes, and Bulgaria and Romania, through continued directed credits and energy price supports to state enterprises, experienced a reversal of stabilization. Annual inflation reached an average of 67 percent during the recovery period, followed by a reversal of growth. Belarus and Uzbekistan, having undertaken limited reform, have seen a return to low-cost directed credits, which have fueled recovery but have also given rise to a return of high inflation, to about 50 to 60 percent in 1997 (and over 150 percent within 1998 in Belarus). This picture raises a concern about the sustainability of growth in these two cases. Indeed, estimates for 1998 (Table 1) show the onset of a sharp slowdown in Belarus and continued slow growth in Uzbekistan.

Timing and Sequencing of Reforms

The timing and pace of reform have perhaps been the most provocative issue in debates about growth in transition economies. Often, the discussion has been reduced to a too-simplistic debate between shock therapy and gradualism. It may be better to think of the issue in more nuanced terms, and ask whether an earlier start or more discrete sharp moves toward reforms that can be done quickly (such as price liberalization) lead to better growth performance. The choice is made more complex by the possibility that it is a package of complementary reforms rather than some "silver bullet" that works best. A separate issue is whether, once the conclusion is accepted that moving faster leads to higher growth, the political will or a political environment exists that enables policymakers to choose to inflict pain up front, knowing improvements will come only later. In a sense, despite eight years of experience, it is still too early to judge which approach has worked better, as some countries may still show late but strong growth surges, while others may yet see a reversal, as indeed has already happened in southeastern Europe. Nevertheless, some illustration of the varied effects of differences in the pace and intensity of reforms can be provided.

A useful way of thinking about the time pattern of reforms and resulting output performance is the "creative destruction" framework developed above. At the outset, rapid reforms including price liberalization have more of a destructive than a creative effect (as Hernández-Catá, 1997, also emphasizes). Indeed, it is notable that for the early period, 1990–93, the regression analysis in the appendix suggests that greater price liberalization results in more decline (see the negative coefficient on the price liberalization variable in equation B2). The top panel of Figure 5, using fitted values from the regression analysis, tells a similar story, depicting a U-shaped relationship between growth performance and the degree of progress in reform in 1990–93. Were the analysis to stop at that point, the conclusion could be drawn—as it often has been—that less reform is better than reform that is intermediate in scope. Moreover, since most of those economies at the right (greater reform) end of the U in 1993 were Central European economies, their performance has often been attributed to geography and history—that is, better initial conditions.

Figure 5. Impact of Reform on Growth: Fitted Regression Values[1]

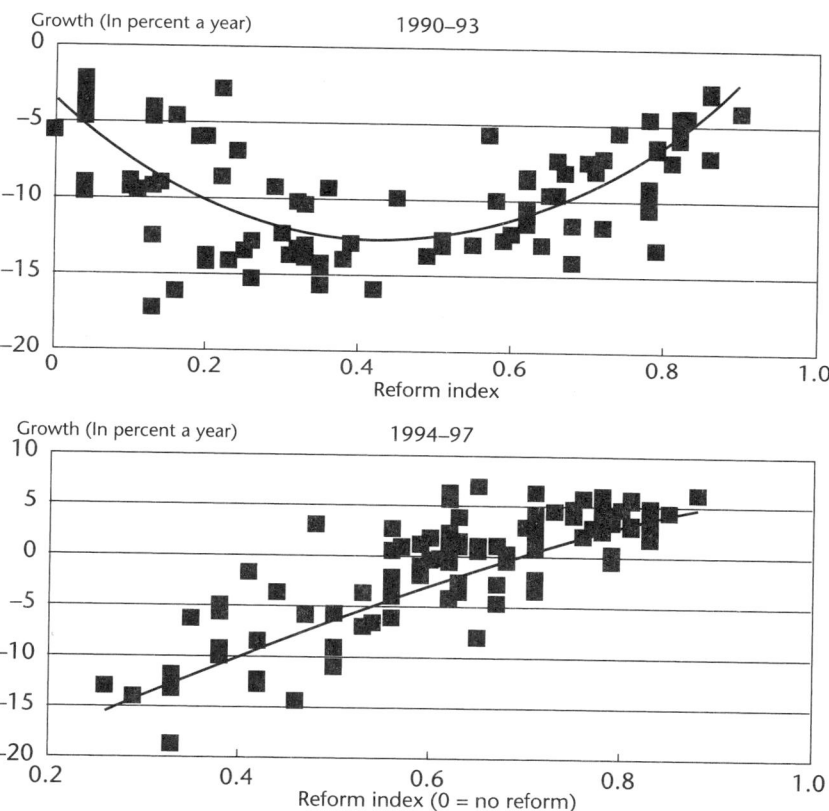

Sources: IMF staff estimates; and EBRD (1997).
[1]The fitted values are obtained from the multivariate panel data regressions B1 (top panel) and C1 (bottom panel) in Table 11 in the appendix. A polynomial trend line has been added to the fitted regression values.

But with the passage of time, one in fact has seen very much what the analytical framework suggests: in the advanced group of countries, as progress in reform continues, the negative, destructive effects of reform come to be strongly outweighed by the positive, creative, and growth-inducing effects. In the bottom panel of Figure 5, which depicts the recovery period, this is now reflected in a very clear positive relation between the degree of reform and growth performance. In the formal regression analysis, the price liberalization variable becomes strongly positive in the second period (see equation C2 in Table 11 in the appendix); indeed, the size of the coefficients for all policy variables tends to be much higher. Of course, a few exceptions remain—Belarus and Uzbekistan again—where limited reform is associated with recovery. But the overwhelming message of the data is that those countries that started early (or started later but moved rapidly) may have paid an initial price in the form of sharper output declines, but are now reaping the benefits in the form of more rapid growth. In contrast, those that have undertaken limited or very moderate reform continue to suffer decline, or at best experience only nascent and fragile recoveries.

Political Economy Factors

In addition to the proximate causes of growth discussed so far, it is useful to consider some factors related to political economy, which, by affecting the nature and effective implementation of economic reforms, indirectly affect growth. At the start of the transition, political support for the transformation of the economy may have been quite widespread, but it was by no means universal. Opposition of varying degrees was to be found among the managerial elite of the Soviet period, the bureaucracy, and many but not all of the Communist Party elite. For most Central European countries and the Baltics, the prospect of eventual accession to the European Union acted as a strong beacon, showing the way to market reform. In those countries, as well as in a few early reformers farther east—Armenia and the Kyrgyz Republic— strong and continued progress on reform created a demonstration effect, as other countries recognized the potential benefits: growth in the service sector, new opportunities for small entrepreneurs, and eventually general recovery. Of course, an early start on comprehensive reform also created opposition to further reform, particularly because of rising unemployment and the removal of privileges. But in many of these countries, the initial goodwill to reform was enough to sustain the reforms politically until the new beneficiaries added their voices to the support for continued reform.[20] It is also notable that even though a wave of elections in Central Europe in the mid-1990s brought many left-oriented governments to power, the main direction of economic policy was little changed.

---

[20]The possible circularity in the causation of reform (reform leads to growth, which leads to more reforms) is not reflected in the ordinary least-squares specification of regression equations. Thus, formally speaking, the coefficients of reform in the growth equation may be overestimated. (We owe this point to Olivier Blanchard.) However, even without a formal test of the hypothesis that growth can lead to reforms, it is evident that so far none of the cases where growth preceded reform (Belarus and Uzbekistan, and Bulgaria and Romania earlier) do we see growth followed by more reform.

In countries where reform did not get off to an early start or was very incomplete (for example, where there was considerable privatization, but continued soft budget constraints and inadequate development of rule-of-law institutions) the policy process was captured by new vested interests. These were especially concentrated in the energy, banking, and heavy-industry sectors. These vested interests often began by accumulating wealth through the economic rents resulting from large price distortions in energy and raw materials, and by borrowing from the central bank during years of inflation. Mass privatization was often captured by such vested interests, who understandably favored this form of privatization. Once their private ownership of former state assets was assured, they supported inflation control, because it would help stimulate recovery and thus the growth of their newly acquired firms. But these insiders continued to strongly oppose the full liberalization of market opportunities, which would bring in new domestic or foreign competition. With the transformation to the market thus frozen in midcourse, the aims of the new vested interests, those of the old, surviving state enterprises, and a political establishment concerned about employment broadly coincided in a status quo. One manifestation of such a political economy equilibrium is the so-called virtual economy.[21] This describes the situation where noncash operations—barter, arrears, in-kind wages, tax offsets—help maintain the status quo and provide a cover of nontransparency for economic operations of low or even negative productivity that are not market based and allow rent seeking and corruption. The potential virtuous circle of reform and growth is replaced by a vicious circle of suspended reform and stagnation.

Which Factors Matter Most?

One can best summarize the implications of all the above evidence by asking whether certain aspects of structural reform are more important determinants of growth than others, and whether some factors deserve greater attention from policymakers. The answer to the first question is no, but the answer to the second is yes. The evidence described so far suggests, if anything, that what is needed is a package of across-the-board policy measures; there is no magic single key to successful growth. In the words of Harberger (1998) in a recent article on growth, it is the "thousand and one" little things that hard-working and innovative managers do that create new output. Aziz and Wescott

---

[21]See in particular Gaddy and Ickes (1998).

(1997) provide a more formal demonstration of the need for a comprehensive package. The early studies of growth in transition found many different policy measures to be important: stabilization, general progress on structural reform (including price liberalization and privatization), reduction of the government budget deficit, a strong legal climate of transparency and fairness (the rule of law), openness to external trade, and a high degree of competitiveness.

Having said this, one can still point to certain areas of structural reform that need more attention from policymakers, since the implementation of policy has not been even and across the board. In some instances (such as Ukraine), structural reforms have not advanced very far beyond financial stabilization and initial (often still partial) price and/or exchange rate liberalization, and even liberalization has been delayed in countries such as Belarus, Turkmenistan, and Uzbekistan.

In many transition countries, in both CEE and elsewhere, privatization is well advanced, but the associated conditions of a hard budget constraint and open competition are by no means fully in place.[22] Admittedly the extent to which this is true varies from the advanced transition cases such as Croatia, Hungary, Poland, Slovenia, and to a lesser extent the Baltics, through moderately advanced cases such as Armenia, Kazakhstan, Kyrgyz Republic, and in some ways Russia, to the least-advanced reformers. Finally, for almost all countries, but again to varying degrees, the effective implementation of strong legal institutions supporting property rights is a key item on the agenda. Some of the critically needed policy actions concern items that, by their nature, take rather more time to accomplish. Among these are the strengthening of legal institutions, privatization of natural monopolies, and the strengthening of banking systems and more generally the system of financial intermediation, in part through improving mechanisms of prudential regulation and supervision. Others are items that should have been done earlier but were not: the list includes privatization of enterprises other than natural monopolies, price liberalization, and fiscal reform. Perhaps a few are items whose importance as bottlenecks was not well understood earlier; these include simple business registration and entry regulations, agricultural land collateral systems, competition in supply and marketing networks related to agriculture, and effective and quick contract law settlement.

---

[22] See Nellis, this volume, and Havrylyshyn and McGettigan (1999).

Conclusion

Lessons on Achieving Recovery

Several lessons emerge from this analysis. The consensus is very clear on the first lesson, namely, that stabilization is a sine qua non. All studies agree that inflation must first be controlled and brought down at least to levels well below 50 percent before sustainable recovery can occur. If inflation is not driven further down and prevented from increasing again, any recovery that occurs is unlikely to be sustained. Cases of early recovery accompanied by still-high or rebounding inflation—such as Bulgaria and Romania—eventually saw a reversal, although lack of continued progress in other reforms also played a role. Similar recoveries accompanied by high inflation and limited reform in Belarus and Uzbekistan may also prove unsustainable.

There is no denying that structural reforms cause a dislocation of resources, including labor, and hence pain to some in the economy. It follows that delaying such reforms can delay the pain. However—and this is the second lesson—such delay imposes a cost: the lost opportunity for a vibrant and sustained recovery that provides economic gains to all. Those cases where recovery has occurred despite delays in reform appear to provide only temporary shelter from the inevitable pain. Of four such cases noted above, two suffered strong reversals, while the other two continued to suffer high inflation and in 1998 already showed much slower (Belarus) or still relatively slow growth (Uzbekistan).

A third lesson is that there is no shortcut to reform. No single reform provides a simple key or panacea—a comprehensive package combining at least minimal progress in all areas is required. This does not mean that all aspects of reform—price liberalization, privatization, establishment of competitive markets, open trade, free entry, and enforced bankruptcy for unviable enterprises—have to be imposed overnight. Nor does it mean that the transformation to a new market environment has to be complete in all these dimensions before recovery will occur. It does, however, mean that the process of reform in each of these areas has to begin and proceed at an appropriate but steady pace, with some reforms perhaps moving faster (price liberalization, open trade), and others more slowly (privatization, establishment of competition, security of property rights).

A fourth lesson is that unfavorable initial conditions should not become an excuse for inaction. Initial conditions such as heavier industrialization or a relative dearth of historical contacts with market economies can hamper recovery, but they are not insurmountable obstacles, for several reasons. First, their negative effects decline over time. Second, the empirical studies clearly suggest that these effects can be compensated by modestly faster progress on reforms. And third, perhaps the main effect is indirect; that is, unfavorable initial conditions result in less political will and capacity for reform, and less reform means less growth. This interpretation leaves untouched the simple conclusion that more reform leads to more growth.

A fifth lesson is that developing institutions that create a market-friendly environment cannot be delayed for too long. Putting in place secure property rights, easy entry into business, enforceable contracts, the rule of law, and the whole network of institutions that support value-creating production activities is essential. When these changes should come about is more difficult to say. They have clearly been coming more slowly than other elements of reform, but that may be their nature. In some of the lagging reformers, these institutions are very much undeveloped; indeed, many recent writings on this topic suggest that, because they were delayed for so long, the environment of criminality and disregard for law that filled this vacuum now hinders efforts to introduce the rule of law.

The major new development during 1998 was the fallout from the financial crisis in Russia in August of that year. As a result, a reversal of stabilization and of the incipient recovery has occurred in Russia itself, with a continued negative impact on growth in neighboring countries with substantial trade ties to Russia. The Russian crisis therefore reinforces two of the key lessons of this study: first, that incomplete structural reforms to strengthen property rights and governance jeopardize the sustainability of financial stabilization; and second, that the costs of incomplete reform in terms of lost output and renewed inflation can be severe. True, there are many differences between Russia and the three previous cases in which stabilization programs were reversed (Albania, Bulgaria, and Romania). Yet all four countries have been characterized by inadequate implementation of structural reforms, major manifestations of which have been the improper use of bank credit and growing problems of nonpayment, offsets, and barter, reflecting a general breakdown of financial discipline. The lesson for other transition countries is that lasting stabilization and recovery are never assured so long as the structural and governance reform process is not finished.

Another recent development has been the sharp reduction in the new capital inflows that can contribute to sustaining growth. This process, of course, began earlier, as financial markets reassessed the prospects for emerging markets after the events in East Asia in 1997 and early 1998. In the case of Russia, the financial markets judged that capital inflows had been used to postpone reforms rather than to finance them. One indicator of how far the turnaround in markets has gone is the increase in spreads; another is the generalized downgrading by private credit rating agencies. But some differentiation among countries is occurring: spreads increased by as little as 60 basis points for the better-performing Central European countries and the Baltics, compared with increases of over 1,000 basis points in some CIS countries. In a few cases in Central Europe and the Baltics, rating agencies have reaffirmed their ratings, or at most posted notices expressing some concern. This still fragmentary evidence suggests that, if countries are to benefit from favorable treatment, they will need to reinforce the macroeconomic and structural policies that lie behind successful performance on disinflation and growth.

Future Prospects and Challenges

The very fact that the great majority of transition economies have begun an economic recovery—and that nearly two-thirds have already sustained their recoveries for at least three years—is evidence that the transition has come a long way. But by the same token, a few countries have faltered, several have seen only a fragile recovery, and a handful have scarcely begun. Thus the agenda for the transition in these countries remains considerable.

For a number of the Central European countries and the Baltics, the transition process is well advanced, and their problems and issues are becoming more similar to those facing middle-income market economies. Already one has seen, at least until mid-1998, in the Czech Republic, Estonia, Hungary, Latvia, Poland, and perhaps Croatia and Slovenia, a strong recovery running ahead of itself and generating risks of overheating, and contagion leading to reversals of capital inflows. In fact, in the case of the Czech Republic, this scenario materialized in 1997. Furthermore, in the future these more advanced transition economies will not be able to rely on the early and substantial efficiency improvements from the elimination of the distortions of central planning. Rather, their growth will depend much more on the mobilization of savings and their efficient intermediation by the financial sector into high investment. Also, much more effort will be needed to rationalize and perhaps still reduce these countries' expensive social programs; otherwise, ironically, these transition economies could find themselves with new labor market distortions quite soon after the removal of the fundamental product market distortions of central planning.

For most of the CIS countries, and to some extent those in southeastern Europe, a large unfinished agenda of market-oriented reforms remains. The extent of the task ranges from the completion of large-scale privatization and a meaningful imposition of hard budget constraints in Bulgaria and Romania, to making a serious start on reform in Belarus and Turkmenistan, to restarting the process in Uzbekistan. In all but the last three countries, the first swallows of a market springtime in fact appeared some time ago. But the winter of an uncertain transition appears to be stubbornly reappearing in other countries, as market signals, institutions, and credible government policies supporting markets are buffeted by a lack of clarity, policy reversals, and lack of follow-through in some reform areas. As a result, the reform agenda (and in a few cases even the stabilization agenda) remains quite extensive in these countries, and in some cases there is danger of further backsliding.

Finally, in all countries there remains the very important task of securely establishing good economic governance—this is perhaps more sorely lacking in the CIS and southeastern Europe, but it is important in the others as well. In many countries (especially in this second group) the government has still not pulled back enough from interventions in economic activity and various types of signaling with respect to resource allocation. But at the same time these governments have perhaps pulled back too far from the crucial task of providing the discipline of law and order, as well as a secure climate for individuals to engage in fruitful economic activity of their choice.

Indeed, in many countries a kind of vicious circle has developed. Poor economic governance delays structural reform, which in turn inhibits the economic recovery and constrains the development—and influence on policies—of a new, more dynamic business sector. This is accompanied by the perpetuation of old economic structures and relationships that tend to inhibit improvements in governance. Clearly, this vicious circle needs to be broken by finding ways to more actively promote good economic governance.

Appendix: Regression Analysis of Key Factors Underlying Growth

As Harberger (1998) observed, growth is, at heart, the sum of "a thousand and one" individual initiatives by entrepreneurs and managers to make improvements in products and processes. Regression analysis cannot explain such growth. Rather, it can at best illustrate its nature by organizing the underlying stylized facts. A background paper for this study (Havrylyshyn, Izvorski, and van Rooden, 1998) attempts such an exercise, in a manner similar to several recent studies on transition, by marshaling the stylized facts of growth in 25 countries over eight years (1990–97), together with values for variables reflecting some of the key factors hypothesized to affect growth. The relationship is formulated as follows:

growth = f (inflation, general structural reform progress, elements of reform, size of government, initial economic conditions, compliance with Fund programs).

With 200 observations for most but not all of these variables, the above relationship can be estimated for both the entire period and the subperiods. Although the distinction is somewhat arbitrary, it is useful to consider separately the period of "decline" (1990–93) and the period of "recovery" (1994–97). During the first period, at most a handful of countries saw the beginnings of recovery; during the second, nearly a dozen countries experienced three or more years of growth, and most others either began to grow or at least saw the decline approaching bottom.

Because data for 1998 were still incomplete at the time of this writing, the sample period comprises the years 1990–97. However, when the sample period is extended to include estimates for 1998, the results remain intact.

By far the dominant statistical association is found for two policy variables: the degree of price stabilization and general progress in structural reforms. The equation's explanatory power is quite high for this type of data set: the adjusted R^2 ranges from about 0.50 for the whole period (equation A1 in Table 11) to about 0.80 for the annual growth observed in the recovery period (equation C1). It is notable that the results are stronger and have higher statistical significance on standard econometric tests in regressions for the recovery period, with 100 observations, than in regressions using the full database of 200 observations for the period 1990–97. This is to be expected, of course, because the factors that explain decline are not exactly the same as those that explain recovery. In particular, one factor—the price liberalization subcomponent of the reform index—has an initial partially negative effect on output (which could be due to the Schumpeterian destruction of the "bad"; equation B2). But as reform and time progress, the price liberalization effect is fully positive (Schumpeterian creation of the new "good"; equation C2), or, put differently, early price reform begins to matter once additional reforms in other areas have taken place.

When separate equations are estimated for the CEE countries and the Baltics on the one hand (equations A2 and A2'), and for the CIS countries on the other (equations A3 and A3'), it is notable that a given amount of reform, as measured by the index, has a stronger impact on growth in the first group of countries. This could reflect the fact that, from the onset of the sample period, the CEE countries and the Baltics were already at a more advanced stage of transition than the CIS countries.

Table 11. Regression Analysis of Growth Determinants

Equation	Sample	Independent variables[1]				Adjusted R²
		LNP	RI	EXP[2]	INCOND	
A1	All	-2.57 (-17.70)	11.21 (10.86)			0.54
A2	CEE + Baltics	-3.27 (-12.56)	14.69 (10.10)			0.58
A3	CIS	-2.22 (-10.91)	8.87 (3.68)			0.46
A4	All	-2.62 (-17.92)	13.01 (10.85)		-2.06 (-3.02)	0.55
A5	CEE + Baltics	-3.26 (-12.23)	15.68 (9.79)		-1.18 (-1.19)	0.58
A6	CIS	-2.28 (-11.68)	9.14 (3.99)		-3.05 (-2.99)	0.50
A7	All	-2.55 (-14.30)	19.93 (8.67)	-0.10 (-2.43)	-2.53 (-3.63)	0.66
A8	CEE + Baltics	-3.07 -10.31)	29.44 (5.44)	-0.20 (-2.45)	-4.00 (-4.15)	0.62
A9	CIS	-1.85 (-4.44)	16.52 (5.17)	-0.17 (-2.17)	-1.47 (-0.93)	0.61

Equation	Sample	Independent variables[3]			Adjusted R²
		LNP	RI	INCOND	
A1'	All	-2.52 (-18.52)	11.14 (12.13)		0.55
A2'	CEE + Baltics	-3.13 (-13.22)	14.14 (11.19)		0.58
A3'	CIS	-2.16 (11.63)	8.11 (3.98)		0.48
A4'	All	-2.58 (-18.77)	12.81 (12.08)	-1.98 (-3.23)	0.55
A5'	CEE + Baltics	-3.13 (-12.95)	15.47 (10.88)	-1.50 (-1.67)	0.59
A6'	CIS	-2.22 (-12.51)	8.15 (4.23)	-3.09 (-3.29)	0.53

Equation	Sample	Independent variables[4]						Adjusted R²
		LNP	RI[5]	LIP	LEN	LEX	LEG	
B1	All	-2.08 (-12.00)	2.51 (1.53)					0.48
B2	All	-1.91 (-11.01)	13.75 (2.99)	-12.40 (-2.58)				0.53
B3	All	-2.00 (-11.67)		1.38 (0.82)				0.51
B4	All	-2.08 (-12.00)	-0.81 (-0.27)		4.42 (1.15)			0.48
B5	All	-2.09 (-12.66)			3.52 (1.76)			0.49
B6	All	-2.02 (-11.36)	-3.03 (-0.57)			4.08 (1.09)		0.50
B7	All	-2.08 (-12.70)				2.28 (1.67)		0.48

Table 11 (*Concluded*)

Equation	Sample	LNP	RI[5]	LIP	LEN	LEX	LEG	PRO	Adjusted R²
				Independent variables[6]					
C1	All	−2.44	14.11						0.81
		(−16.05)	(21.12)						
C2	All	−2.84	3.01	12.47					0.77
		(−11.88)	(1.10)	(3.45)					
C3	All	−2.30		16.00					0.76
		(−14.04)		(17.15)					
C4	All	−2.64	13.08		−0.43				0.74
		(−12.21)	(3.73)		(−0.12)				
C5	All	−2.30			13.91				0.80
		(−16.01)			(20.41)				
C6	All	−2.39	5.75			6.09			0.75
		(−13.47)	(1.38)			(1.93)			
C7	All	−2.34				10.26			0.74
		(−13.00)				(16.73)			
C8	All	−2.05	15.37				−2.25		0.87
		(−12.43)	(10.08)				(−1.97)		
C9	All	−1.42					9.78		0.74
		(−6.77)					(12.91)		
C10	All	−2.50						0.11	0.65
		(−10.94)						12.61	(12.61)

Sources: National authorities; de Melo, Denizer, and Gelb (1996); de Melo and others (1997); EBRD, *Transition Report*, various issues; and IMF staff estimates.

Note: Dependent variable in all equations is real GDP growth; independent variables are as follows (t-statistics in parentheses):

LNP	Natural logarithm of inflation (CPI, year-on-year).
RI	Structural reform index.
EXP	Government expenditure as a percentage of GDP.
INCOND	Initital conditions (structural indicators from de Melo and others, 1997).
LIP	Structural reform subindex for liberalization of internal prices.
LEN	Structural reform subindex for private entry in markets.
LEX	Structural reform subindex for liberalization of trade and foreign exchange systems.
LEG	Structural reform index for legal reform.
PRO	IMF-supported program implementation indicator (percentage of performance criteria met).

[1]Data are for 1990–97 except where noted otherwise.
[2]Equations including this variable are estimated using 1992–97 data.
[3]Data are for 1990–98.
[4]Data are for 1990–93.
[5]This variable excludes those subcomponents that are included sepearately in the specification.
[6]Data are for 1994–97.

Of the reform subcomponents, price liberalization stands out, as noted, as does its statistical explanatory power when included together with the general reform index, which then excludes the price liberalization subcomponent (equations B2 and C2). The other components (trade and foreign exchange reform, privatization and ease of new entry, legal reform) are each close substitutes for the general index. However, they do not have strong additional separate significance in the statistical analysis, except for trade and foreign exchange liberalization in the recovery period, which has a positive effect (equation C6). The generally very close association of the various subcomponents of reform is similar to the results for other economies in Aziz and Wescott (1997), in that a *combination* of policies is more critical for growth than any single type of policy.

Two factors that usually play a large role in statistical studies of long-term growth in other economies—the investment-GDP ratio and the degree of economic openness (or a proxy for export growth)—were not found to show a significant statistical association with growth in this study (results not shown). For investment, the reason was noted in the text: the nature of transition is such that efficiency improvements are a particularly important potential source of early growth, and large new investments may not be necessary. They may, of course, be necessary to some degree for the growing portions of the economy, but this may be accompanied by the shrinking of investment in other areas. Openness of an economy is difficult to measure, and export growth is as much an effect or reflection of early, efficiency-based growth as it is a cause; for these reasons, its explanatory power may not be great. Foreign direct investment is generally unlikely to contribute to the early recovery, for it will not be forthcoming until after the conditions that generate growth (stabilization and structural reforms) are well in place.

Initial conditions, including overindustrialization, do matter and show a statistically significant negative effect on growth for the sample as a whole (equations A4 and A7). But the magnitude of this effect is very small compared with that of the main policy variables; it requires relatively little additional improvement in macroeconomic and structural policies to compensate for more adverse initial conditions. For example, an industry share 10 percentage points higher in 1990 (say, 40 rather than 30) would have lowered the growth rate by 0.8 percentage point, but this could have been fully offset by a small increase in the reform index (which is scaled 0.0 to 1.0) from, say, 0.2 to 0.24, or from 0.3 to 0.34. From this, we may conclude that policies are the most important factor explaining differences in growth performance among countries.

Equations A6 and A6' suggest that initial conditions have had a more pronounced adverse impact on growth in the CIS countries than in CEE and the Baltics. However, this again may reflect the more advanced stage of the transition process in the latter group, as the impact of initial conditions can be expected to diminish over time. Moreover, when the equation controls for the size of the government (equations A7, A8, and A9), the impact of initial conditions is actually less strong in the CIS countries.

Finally, turning to the association with Fund programs, it is found that an index of effective program implementation (based on compliance information in the IMF's database and described in a background paper by Mercer-Blackman and Unigovskaya, 2000) is positively correlated with growth in the regressions (equation C10). In effect, the program implementation variable is closely correlated with the reform index, and both have very similar effects in the regression equations; when both variables are included in the equation for 1994–97, the program implementation variable displaces the structural reform indicator. This stylized fact might be interpreted as reflecting an underlying (and unmeasurable) factor, namely, commitment of the authorities. Where authorities are committed to reform, they know what needs to be done or how to design a policy program, and they ensure that it is implemented. Therefore, one observes early stabilization, early and strong progress on reforms, and effective implementation of Fund programs (all of the sustained growth transition economies except Slovenia have had—and generally still have—Fund programs), and finally, as a result, good growth performance. Thus the variable that is missing in the econometrics may be the most important variable in practice.

Bibliography

Aghion, Philippe, and Olivier Jean Blanchard, 1993, "On the Spread of Transition in Central Europe," EBRD Working Paper No. 6 (London: European Bank for Reconstruction and Development).

Åslund, Anders, Peter Boone, and Simon Johnson, 1996, "How to Stabilize: Lessons from Post-Communist Countries," *Brookings Papers on Economic Activity: 1*, Brookings Institution, pp. 217–313.

Aziz, Jahangir, and Robert F. Wescott, 1997, "Policy Complementarities and the Washington Consensus," IMF Working Paper 97/118 (Washington: International Monetary Fund).

Barro, Robert J., and Xavier Sala-i-Martin, 1994, *Economic Growth* (New York: McGraw Hill).

Berg, Andrew, Eduardo Borensztein, Ratna Sahay, and Jeromin Zettelmeyer, 1999, "The Evolution of Output in Transition Economies: Explaining the Differences," IMF Working Paper 99/73 (Washington: International Monetary Fund).

Blanchard, Oliver, 1997, *The Economics of Transition in Eastern Europe* (Oxford: Clarendon Press).

Bloem, Adriaan M., Paul Cotterell, and Terry Gigantes, 1996, "National Accounts in Transition Countries: Distortions and Biases," IMF Working Paper 96/130 (Washington: International Monetary Fund).

Broeck, Mark de, and Vincent Koen, 2000, "The 'Soaring Eagle': Anatomy of the Polish Take-off in the 1990s," IMF Working Paper 00/6 (Washington: International Monetary Fund).

Brenton, Paul, and Daniel Gros, 1997, "Trade Reorientation and Recovery in Transition Economies," *Oxford Review of Economic Policy*, Vol. 13, No. 2, pp. 65–76.

Brunetti, Aymo, Gregory Kisunko, and Beatrice Weder, 1997a, "Credibility of Rules and Economic Growth: Evidence from a Worldwide Survey of the Private Sector," Policy Research Working Paper No. 1760 (Washington: World Bank).

———, 1997b, "Institutional Obstacles to Doing Business: Region-by-Region Results from a Worldwide Survey of the Private Sector," Policy Research Working Paper No. 1759 (Washington: World Bank).

———, 1997c, "Reliability of Rules and Economic Performance in Former Socialist Countries," Policy Research Working Paper No. 1809 (Washington: World Bank).

Bruno, Michael, and William Easterly, 1998, "Inflation Crises and Long-Run Growth," *Journal of Monetary Economics*, Vol. 41, pp. 3–26.

Carlin, Wendy, 1995, "Enterprise Restructuring in Early Transition: The Case Study Evidence from Central and Eastern Europe," *Economics of Transition*, Vol. 3 (December), pp. 427–58 (London: European Bank for Reconstruction and Development).

Christophersen, Peter, and Peter Doyle, 1998, "From Inflation to Growth: Eight Years of Transition," IMF Working Paper 98/99 (Washington: International Monetary Fund).

de Melo, Martha, Cevdet Denizer, and Alan Gelb, 1996, "From Plan to Market: Patterns of Transition" (Washington: World Bank, Policy Research Department, Transition Economics Division).

de Melo, Martha, Cevdet Denizer, Alan Gelb, and Stoyan Tenev, 1997, "Circumstance and Choice: The Role of Initial Conditions and Policies in Transition Economies" Policy Research Working Paper No. 1866 (Washington: World Bank).

Dhonte, Pierre, and Ishan Kapur, 1997, "Towards a Market Economy: Structures of Governance," IMF Working Paper 97/11 (Washington: International Monetary Fund).

Djankov, Simeon, and Bernard M. Hoekman, 1996, "Fuzzy Transition and Firm Efficiency: Evidence from Bulgaria, 1991–94," CEPR Discussion Paper No. 1424 (London: Center for Economic Policy Research).

———, 1997, "Trade Reorientation and Post-Reform Productivity Growth in Bulgarian Enterprises," World Bank Policy Research Working Paper No. 1707 (Washington: World Bank).

Earle, John, and Saul Estrin, 1997, "After Voucher Privatization: The Structure of Corporate Ownership in Russian Manufacturing Industry," CEPR Discussion Paper No. 1736 (London: Centre for Economic Policy Research).

Easterly, William, and Stanley Fischer, 1995, "The Soviet Economic Decline," *World Bank Economic Review*, Vol. 9, No. 3 (September), pp. 341–71.

European Bank for Reconstruction and Development, 1996, 1997, 1998, *Transition Report* (London).

Fischer, Stanley, 1993, "The Role of Macroeconomic Factors in Growth," *Journal of Monetary Economics*, Vol. 32, pp. 458–512.

Fischer, Stanley, and Alan Gelb, 1991, "The Process of Socialist Economic Transformation," *Journal of Economic Perspectives*, Vol. 5, No. 4, pp. 91–105.

Fischer, Stanley, Ratna Sahay, and Carlos A. Végh, 1996, "Stabilization and Growth in Transition Economies: The Early Experience," *Journal of Economic Perspectives*, Vol. 10, No. 2, pp. 45–66.

———, 1998, "From Transition to Market: Evidence and Growth Prospects," IMF Working Paper 98/52 (Washington: International Monetary Fund).

Frydman, Roman, Cheryl Gray, Marek Hessel, and Andrzej Rapaczynski, 1997, "Private Ownership and Corporate Performance: Some Lessons from Transition Economies," Policy Research Paper No. 1830 (Washington: World Bank).

Gaddy, Clifford G., and Barry W. Ickes, 1998, "Beyond Bailout: Time to Face Reality About Russia's 'Virtual Economy,'" *Foreign Affairs*, Vol. 77 (September–October), pp. 53–67.

Galal, Ahmed, Leroy Jones, Pankaj Tandon, and Ingo Vogelsang, 1994, *Welfare Consequences of Selling Public Enterprises: An Empirical Analysis* (London: Oxford University Press).

Ghosh, Atish, and Steven Phillips, 1998, "Inflation, Disinflation, and Growth," IMF Working Paper 98/68 (Washington: International Monetary Fund).

Harberger, Arnold C., 1998, "A Vision of the Growth Process," *American Economic Review*, Vol. 88, No. 1, pp. 1–32.

Havrylyshyn, Oleh, and Hassan Al-Atrash, 1998, "Opening Up and Geographic Diversification of Trade in Transition Economies," IMF Working Paper 98/22 (Washington: International Monetary Fund).

Havrylyshyn, Oleh, Ivailo Izvorski, and Ron van Rooden, 1998, "Recovery and Sustained Growth in Transition Economies 1990–1997—A Stylized Regression Analysis," IMF Working Paper 98/141 (Washington: International Monetary Fund).

Havrylyshyn, Oleh, and Donal McGettigan, 1999, "Privatization in Transition Countries: A Sampling of the Literature," IMF Working Paper 99/6 (Washington: International Monetary Fund).

Havrylyshyn, Oleh, and others, 1999, *Growth Experience in Transition Countries, 1990–98*, IMF Occasional Paper No. 184 (Washington: International Monetary Fund).

Hernández-Catá, Ernesto, 1997, "Liberalization and the Behavior of Output During the Transition from Plan to Market," *Staff Papers*, International Monetary Fund, Vol. 44 (December), pp. 405–29.

Hu, Zuliu F., and Mohsin S. Khan, 1997, "Why Is China Growing So Fast?" *Staff Papers*, International Monetary Fund, Vol. 44 (March), pp. 103–31.

International Monetary Fund, 1994, "Financial Relations Among Countries of the Former Soviet Union," *Economic Review* (Washington).

———, 1995, "World Economic Outlook, October 1995," *World Economic and Financial Surveys* (Washington).

———, 1997, *The ESAF at Ten Years: Economic Adjustment and Reform in Low-Income Countries*, IMF Occasional Paper No. 156 (Washington).

———, 1998, "Cambodia: Recent Economic Developments," SM/98/82 (Washington).

Johnson, Omotunde E.G., 1997, "Cooperation, Emergence of the Economic Agency Role of Government, and Governance," IMF Working Paper 97/150 (Washington: International Monetary Fund).

Johnson, Simon, Daniel Kaufmann, and Andrei Shleifer, 1997, "The Unofficial Economy in Transition," *Brookings Papers on Economic Activity: 2*, Brookings Institution.

Kaufmann, Daniel, 1997, "Corruption: Some Myths and Facts," *Foreign Policy* (Summer), pp. 114–31.

Koen, Vincent, and Paula de Masi, 1997, "Prices in the Transition: Ten Stylized Facts," IMF Working Paper 97/158 (Washington: International Monetary Fund).

Koning, Jozef, 1997a, "Competition and Firm Performance in Transition Economies: Evidence from Firm Level Surveys in Slovenia, Hungary and Romania," CEPR Discussion Paper Series No. 1770 (London: Centre for Economic Policy Research).

———, 1997b, "Firm Growth and Ownership in Transition Countries" (unpublished; Leuven, Belgium: Leuven Institute for Central and East European Studies of the University of Leuven).

Kornai, János, 1994, "Transformational Recession: The Main Causes," *Journal of Comparative Economics*, Vol. 19, pp. 39–63.

Lau, Lawrence J., Yingyi Qian, and Gérard Roland, 1998, "Reform Without Losers: An Interpretation of China's Dual-Track Approach to Transition," CEPR Discussion Paper No. 1798 (London: Centre for Economic Policy Research).

Lilien, David M., 1982, "Sectoral Shifts and Cyclical Unemployment," *Journal of Political Economy*, Vol. 90, pp. 777–93.

Mauro, Paolo, 1997, "Why Worry About Corruption?" *Economic Issues*, Vol. 6 (Washington: International Monetary Fund).

Mercer-Blackman, Valerie, and Anna Unigovskaya, 2000, "Compliance with IMF Program Indicators and Growth in Transition Countries," IMF Working Paper 00/47 (Washington: International Monetary Fund).

Olson, Mancur, 1997, "Big Bills Left on the Sidewalk: Why Some Nations Are Rich and Others Poor," *Journal of Economic Perspectives*, Vol. 10, pp. 3–24.

Olson, Mancur, Naveen Sarna, and Anand V. Swamy, 1997, "Governance and Growth: A Simple Hypothesis Explaining Cross-Country Differences in Productivity Growth" (unpublished; Washington: Economic Growth Center of the U.S. Agency for International Development).

Pinto, Brian, Marek Belba, and Stefan Krajewski, 1993, "Transforming State Enterprises in Poland: Evidence on Adjustment by Manufacturing Firms," *Brookings Papers on Economic Activity: 1*, pp. 213–70.

PlanEcon, 1998, *Review and Outlook for the Former Soviet Republics* (Washington).

Pohl, Gerhard, Robert Anderson, Stijn Claessens, and Simeon Djankov, 1997, "Privatization and Restructuring in Central and Eastern Europe: Evidence and Policy Options," World Bank Technical Paper No. 368 (Washington: World Bank).

Roberts, Bryan, Yevgeny Gorkov, and Jay Madigan, 1998, "Is Privatization a Free Lunch? New Evidence on Ownership Status and Firm Performance" (Washington: U.S. Agency for International Development).

Romer, Paul, 1990, "Endogenous Technological Change," *Journal of Political Economy*, Vol. 98, No. 5, pp. S71–S102.

Sachs, Jeffrey, 1996, "The Transition at Mid Decade," *American Economic Association, Papers and Proceedings*, Vol. 86, No. 2, pp. 128–33.

Sachs, Jeffrey, and Wing Thye Woo, 1997, "Understanding China's Economic Performance," HIID Development Discussion Paper No. 575 (Cambridge, Massachusetts: Harvard Institute for International Development).

Sala-i-Martin, Xavier, 1997, "I Just Ran Four Million Regressions," NBER Working Paper No. 6252 (Cambridge, Massachusetts: National Bureau of Economic Research).

Sarel, Michael, 1996, "Nonlinear Effects of Inflation on Economic Growth," *Staff Papers*, International Monetary Fund, Vol. 43 (March), pp. 199–215.

Schaffer, Mark, 1998, "Do Firms in Transition Economies Have Soft Budget Constraints? A Reconsideration of Concepts and Evidence," *Journal of Comparative Economics*, Vol. 26, pp. 157–79.

Selowsky, Marcelo, and Ricardo Martin, 1996, "Policy Performance and Output Growth in the Transition Economies," *American Economic Association, Papers and Proceedings*, Vol. 87, No. 2, pp. 349–53.

Smith, Stephen C., Beam-Cheol Cin, and Milan Vodopivec, 1997, "Privatization Incidence, Ownership Forms, and Firm Performance: Evidence from Slovenia," *Journal of Comparative Economics*, Vol. 25, pp. 158–79.

Tarr, David G., 1994, "The Terms-of-Trade Effects of Moving to World Prices on Countries of the Former Soviet Union," *Journal of Comparative Economics*, Vol. 18, No. 1, pp. 1–24.

Vienna Institute for Comparative Economic Studies, 1997, "Countries in Transition," in *Handbook of Statistics* (Vienna).

Westin, Peter, 1998, "Comparative Advantage and Characteristics of Russia's Trade with the European Union," *Review of Economies in Transition*, No. 2., pp. 5–30 (Bank of Finland: Institute for Economies in Transition).

Wolf, Holger C., 1997, "Transition Strategies: Choices and Outcomes" (New York: Stern Business School).

World Bank, 1996a, *World Development Report 1996: From Plan to Market* (Washington).

————, 1996b, *Statistical Handbook 1996—States of the Former USSR*, Studies of Economies in Transformation (Washington).

Zettelmeyer, Jeromin, 1999, "Uzbek Growth Puzzle," *Staff Papers*, International Monetary Fund, Vol. 46 (September–December), pp. 274–92.

Inflation and Growth in Transition: Are the Asian Economies Different?   5

Sanjay Kalra and Torsten Sløk

This chapter assesses progress made by China, the Lao People's Democratic Republic (henceforth Laos), Vietnam, and Mongolia in their transition to a market-based system. It compares their progress to that of the economies of Central and Eastern Europe (CEE) as well as of the Baltics and the former Soviet Union (BRO). It also outlines future challenges to these economies. These countries have liberalized prices and exchange rates and are now firmly integrated into the world economy. Although they are very far from their initial positions, much still remains to be accomplished, especially in structural reform. But these economies are now on an irreversible path.[1]

The contribution of initial conditions to subsequent stabilization and reform in the transition economies has been widely discussed in the literature (e.g., de Melo and others, 1998). A broad consensus suggests that while favorable initial conditions have a salutary effect on the success of transition, a willingness to stabilize and to undertake structural reforms is critical to ensuring sustained growth and low inflation. Nevertheless, it has been suggested that the more favorable conditions of the Asian economies at the outset of the transition process, compared with those in the CEE-BRO economies, may have smoothed the transformation for them. (See Table 1.) Among the conditions favoring the Asian economies were the following:

- A more settled political situation allowed institution building to focus on economics without also having to establish a new political order. Reforms took place in China, Laos, and Vietnam without the collapse of their political structures. Mongolia is the exception, since it undertook far-reaching, but peaceful, political reforms in 1992 after the dissolution of the Soviet Union.
- A relatively large agricultural sector and rural labor surpluses facilitated growth without wholesale dismantling of the "overindustrialized" state-owned sector as in the CEE-BRO countries. In China, agriculture accounted for about 40 percent of GDP in the late 1970s, employing 70 percent of the economically active

---

[1]For earlier cross-country transitional experiences, see Bruno (1992), Aghevli (1992), and McKinnon (1992). More recent developments are discussed in Fischer and others (1998).

population. The share of agriculture in output in Laos, Mongolia, and Vietnam in the late 1980s was similar or higher. In CEE-BRO economies, the share of agricultural output tended to be lower.

- Varying, but generally looser, integration in the Council for Mutual Economic Assistance (CMEA) system (except for Mongolia) cushioned the Asian economies against the large external shocks associated with the collapse of the former Soviet Union.
- A collective memory of market-oriented systems was alive, particularly in Indochina. In Vietnam, a significant nonstate sector continued to exist, because about 40 percent of industrial production and a large part of the service sector were in private hands. Moreover, agriculture in the south had never been fully collectivized. In Laos, central planning had held sway only since the mid-1970s, and a strong market legacy remained. This was, however, less the case in China and Mongolia, where central planning had existed for decades.

However, not all initial conditions in the Asian economies were favorable:

- Consistent with the dominance of agriculture were low per capita income, extreme poverty, rudimentary infrastructure, and weak administrative capacity. Also, in China and Mongolia, a larger state industrial sector paralleled the experience of the CEE-BRO economies.
- The external environment was often unfavorable for these countries. While reforms in Laos and Mongolia, undertaken in the context of Fund-supported programs, paved the way for external assistance, Vietnam's isolation from the international community made arranging external assistance more problematic (though these difficulties were somewhat cushioned by oil exports and remittances).

Just as the initial conditions differed among the four countries, reform strategies also differed. China's reforms have often been characterized as gradualist (although, as argued below, early and rapid reforms were made, especially in agriculture). In contrast, Mongolia set out on a road to rapid reforms. Laos and Vietnam are intermediate cases, mirroring some features of the advanced CEE transition economies.

Disinflation and Inflation Stabilization[2]

This section examines the Asian economies' efforts to stabilize inflation. Using a panel data set of 29 transition economies, the chapter ex-

---

[2]For a distinction between "disinflation" and "moderate inflation" see Cottarelli and Doyle in this volume.

Table 1. Macroeconomic Performance in Four Asian Transition Economies at the Start of Reforms and in Recent Years

Indicator	China Initial condition 1979	China Recent outcome 1998	Vietnam Initial condition 1985	Vietnam Recent outcome 1998	Laos Initial condition 1987	Laos Recent outcome 1998	Mongolia Initial condition 1992	Mongolia Recent outcome 1998	CEE-BRO Initial condition	CEE-BRO Recent outcome 1997–98
Real GDP growth (percent)[1]	7.6	8.3	3.6	5.9	−3.2	5.8	−9.5	3.7	−10	4
Inflation (percent, end period)	1.9	−1	223.3	9.2	40	141.88	325.5	6.5	788.5	15.9
					Median					
					(In percent of GDP)					
Overall budget deficit (excluding grants)	4.2	3	6.1	4.5	15.4	2.7	12.7	11.2	...	...
Current account deficit	−0.1	3.4	1.4	10.4	16	10.4	6.7	11.3	...	...
Official reserves (in weeks of imports)	9.4	43.2	0	8.9	0	2.1	0.6	11.5	...	...
Broad money	22.6	53.1	26	22.7	8.4	26.7	27.6	19.1	...	...

Source: *IMF Recent Economic Developments* (various issues); and Christoffersen and Doyle (1998).
Note: CEE = Central and Eastern Europe; BRO = Baltics, Russia, and other former Soviet Union countries.
[1]Average 1997–98.

amines the experience of the Asian economies in disinflating and stabilizing inflation. Since the CEE-BRO countries, used in Christoffersen and Doyle (1998), form part of this augmented data set, the experience of the Asian economies can be compared with the results reported elsewhere (e.g., Cottarelli and Doyle, in this volume).

Prior to the reforms, with the exception of China, all the Asian transition economies faced fiscal imbalances similar to, or larger than, those of the CEE-BRO economies. These imbalances, whose true size was masked by the lack of transparency in public sector accounts, were made worse by such early reforms as wage adjustments, price liberalization, exchange rate devaluation, and monetization of in-kind payments. At the same time, revenues from the rudimentary tax systems fell off as state enterprise performance declined because of reductions in budgetary transfers.

With the collapse of the former Soviet Union and the drying up of external assistance from the CMEA countries, the resulting deficits had to be monetized. Inflation escalated into hyperinflation, accompanied by substantial currency substitution and a sharp decline in the broad money-GDP ratio. The need for large relative price changes generated further price pressure. Relative price adjustments were particularly dramatic in the early phases of price liberalization, but became less so over time. Relative prices were adjusted fairly rapidly, partly reflecting limited indexation.

The initial inflation experience of the individual countries varied. With the exception of China, where inflation never rose above 30 percent, all other countries experienced high inflation at the onset of the transition. Figures 1 and 2 show inflation in the Asian transition economies within the time it took to stabilize. Inflation in Laos peaked at 100 percent in mid-1989, the result of an initial jump in prices after they were liberalized. In Vietnam, inflation reached 500 percent in 1986 and continued above 300 percent in 1987–88. In Mongolia, inflation peaked at 420 percent in early 1993. Even in China, measured inflation became higher and more variable during the transition.

Policies To Combat High Inflation

This section takes a close look at the role of structural reform in growth and assesses the progress made in the Asian economies. Some conclusions follow.

Fiscal consolidation and early, extensive agricultural reform were key to successful disinflation in the Asian economies. The fiscal consolidation-disinflation nexus witnessed in the CEE-BRO economies was repeated. China's fiscal position, already strong at the outset, required

Figure 1. Growth and Inflation in Four Asian Transition Economies
(In transition time)[1]

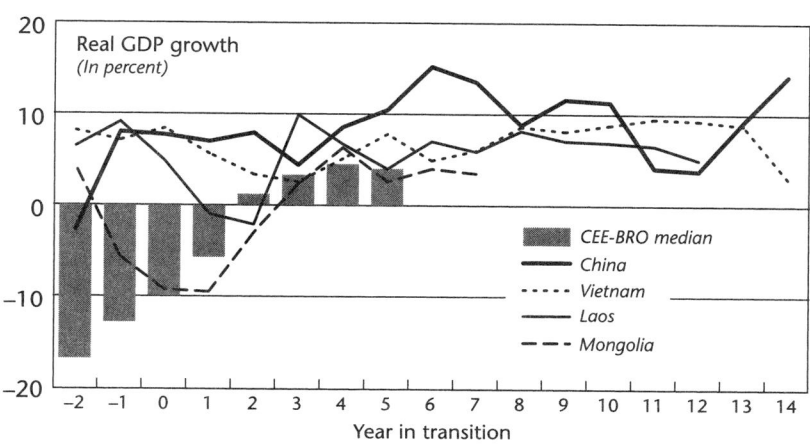

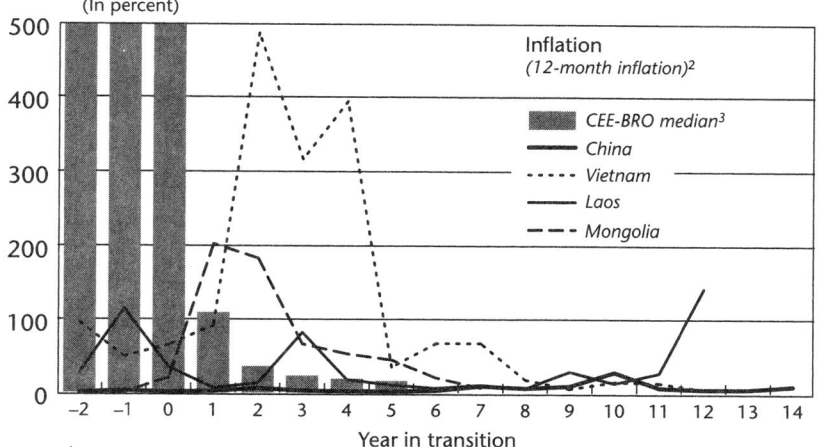

Sources: *World Economic Outlook* and IMF staff estimates.
Note: CEE is Central and Eastern Europe; BRO is Baltics, Russia, and other former Soviet Union countries.
[1]Period 1 is the first year of significant steps to transition: China (1979), Vietnam (1985), Laos (1987), and Mongolia (1992).
[2]Period average is used when 12-month inflation is unavailable.
[3]CEE-BRO median for periods –2, –1, and 0, are 892, 1021, and 789, respectively.

Figure 2. Inflation in Four Asian Transition Economies, 1993–98
(12-month percent change)

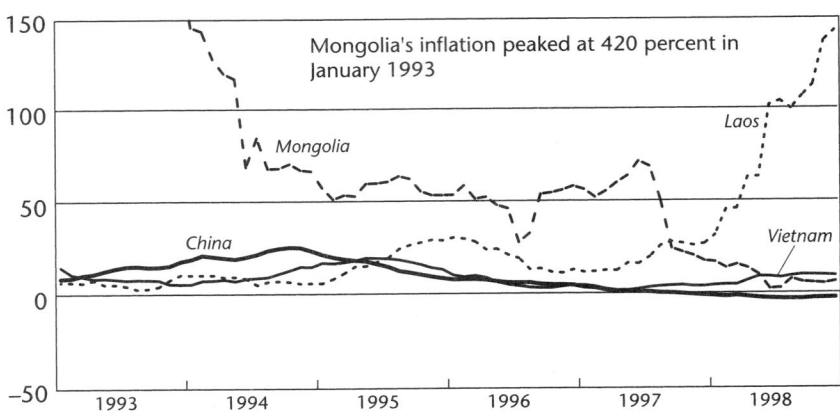

Sources: IMF Institute and staff estimates.

only modest adjustment. Sizable fiscal tightening undertaken in Laos and Vietnam initially focused on expenditure cuts and later on revenue enhancement (Dodsworth and others, 1996b). In Mongolia, the availability of substantial external assistance reduced the need for domestic financing to bring the budget deficit down to a reasonably low level.

Exchange rate policy in all the Asian countries was flexible, with movements in the free market rate a key indicator for the official exchange rate. None of these countries used the exchange rate as a nominal anchor for stabilization, a feature that parallels the limited use of formal exchange rate and monetary targets in the CEE-BRO countries. The Asian economies, known to be undertaking structural change, with its attendant uncertainty, clearly had inadequate international reserves to make official pegs credible. The monetary framework in each country was discretionary. Laos and Mongolia relied on Fund-supported programs to enhance credibility.

Disinflation and Inflation Stabilization

Tight financial policies were successful in reducing inflation in Laos, Mongolia, and Vietnam (Figures 2 and 3). Inflation in Laos was held to 10 percent during 1991 and remained in single digits until the end of 1994, but rose steadily during 1995 and the first half of 1996, to settle

Figure 3. Fiscal Indicators in Four Asian Transition Economies, 1989–98
(In percent of GDP)

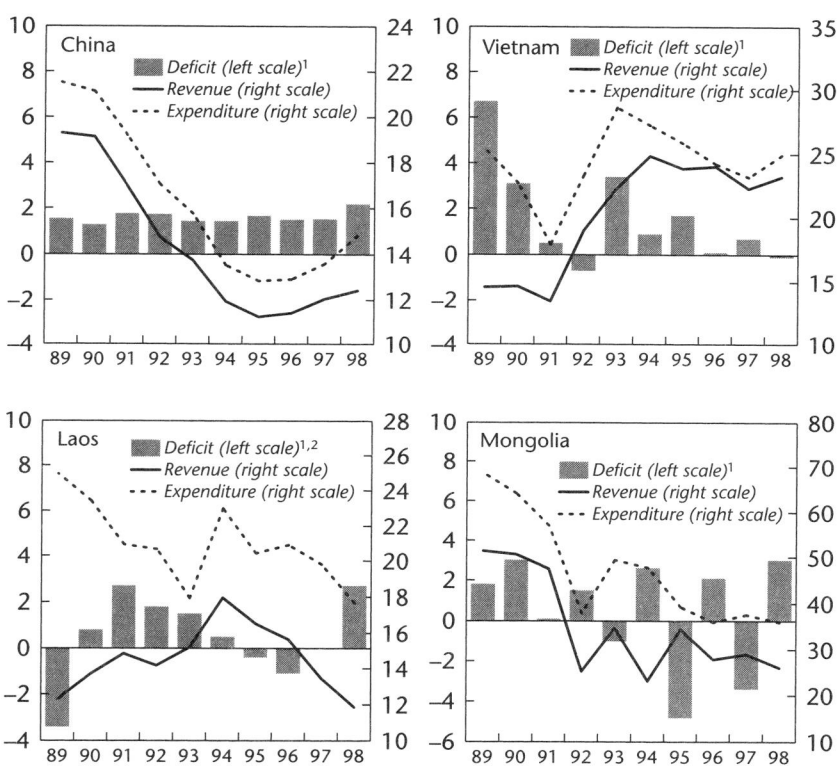

Sources: *World Economic Outlook* and IMF staff estimates.
[1] Domestically financed deficit.
[2] The fiscal year was changed from a calendar year basis to an October–September basis in 1992.

in the 10–25 percent range. In Vietnam, inflation was reduced to 35 percent during 1989, and after increasing again to almost 70 percent in 1990–91, declined to single digits during 1993–94. It rose to 15–20 percent during 1994–95, before falling again to single digits during 1996–97. In Mongolia, inflation was reduced to single digits in 1998. In China, inflation never crossed moderate double-digits levels.

Notwithstanding successful disinflation, the experience of the Asian economies exemplifies the difficulties in keeping inflation consistently low over a long period. The disinflation gains in Laos were reversed in 1997; inflation in China has persisted at moderate levels for some time and has displayed a significant cyclical pattern. These developments and the experience of some advanced transition economies of CEE suggest that inflation performance may remain variable and moderate inflation may persist in transitional economies for a long time. Advanced transition economies may already be subject to inflation cycles of the type witnessed in market economies. Furthermore, as the transition progresses and inflation falls to more moderate levels, the link between fiscal tightening and disinflation may grow weaker.

Inflation and Growth in Transition

Strong output growth in the Asian transition economies (excluding Mongolia) during the disinflation period contrasted sharply with CEE-BRO experience. This growth was buoyed by a significant supply response from agriculture. In addition, contrary to deteriorating current account balances experienced in the CEE-BRO, the Asian economies benefited from improved external accounts and a rapid buildup of reserves associated with high export growth and low fiscal deficits. Moreover, import growth was relatively modest and often driven by investment needs.

Recent analyses have suggested threshold levels may exist in the relationship between inflation and growth (Sarel, 1996, and Ghosh and Phillips, 1998). This hypothesis is tested for the CEE-BRO transition economies by Christoffersen and Doyle (1998), who estimate the threshold level of inflation at about 13 percent, higher than in industrial market economies. Cottarelli and Doyle (in this volume) suggest that this higher threshold inflation may indicate that the threshold level falls during transition and may be lower for the advanced reformers. For the Asian countries, no clear indication of a threshold level of inflation is evident (Box 1). Adding the four Asian transition economies to Christofferson and Doyle's panel data set reduces the inflation threshold to about 8 percent.

These results suggest that, while inflation has inhibited growth in Asian transition countries, no evidence supports the view that the size of the negative effect increases when inflation passes a certain point. More work needs to be done to explain this phenomenon, which may in part reflect more moderate relative price distortions because of the larger share of agriculture in total output (Coorey and others, 1998). Also, the estimated fixed effects for the Asian transition countries are higher than those of the CEE-BRO economies, indicating that growth in the Asian countries has been stronger than in non-Asian transition countries for given levels of inflation.

Box 1. Inflation and Growth in Transition Economies

Recent analyses have suggested that threshold levels may exist in the relationship between inflation and growth: above the threshold inflation and growth may be negatively related, but below this level there may be no clear (or even a positive) relationship between growth and inflation (Sarel, 1996; and Ghosh and Phillips, 1998). Using Sarel's methodology, Christoffersen and Doyle (1998) test this hypothesis for the CEE-BRO transition countries and find a threshold level of inflation of about 13 percent, higher than in industrial market economies (Ghosh and Phillips). For the Asian transition economies, no clear threshold level of inflation is apparent. Using an augmented data set that includes Asian transition economies, the threshold level of inflation falls to 8.

The simplest version of the equations estimated in Christoffersen and Doyle is:

$$g_y = b_1 * \log\pi + b_2 * (\log\pi - \log\pi^*) + \text{fixed effects and control variables, (1)}$$

where g_y is growth rate of GDP, π is inflation, and π^* is the threshold level of inflation. The threshold value of inflation is defined as the value that maximizes R^2 for (1). For the variable inflation minus threshold, negative values are assigned the value zero. The coefficients are interpreted as follows: if inflation is below the threshold level then inflation has the coefficient b_1, whereas if inflation is above the threshold the coefficient becomes $b_1 + b_2$. Cottarelli and Doyle (chapter 3 in this volume) suggest that differences between transition and industrial countries may suggest that threshold levels of inflation may fall in "transition" time, and may be lower for the advanced reformers.

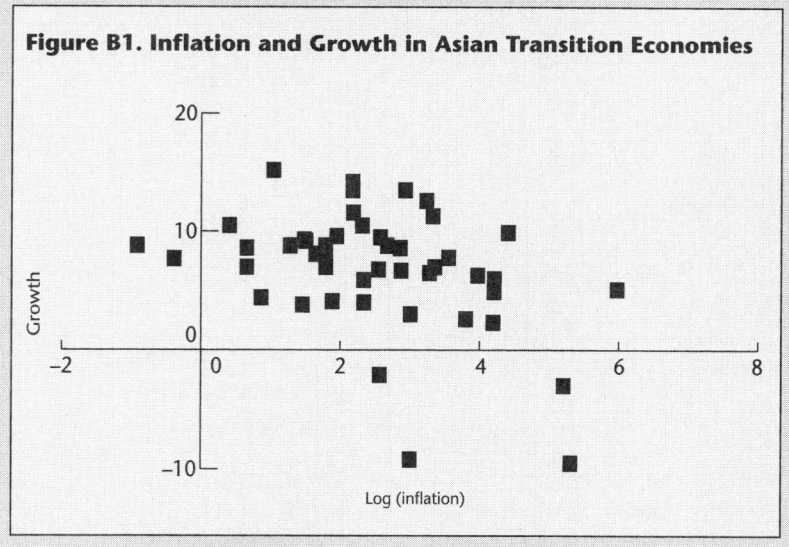

Figure B1. Inflation and Growth in Asian Transition Economies

Box 1 (*Concluded*)

Figure B1 shows a cross-plot of growth and inflation for the four Asian countries; no clear indication of a threshold level of inflation is apparent. The four Asian transition economies were added to Christoffersen and Doyle's panel data set and equation (1) was estimated using fixed effects, allowing the two groups of countries (Asian and non-Asian) to have different fixed effects. The reestimated equation is:

$$g_y = 1.66^*\log\pi - 5.55^* (\log\pi - \log\pi^*) \qquad (2)$$
$$\quad (2.40) \qquad (5.81)$$

$$R^2 = 0.54 \ \ S.E. = 7.64$$

Two results follow this reestimated equation: First, the fixed effects of equation (2) is 7.0 for the Asian transition countries and 1.6 for the non-Asian transition countries. This indicates that for the same level of inflation, growth was higher in the Asian transition countries. Second, the inflation threshold for the augmented data set is 8. (The R^2 from the estimation using the Christofferson and Doyle augmented panel data set is shown in Figure B2.)

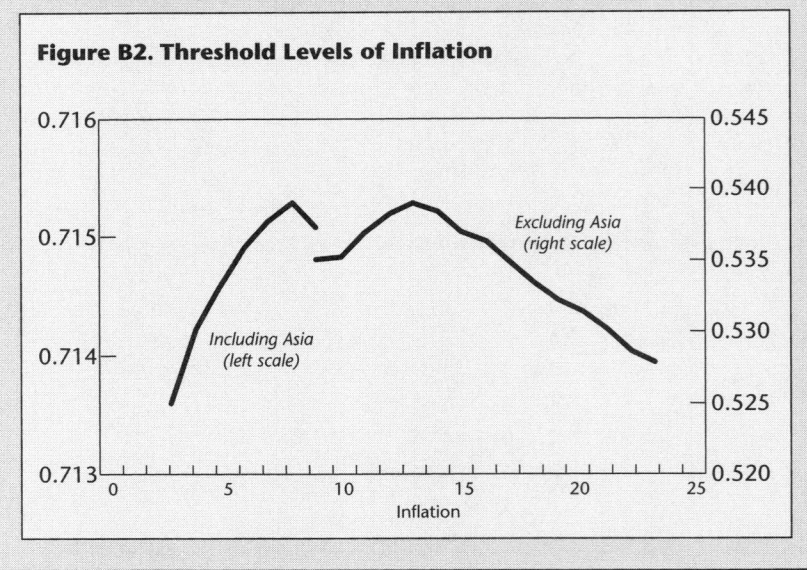

Figure B2. Threshold Levels of Inflation

Excluding Asia (right scale)

Including Asia (left scale)

Inflation

Growth and Structural Reform

The output performance of the Asian transition economies has, on the whole, been remarkably good. With the exception of Mongolia, these countries avoided the large output declines seen in the CEE-BRO economies.[3] China's economic performance over the past two decades has been particularly impressive.[4] Rapid growth in the Asian countries, such as China, that are perceived to have followed a gradualist approach to reform has raised questions about whether rapid reforms are the best path to sustained growth.[5] The remainder of this section reviews this debate, with particular reference to China where it has been most heated.

The Chinese Experience: Does Gradualism Pay?

China's strong economic performance since the onset of reforms has been the center of a lively debate about alternative approaches to structural reforms. Sachs and Woo (1997) divide the debate neatly into two camps: the experimentalists, who explicitly attribute China's success to the evolutionary, experimental, and incremental nature of the reform process (see Naughton, 1994, and Rawski, 1994), and the convergence school, including Sachs and Woo themselves, who view gradualism not as a strategy but as a result of continuing political conflict and other difficulties. The experimentalists argue that China is groping toward a unique economic model, and that a faster approach to reforms would have led to worse results. The convergence school, in contrast, believe that favorable outcomes have occurred despite gradualism, not because of it, and that the best results have been achieved precisely where reforms have been fastest. While a full assessment of this debate is beyond the scope of this chapter, the following is a brief summary of some key issues.

China's approach to economic reform needs first to be set in a historical context. Reforms began in late 1978, just two years after the end of the Cultural Revolution, a time of political and economic upheaval. As Fan Gang (1994) points out, economic conditions were improving fast, but neither the economic nor the political conditions were in place for shock therapy, even if that had been envisioned at the time. The objective of a "socialist market economy with Chinese characteristics" was not adopted until 1992, nearly 15 years after the reforms had begun. For these reasons a gradual approach to reform was inevitable in China.

---

[3]See Fischer and others (1998) for evidence on differences in output performance across countries in the CEE-BRO countries, and Mongolia during 1992–95.

[4]Strong overall growth performance in China has been associated with considerable variation across provinces. These variations provide useful information about the determinants of growth, including the importance of agriculture, state enterprises, and nonstate sector activity.

[5]See, for example, Fischer and others (1998) where an index of economic liberalization is found to be statistically significant in explaining growth performance.

Gradualism, however, is a crude way to describe reform in China. In very broad terms, this reform could be characterized as having at least four elements. First, China has followed what Fan Gang called an "easy to hard" reform sequence starting with the sectors in which gains were easiest and most productive. The development of the household responsibility system in agriculture gave families the right to most revenue from farming (although production controls remained and a substantial part of their output had to be sold at below-market prices). The relaxation of entry into industry in rural areas led to the development of the Township and Village Enterprises (TVEs), which have grown very rapidly, nourished by the large rural labor surplus. Setting up Special Economic Zones proved a magnet for foreign direct investment in the coastal provinces and had major spillover effects on local economies. Second, reform in China followed a "dual track" approach, aimed at having the old gradually give way to the new. This has been particularly evident in the case of prices and the foreign exchange market, where marginal prices and administered prices coexisted for some time before the systems were finally unified.

While this dual approach clearly had costs, especially in encouraging illegal arbitrage between the market and administered sectors, it had the important advantage of allowing market forces to operate at the margin. Third, the pattern of implementation has been cyclical, with periods of advance giving way to periods of consolidation in response to such economic problems as excess demand or inflation. This pattern has partly reflected the authorities' determination to maintain overall macroeconomic stability and partly the lack of effective indirect instruments for macroeconomic control. Fourth, the reforms have been carried out with considerable pragmatism and flexibility. The Chinese have often allowed different norms to coexist and compete (embodied in the phrase "seeking to cross the river by feeling the stones"—a phrase that contrasts interestingly with the Eastern European reformers slogan that "one can only cross a chasm in one jump"). A number of the most important initiatives, such as the household responsibility system in agriculture and the growth of TVEs, developed locally rather than being introduced by the central government.

Has gradualism succeeded in China or would a faster approach have been better? It is difficult, of course, to argue with success. China's growth rate during reform has been remarkably high, resulting in an enormous improvement in welfare for one quarter of the human race. But as Sachs and Woo cogently argue, it is far from clear that this was the *result* of gradualism. Indeed, the fastest growth took place in the sectors where reforms were most comprehensive. Rather, China's initial conditions—including the large rural labor surplus and the relatively large agricultural sector—permitted rapid growth without requiring politically difficult reform of state enterprises. In addition, starting from a position of near autarky, significant gains from trade were to be had as well. These conditions did not, of course, exist in the CEE-BRO economies.

The gradual pace of reform in public enterprises and in the financial sector has helped maintain social stability in China, but this has been bought at a price. While the share of state enterprises in output has steadily declined in China, these enterprises continue to use a disproportionate share of inputs. This has resulted in growing waste and financial loss, exacerbated by competition from the TVE and foreign enterprise sectors. These losses have been financed by the banks, resulting in a rising level of nonperforming loans and contingent fiscal liabilities that are unsustainable over the medium term (Lardy, 1998). Now that China has completed the "easy" phase of reforms, success in addressing these difficult issues holds the key to its continued success over the medium term.

Other Asian Transition Economies: The Pitfalls of Partial Reform

The experience of other Asian transition economies echoes themes heard in the case of China and the CEE-BRO economies (see appendix for details):

- Exogenous shocks and domestic discontent with the performance of centrally planned systems provided the initial impetus for the move to market-based systems. This sequence was perhaps clearest in Mongolia where the disruption stemming from the loss of transfers from the former Soviet Union and the breakdown of the CMEA system was most debilitating, and the collapse of the former Soviet Union provided the opportunity to break away from a grudgingly accepted economic system. Ironically, Laos initiated a move to decentralized decision making in 1979 when the loss of Western aid and an economic embargo combined with poor weather conditions to precipitate economic collapse.
- The large agricultural sector, perceived as an advantageous initial condition for many reasons, is often suggested as a factor in avoiding output collapse in the transition economies of Indochina (Dodsworth and others, 1996a and b; Woo and others, 1997). Institutional structures in agriculture are, or can rapidly

become, more flexible than those in state-owned industrial enterprises and thus permit a more rapid supply response to price incentives.[6] Other advantages have also been cited. Agricultural growth is a natural developmental process, and in the Asian economies it helped absorb rural labor surpluses. Agriculture also helped alleviate redundancies from the industrial sector because it had less pronounced wage and price rigidities. In contrast, the transition in the CEE-BRO economies involved reversing overindustrialization and costly, socially painful labor retrenchment.

- The choice of speed and scope of the transition—in the initial stages and as the transition progressed—was heavily influenced by initial conditions, political acceptance of the market mechanism, the ease with which difficulties associated with partial reforms could be contained initially and eventually remedied, and the availability of external financial assistance and foreign direct investment flows.

- Within the Asian economies, the experience of Vietnam was similar to that of China: the market was seen as an instrument for higher growth and was introduced selectively and in stages. Administrative measures continue to play an important role in the nonagricultural sector, and the trade regimes remain relatively restrictive. Laos and Mongolia also have similarities: there is an acceptance of the market, the role of administered prices is minimal, and outward orientation is strong. Greater reliance on decentralized decision making and market forces is also reflected in privatization, which is quite advanced in both countries, even in the nonagricultural sector.

- Decentralization was often initiated in response to popular unrest with central control (as in Laos). Furthermore, once initiated, the process was not always fully controllable. Many "spontaneous" privatizations took place in Mongolia, decision making was often under weaker control in the agricultural sector in Vietnam than had been envisaged, and asset stripping was often encountered in state-owned enterprises. These developments underline the need for a transparent and effective legal and regulatory framework to assist the transition.

---

[6]The claim of a more favorable supply response in agriculture is perhaps not as tight as may appear. In particular, it is difficult to disentangle the extent to which price liberalization may have increased overall supply and to which it merely reflected an increase in the *marketed* surplus, and hence *measured* output. This parallels the argument for the CEE-BRO economies where underreporting of private sector activity may be substantial.

- China's and Vietnam's selective and gradualist strategy appears to have provided rich dividends, but cannot be seen as unambiguously validating gradualism. Indeed, high growth came from agriculture in which reforms were the fastest. The speed and depth of the reforms in this sector were akin to the shock therapy applied in many CEE-BRO countries. Furthermore, as the scope for further efficiency gains in agriculture is narrowed, the need to widen the range of reforms is becoming more apparent.

- As the transition unfolds, the response to impending instability has been unpredictable. At times, macroinstability has spurred liberalization and reform (as in Vietnam in the mid-1980s); at other times, most recently in Laos and Vietnam in the wake of the Asian crisis, some backtracking and recourse to old methods of control and command have occurred.

- Partial reforms inevitably generated tension and macroeconomic imbalance, suggesting the need to continue, and often spurring, the reform process. The dual track pricing and exchange rate systems in Laos and Vietnam were useful in providing market signals at the margin, but they also produced macroimbalances when market and official rates were unsynchronized and generated considerable scope for corruption and rent-seeking activity. Similarly, continuing weakness in the financial system, governance problems, and absence of controls over access to bank credit by enterprises encouraged inflation. Such factors generated a crisis in Vietnam in the late 1980s and price and exchange-market instability in Laos in late 1994, and they threatened to reverse inflation reduction in Mongolia in 1998.

- The need for reform of state-owned enterprises and of the financial sector is increasingly apparent in the Asian transition economies. Because the growth impetus from agriculture appears to have diminished, further sustained growth will have to come from elsewhere, perhaps from a combination of light, export-oriented manufacturing and further development of services. To provide room for these sectors, the claim of state-owned industrial enterprises on resources would have to be progressively reduced. The inefficiency of enterprises is only masked by budgetary subsidies, quasi-fiscal deficits, and state support through protectionist trade policies. The adverse effects are manifest in the weak commercial bank balance sheets and reflect poor managerial and risk assessment skills. Reforms in the financial sector are urgently required to maintain macrostability and to provide efficient financial intermediation to support growth.

Conclusion

Overall, the experience of the Asian transitional economies appears to have been somewhat happier than that of the CEE-BRO economies. Inflation remained low, as in the case of China, or was rapidly brought down to more favorable levels in the other economies. In addition, output performance was generally better than in the CEE-BRO economies, and—except in Mongolia—the large declines in output experienced by the CEE-BRO economies were avoided. Substantial progress has also been made in moving toward market-based systems, though much remains to be accomplished. These overall outcomes resulted from fairly different initial conditions and were achieved at a differing pace in each economy.

Initial conditions, similar to those in the economies of the CEE-BRO, were perhaps most unfavorable in Mongolia. Economies affected most directly by the collapse of the CMEA system experienced a significant worsening of their fiscal positions as the large external transfers vanished almost overnight. China may have had the best starting point, with a relatively favorable fiscal position, and with the least amount of political strife. Laos and Vietnam could be considered intermediate cases, somewhat removed from the difficulties associated with the CMEA system, and located in the still fast-growing East Asian region.

The pace of stabilization and reform has also differed among the Asian economies. Mongolia appears to have taken the fastest strides in liberalizing prices, reforming trade, and privatizing enterprises. The pace was more differentiated in the other economies. China, Laos, and Vietnam undertook early and quick reforms of agriculture, but the pace of price, exchange, and trade system liberalization was selective and moderate. Reforms in state-owned enterprises and the financial sector were either relatively slow or lagged significantly.

What are the lessons of the transitional experiences of the Asian countries? For one, these experiences confirm that while favorable initial conditions do have an important bearing on the subsequent course of the transition, implementation of difficult stabilization policies and fundamental structural reform is critical to ensuring sustained growth and low levels of inflation. This was also true in China, where growth has been fastest in sectors where liberalization is most advanced and where the risks to future growth are largest in sectors where the most remains to be done. Economic transactions, even in tight, centrally controlled economies, begin to reflect market forces soon after decentralized decision making is permitted. What cannot be quickly replicated is a full complement of efficient institutions to support these market transactions.

The stabilization experience of the Asian transition economies indicates that external deterioration and spiraling inflation can be checked through appropriately tight financial policies, even in a period of rapid structural economic reforms. Prior to the reforms (barring China) all other countries faced major fiscal imbalances. Tight financial policies were successful in reducing inflation in Laos, Mongolia, and Vietnam. While fiscal reforms provided new sources of revenue when enterprise surpluses were no longer available to government, the authorities maintained tight monetary control and ensured that interest rates remained positive in real terms. The experience also points to the need for vigilance to ensure that the fruits of stabilization are not lost, as temporarily occurred in Vietnam in 1990 and 1991, and in Laos in 1995 and 1997.

The Asian experience also highlights the importance of liberal price and exchange markets to ensure market-based resource allocation. Liberalization was crucial in reducing economic distortions, and liberalized prices were critical to generating the supply response in the agricultural sector. In this context, the dual price and exchange rate systems in China, Laos, and Vietnam, while leading to much inefficiency and rent seeking, had the important advantage of providing market signals at the margin.

How does the experience of the Asian economies stand in light of the so-called orthodoxy—the more the better, the faster the better? Undoubtedly, early clarification of property rights in the agricultural sector was key to the strong output response enjoyed by all the Asian economies. While this resilience of output is often associated with the large share of agriculture in the economy, it should be borne in mind that decentralized and privatized economic decision making brought about institutional changes in this sector in all these economies at an early stage. And the gains were substantial. Indeed, even in the case of China, often viewed as the model of gradualist success, agricultural reform was rapid and approximated the shock therapy approach of some CEE-BRO economies. By the same token, however, the slow pace of reform in the small-enterprise sector did not act as a constraint on growth in the initial stages. The lack of extensive financial sector reform may also not have acted as a brake on agricultural growth because of the weak links between the two sectors.

The relatively slow pace of reform of state-owned enterprises and continued weakness in the financial sector in all the Asian economies is a matter of increasing concern. As further gains from reform in the agricultural sector become harder to come by, sustained growth will have to come from fundamental reforms in industry, where the state-owned enterprises still play a dominant role. The weak performance and inefficiency of these enterprises continue to be a drag on overall growth and have spilled over into the banking sector where the recurring losses have accumulated in large portfolios of nonperforming loans and are reflected in high interest rate levels and spreads. As is also becoming evident in the CEE-BRO economies, the more difficult reforms in the industrial and financial sectors are likely to be the binding constraint, and vigorous pursuit of reforms in these areas holds the key to future sustained growth.

Appendix: Country Experiences

Vietnam

Favorable conditions at the outset facilitated Vietnam's transition. Agriculture accounted for almost 40 percent of output. The economy was only loosely integrated with the CMEA system. Furthermore, substantial foreign savings available from fast-growing neighbors combined with the fortuitous coming-on-stream of domestic oil production in the early 1990s to relieve important growth constraints. On overall objectives, the official position has been that Vietnam does not aspire to become a full-fledged market economy; instead the market mechanism is intended to promote growth and ensure overall stability (Reidel and Comer, 1997, and Mihaljek, 1998). Reflecting these overall objectives, the pace of reforms has varied. Reforms in agriculture have been substantial with extensive, progressive decentralization, and liberalization. Reforms in the financial and enterprise sectors have lagged behind, and the Asian crisis has led to some backtracking.

Reforms were first undertaken in late 1979 after the Sixth Plenum of the Fourth Party Congress. The most important steps were taken in agriculture, where responsibility for output targets was shifted from the cooperatives to households. Surpluses above the targets could be retained and traded. This change in the contractual arrangement was very successful and agricultural growth increased sharply. These reforms were carried further in 1986 under *doi moi* (economic renovation), in which quota obligations were eliminated and all agricultural produce could be sold in the market. Still deeper reforms came in 1988 with the introduction of long-term land leases, which were transferable under specified circumstances. With this important step, almost all operational control over the dominant sector of the economy had moved to private hands. Other reforms were also undertaken: the state monopoly over international trade was dismantled, quotas were replaced by import duties (albeit at high levels), and steps were made to attract foreign investment.

The onset of a macroeconomic crisis in early 1989, following the collapse of the former Soviet Union and the CMEA, spurred price liberalization, exchange rate unification, and the dismantling of extensive state controls over internal trade. By then, the system of administered prices and exchange rate controls had resulted in widespread parallel markets, broad divergences between official and black market prices, and a grossly overvalued dong. The stabilization program included a sharp fiscal contraction, unification of the multiple exchange rates at the level of the parallel market (entailing a fivefold increase in the official rate), and a substantial increase in interest rates. By mid-year, the program was successful in reducing inflation significantly. The fiscal consolidation continued during 1989–91 as government lowered its spending by 6 percent of GDP through large reductions in budgetary subsidies, capital outlays, and the wage bill, including an extensive demobilization of the armed forces.

Reflecting the philosophical basis of the reform strategy, as the macroeconomy stabilized and a balance of payments crisis was averted through large rice and oil exports, the reform imperative receded after 1992, and a large unfinished agenda remains. Significant obstacles remain in the path of an open and liberal trading regime, including continued targeted support to import-substituting state industries and control over the exchange rate and trade flows through rationing of foreign exchange in the interbank market. While a two-tiered banking system has been established, the central bank needs to assume its role as guardian of macroeconomic stability by developing the necessary market-based instruments of monetary management. Restrictions on commercial banks have been reduced over time and a growing number of foreign banks have been permitted to open branches. Nevertheless, domestic commercial banks remain large public institutions, dependent on the central bank and accustomed to lending to state enterprises without credit-risk appraisal. Progress in the reform of state enterprises has been minimal and loss-making enterprises continue to remain afloat through protectionist measures and directed credit from the banking system.

Laos

In Laos, the disappointing performance of the centrally planned economy, established in 1975 after two decades of protracted civil war, provided the impetus to a market-based system in 1979 (Otani and Pham, 1996). The overall commitment to a market economy has been strong, even though implementation of reforms has lagged at times.

The seeds for transition to a decentralized system may have been sown when already low living standards deteriorated because of poor output performance and high inflation soon after central planning was introduced. External and internal resistance to central planning was strong. Aid from Western nations, especially the United States, came to an abrupt end. The economic blockade of the country disrupted trade flows. Internally, resistance in the agricultural sector to forced collectivization and taxation was lively and dissent from the new system was reflected in a flight of skilled human and financial capital. Stagnant exports and the loss of import financing combined to generate considerable pressure on the balance of payments. Widespread parallel markets mirrored the shortage of goods.

Substantive progress was made in economic liberalization and structural reform over the first decade (1979–88), creating a foundation for private sector activity. The reform process gathered momentum under the New Economic Mechanism as the system of official prices based on "cost plus pricing" was abandoned in favor of the principle of "one market, one price" in mid-1987. Almost all retail prices were liberalized, eliminating the distortions created by a two-track pricing system. The progressive easing of restrictions on internal and external trade starting mid-1987 also facilitated the process. The unification of multiple exchange rates at a level close to the prevailing parallel market rate in early 1988 helped in eliminating distortions. Moreover, starting in 1983, larger numbers of public enterprises were free to make production, pricing, employment, and wage decisions and were held accountable for their budgetary obligations. However, banking sector reforms lagged and negative real deposit interest rates continued to hinder resource mobilization.

Since 1988, reforms have focused on raising domestic savings through fiscal consolidation and positive real interest rates, and on inflation reduction through limits on credit expansion to state-owned enterprises. Fiscal consolidation has been centered on a fundamental reform of tax administration, elimination of budgetary subsidies, and rationalization of expenditure priorities. The final steps in external sector liberalization, which had contributed to substantial export growth, were taken in mid-1994 with the elimination of all restriction on international current account transactions. Progress was also made in financial sector reforms, including the opening up of private banks and improvements in monetary control. However, monetary management continued to be complicated by the financial sector's tendency to accommodate credit demands passively, resulting in excessive wage increases by the enterprises.

A lax monetary stance in late 1994 and early 1995, combined with the initial effects of import liberalization, led to a strong surge in demand. A period of inflation and exchange market instability ensued. The initial policy response—small depreciation in the official exchange rate and administrative controls—proved inadequate as transactions shifted to the parallel markets, widening the divergence between the parallel and official rates.

As remedial fiscal measures were undertaken and monetary conditions tightened, in conjunction with the removal of exchange restrictions and the abolition of the official exchange rate in mid-year, macroeconomic stability returned and inflation receded. Simultaneously, curtailment of budgetary subsidies and the privatization of state-owned enterprises hardened enterprise budget constraints. Since, however, these enterprise reforms met with limited success, the government embarked on a broad program of disengagement from all nonstrategic enterprises. Later divestment from strategic enterprises was initiated and, by early 1997, the privatization process was nearing completion. With the basis for a market economy well-entrenched by the end of 1998, the reform agenda now calls for improvements in the banking framework to promote efficient financial intermediation, resolution of insolvency among banks, and greater flexibility in the foreign exchange market to reduce dollarization and enhance confidence in domestic financial assets.

Mongolia

Among the Asian transition economies, the commitment to a market-based economy was perhaps strongest in Mongolia, where long-standing unease with Soviet planning is often cited for the relatively readier acceptance of a market orientation (Boone and others, 1997). In addition, the age structure of the young population favored a move to a new system. Concerted efforts to install a democratic system of government with general elections at an early stage supported this favorable climate. The broad consensus in favor of the required transformation was reflected in the inclusion of important opposition members in the coalition government formed by the former communist party (the MPRP) in 1990. When the former Soviet Union and the CMEA system finally collapsed in 1991, the external shock—a substantial loss in transfers from the former Soviet Union and a sharp decline in trade volumes—was large even by comparison with the dislocation affecting the CEE-BRO countries. Western donors filled the budgetary and external financing gaps, providing foreign financing of the budget through project and cash loans in the range of 10–15 percent of GDP.

Favorable conditions for change notwithstanding, only partial reforms were undertaken initially, reflecting differences within the government on the speed and scope of reform. Some price and trade liberalization was undertaken, a voucher privatization program—the
first in a transition country—was initiated, and the banking system
was deregulated. Partial reforms soon resulted in a loss of monetary
control and near hyperinflationary conditions in 1992–93. Macroeconomic instability was closely associated with a lack of significant reform in the enterprise and financial sectors, which permitted commercial banks to start operations under weak bank supervision, poor bank
management, and considerable insider lending.

Conditions for macroeconomic stability were restored only in mid-
1992 after fresh elections returned a clear parliamentary majority for
the MPRP. The new government made significant progress in unifying
the exchange rate, eliminating all quantitative export and import controls by mid-1993, and improving tax administration and budget management. Together with progress in macroeconomic stabilization,
these initiatives led to real GDP growth in 1994 after a prolonged decline, reflecting a rebound in the livestock sector, higher exports in response to a recovery in export prices, and accelerated growth in the
construction and service sectors.

The pace of structural reforms accelerated during 1994–95 and received fresh impetus from the electoral victory of the reform-minded
coalition of opposition parties in mid-1996. Progress in privatization
was especially noteworthy. By the end of 1994, livestock was almost entirely in private hands and the voucher-based privatization program
was complete. By the end of 1995, through a cash privatization program,
most small and medium-sized enterprises had been privatized. A thriv-
ing secondary market in private housing developed by the end of 1997.
A notable development, which reflected the boldness of the reform policies, was the complete elimination of import duties in early 1997, which
enhanced the already substantial outward orientation of the economy. A
major bank restructuring was initiated at the end of 1996, and tax reform, including the introduction of VAT, was undertaken in mid-1997.

The reform effort stalled in 1998. As principal export prices fell, the
deterioration in the external environment exposed weakness in the financial system, including poor supervision, bad commercial bank
management practices, and corruption in large state-owned enterprises. Domestic political turmoil further delayed the implementation
of corrective fiscal measures.

With political conditions more settled starting at the end of 1998, the
current challenge is to restore the reform momentum while locking in
the low inflation and resilient growth performance of 1998. In particu-

lar, substantial efficiency gains could be garnered from comprehensive bank restructuring to resolve insolvency of commercial banks and from further reduction in the size of government, more transparency in the enterprise sector, and the completion of state divestment of the large enterprises and utilities.

Bibliography

Aghevli, B. B., 1992, "Centrally Planned Economies in Transition: An Asian Perspective" (unpublished; Washington: International Monetary Fund).

Bell, M.W., H.E. Khor, and K. Kochhar, 1993, *China at the Threshold of a Market Economy*, IMF Occasional Paper No. 107 (Washington: International Monetary Fund).

Berg, A., and others, 1998, "The Evolution of Output in Transition Economies: Explaining the Differences" (unpublished, Washington: International Monetary Fund).

Boone, P., B. Tarvaa, A. Tsend, E. Tsendjav, and N. Unenburen, 1997, "Mongolia's Transition to a Democratic Market System," in *Transition: Comparing Asia and Europe Economies*, ed. by W.T. Woo and others (Cambridge, Massachusetts: MIT Press).

Bruno, M., 1992, "Stabilization and Reform in Eastern Europe: A Preliminary Evaluation," IMF Working Paper 92/30 (Washington: International Monetary Fund).

Christoffersen, P. and P. Doyle, 1998, "From Inflation to Growth: Eight Years of the Transition," IMF Working Paper 96/100 (Washington: International Monetary Fund).

Coorey, S., M. Mecagni, and E. Offerdahl, 1998, "Disinflation in Transition Economies: The Role of Relative Price Adjustment," in *Moderate Inflation: The Experience of Transition Economies*, ed. by C. Cottarelli and G. Szapáry (Washington: International Monetary Fund and National Bank of Hungary).

Dodsworth, J.R., and others, 1996a, *Vietnam: Transition to a Market Economy*, IMF Occasional Paper No. 135 (Washington: International Monetary Fund).

———, 1996b, "Macroeconomic Experience of the Transition Economies in Indochina," IMF Working Paper 96/112 (Washington: International Monetary Fund).

de Melo, M., C. Denizer, A. Gelb, and S. Tenev, 1998, "Circumstances and Choice: The Role of Initial Condition and Policies in Transition Economies" (unpublished; Washington: World Bank).

Fan Gang, 1994, "Incremental Change and Dual-Track Transition: Understanding the Case of China," *Economic Policy*, Vol. 19 (Supplement), pp. 99–122.

Fischer, S., and A. Gelb, 1991, "The Process of Socialist Economic Transformation," *Journal of Economic Perspectives*, Vol. 5, No. 4, pp. 91–106.

Fischer, S., R. Sahay, and C. Vegh, 1996, "Stabilization and Growth in Transition Economies: The Early Experience," *Journal of Economic Perspectives*, Vol. 10, No. 2, pp. 45–66.

———, 1998, "From Transition to Market: Evidence and Growth Prospects," IMF Working Paper 98/52 (Washington: International Monetary Fund).

International Monetary Fund, various issues, *Recent Economic Developments* (Washington).

Ghosh, A.R., and S. Phillips, 1998, "Inflation, Disinflation, and Growth," IMF Working Paper 98/68 (Washington: International Monetary Fund).

Lardy, N.R., 1998, *China's Unfinished Revolution* (Washington: Brookings Institution).

McKinnon, R., 1992, "Macroeconomic Control in Liberalizing Socialist Economies: Asian and European Parallels," Working Paper No. PB92–05, Center for Pacific Basin Monetary and Economic Studies (San Francisco: Federal Reserve Bank of San Francisco).

Mihaljek, D., 1998, "Transition to a Market Economy: Where Does Vietnam Stand?" (unpublished; Washington: International Monetary Fund).

Naughton, B., 1994, "What Is Distinctive about China's Economic Transition? State Enterprise Reform and the Overall System Transformation," *Journal of Comparative Economics*, Vol. 18, No. 3, pp. 470–90.

Otani, I., and Chi Do Pham, 1996, *The Lao Peoples' Democratic Republic: Systemic Transformation and Adjustment*, IMF Occasional Paper No. 137 (Washington: International Monetary Fund).

Rawski, T., 1994, "Progress Without Privatization: The Reform of China's State Industries," in *The Political Economy of Privatization and Public Enterprise in Post-Communist and Reforming Communist States*, ed. by V. Milor (Boulder, Colorado: Lynne Rienner), pp. 27–52.

Reidel, J., and R. Comer, 1997, "Transition to a Market Economy in Vietnam," in *Economies in Transition: Comparing Asia and Europe*, ed. by W. T. Woo and others (Cambridge, Massachusetts: MIT Press).

Sachs, J., and W. T. Woo, 1997, "Understanding China's Economic Performances" (unpublished; Cambridge: Harvard Institute for International Development).

Sarel, M., 1996, "Nonlinear Effects of Inflation on Economic Growth," *Staff Papers*, International Monetary Fund, Vol. 43, No. 1, pp. 199–215.

Tseng, W., and others 1994, *Economic Reform in China*, IMF Occasional Paper No. 114 (Washington: International Monetary Fund).

Woo, W.T., and others, eds., 1997, *Economies in Transition: Comparing Asia and Europe* (Cambridge, Massachusetts: MIT Press).

World Bank, 1996, *From Plan to Market*, World Development Report (Washington: World Bank).

Lessons of the Russian Crisis for Transition Economies 6

Yegor Gaidar

What lessons does the Russian financial crisis hold for other economies in transition? I could approach the topic by providing an avalanche of details about exchange rate, interest rate, and budgetary policies, or, perhaps more interesting, details about errors committed by the Russian government, the Russian central bank, and, yes, even the IMF. I will not do so, however, but will instead focus on the problem of soft and hard budget constraints.

Soft Budget Constraint

The concept of the soft budget constraint—essentially a lack of financial accountability by enterprise managers—was first elaborated by nonsocialist economists for enterprises under the socialist system. The application of the term to enterprises in transition economies and in postsocialist economies is, in my view, entirely appropriate. Under the socialist system, the authority of the enterprise manager had nothing to do with whether or not the enterprise was profitable. The soft budget constraint was normally the result of a state budget process far removed from considerations of efficiency or profit. Under market conditions, because profits are the very essence of a manager's authority, the soft budget constraint is rare and always temporary. The market economy, as you well know, is founded on very tough budgetary discipline. A manager whose indifference to budgetary considerations allows an enterprise to fall into bankruptcy suffers a swift and unpleasant fate.

Hard Administrative Constraint

On the other hand, under the socialist system, soft budget constraints coexisted with hard administrative constraints. Since each enterprise was part of a comprehensive hierarchy, the state exercised rigid control over the appointment of managers and made sure that they fulfilled the tasks assigned to them, including the achievement of wide-ranging social aims. When, however, the totalitarian socialist regimes began to disintegrate, administrative control over the enterprise managers also fell apart. In some stage of development in all postsocialist economies, this phenomenon led to a fatal combination of soft budget controls and soft or nonexistent administrative controls.

To understand the attitude of managers in the socialist system, try to imagine an economy in which an enterprise owner has no need to be concerned when the enterprise fails to turn a profit. He knows that a weak bottom line will be compensated by various budgetary understandings, such as subsidies, loans on easy terms, and the possibility of allowing tax arrears to build up without untoward consequences. Imagine what this would mean for the general efficiency of the market mechanism!

First, it would mean that the usual market instruments for redistributing resources from poorly functioning, inefficient enterprises to better-functioning, efficient ones would not work. The discipline of the market would be rendered ineffectual.

Second, because soft budget constraints are incompatible with an equitable and efficient tax system, the enterprise's tax obligation would be determined in practice not by tax law but by the terms of a contract negotiated between the enterprise and the state authorities. Such negotiations invariably lead to corruption.

Worst of Both Worlds

As I just mentioned, practically all postcommunist countries have experienced problems with this combination of soft budget constraints and soft administrative constraints. What is the difference between "market socialist" economies before the start of serious reform and in the postcommunist reality? Before the reforms, enterprise managers were firmly under a system of totalitarian political control. They had to behave. They had to show that they were loyal members of the party. It is also unfortunately true that many managers skimmed off funds from the enterprises, enriching themselves and their families. There were limits to such transgressions, however. The enterprise still had to meet the requirements of the central plan and still had to provide for the welfare of its workers. Failure to carry out fundamental managerial duties would be regarded as breaking the manager's contract with the political establishment. This was simply not done and could result in serious repercussions for the offending manager.

After the crash of communism, the totalitarian regime, with all its social and administrative restraints, ceased to exist. Then, the combination of easy budget constraints and easy administrative constraints produced most undesirable consequences for the enterprises, for society, and for the economy as a whole. These developments were entirely to be expected, given the social environment that emerged after the breakup of the totalitarian regime. Why? First, because of a mind-set deeply ingrained over 70 years of socialism. Far from being distinct entities, enterprises were regarded as part of the state, a result of socialist industrialization. How could an enterprise be disciplined on the trivial grounds that for a time it was unable to fulfill its tax obligations? It would be absurd: the duty of the state was to provide for the enterprise, not the other way around.

Second, because enterprise managers were part of the social infrastructure of the totalitarian society, they were in no way different from other officials in the state administration. They had gone to university together, they worked together, they socialized with one another. They could also collude together. Unless there were countervailing political and legal safeguards—and over the past decade there have been few—this combination of feeble budgetary controls, weak administrative controls, and "old boy" cronyism engendered an inefficient, stagnant, and extremely corrupt environment.

Remedies

What could change this situation? What forces could nudge the economy in the direction of tighter restraints on the enterprises? The first prerequisite is to deal with the huge budget imbalances and monetary overhang that remain as the macroeconomic legacy of the socialist era. Aspirations on the part of the political elite to conform to Western norms of macroeconomic stabilization require a slowdown in the rate of money creation, a reduction in the budget deficit, and the elimination of soft budgetary constraints (including a very hard stand against tax arrears). In Central European countries, such as Hungary and Poland, that found themselves in a similar situation, and where these aspirations were reinforced by the elite's commitment to join the European Union, governments acted resolutely and quickly to impose serious, not to say harsh, financial discipline on enterprises during the early stages of the transition. Their resolution was such that they were able to eradicate the institutionalized culture of the soft budget constraint soon after the transition began.

The Czech Republic provides an interesting example because, of all the socialist countries, it found itself in the best financial condition at the moment of the crash of the socialist economy, and its financial condition remained strong during the first years of transition. Lulled into complacency as a result of its financial advantages, the government failed to push seriously to harden budget constraints on enterprises. Despite the Czech Republic's vaunted macroeconomic efficiency, the government delayed restructuring, allowing the large state enterprises to continue to enjoy soft budget constraints during the first three years of transition and implementing a bankruptcy law only in 1993. The result of the delay was the loss of three precious years of development.

In the majority of cases, macroeconomic stabilization in the postsocialist countries is inseparable from the microeconomy. Stabilization cannot go forward without budgetary restraint at the enterprise level and a wholesale restructuring of inefficient operations. In Russia, of course, macroeconomic policy during the first years of transition was extremely weak, mainly because of a lack of political consensus and a division of political power (as evidenced by rampant inflation during those years). Inadequate budgetary and monetary constraints at the macroeconomic level combined with inadequate budgetary constraints at the enterprise level.

Financing the Budget

By the time monetary stabilization was attempted in Russia, inflation had eroded cash balances and made the financing of budget deficits all but impossible. People were sick of the prolonged inflation. The situation was quite different from what it had been at the moment of the collapse of the socialist economy and demonstrated the folly of delaying reform.

The erosion of monetary balances by inflation made the ratio of money to GDP much lower than it would have been if disinflation had been attempted at an earlier stage. Moreover, the freedom of enterprises to accumulate tax arrears also contributed to an erosion of budgetary receipts. It was very difficult to challenge, let alone change, this firmly established habit.

The government's ability to borrow in the domestic Russian market to finance the deficit was severely limited by the lack of cash balances in the economy. Its budgetary revenues were low, both absolutely and relative to revenues in those transition economies that had begun the reform process earlier. And it seemed unable to legislate the drastic cuts in expenditures necessary for monetary stabilization. Between 1995 and the first half of 1998, the government struggled against easy budgetary restraints at the enterprise level, huge budgetary imbalances at the macroeconomic level, and weak monetary policy. It succeeded in tightening monetary policy, but it continued to struggle with its microeconomic and macroeconomic budgetary problems.

During 1995–98, the problem of tax collection was not a problem of tax administration in the usual sense. It was more a political struggle about what constituted the essence of the emerging economic system, whether it was to be a system in which the relationship between the state and the enterprises was to be regulated by law or whether it would be business as usual, based on political influence and personal contacts. The result of the struggle was what I would call a semi-equilibrium in which the budget deficit was stabilized at around 6 or 7 percent of GDP, but there was not enough political support to reduce this figure. Obviously, deficits of this magnitude are unsustainable in the long run. They can continue perhaps for a year or two, but then the government must either cut expenditures and restructure the interface between the state and the enterprises or forget about monetary stabilization. The choice is clear.

Present Dangers

Radical changes in the international financial climate since 1997 have posed a considerable threat to the Russian economy with its weak financial policies. Unable to reduce the budget deficit, the Russian government is finding it extremely difficult to finance the gap entirely by borrowing from the IMF and the World Bank. Needless to say, it is experiencing even more difficulty in finding commercial credits to finance the deficit. Its ability to borrow commercially depends on swings in the mood of the international financial markets. If these markets are optimistic and expansive, there is some breathing space, but if the mood changes, the borrower is caught in a very serious trap. Foreign investors are extremely wary of taking chances with an unpredictable exchange rate policy: to attract capital, you must have a transparent and stable exchange rate. Capital inflows will not occur if currency risks are not hedged.

Between the autumn of 1997 and August 1998, the Russian government faced a choice between two possible strategies. The first was to demonstrate that it had the political will to tighten the budget by reforming its relationship with large enterprises, such as those in the oil and gas sectors, through the imposition of hard budget constraints. The second was to give up, abandoning the attempt to promote anti-inflation policies. Unfortunately, the attempt to tighten budgetary policy received insufficient political support. The result was inevitable: the continuation of soft budget constraints, soft budget policy, and soft monetary policy.

The first steps of the new government formed in September 1998 showed that it, too, very much preferred the soft budget alternative. What were these first steps? First, it negotiated tax agreements with the largest Russian taxpayers, thus institutionalizing the practice of defining tax obligations not by law but by agreement. Second, it also institutionalized a system of monetary offsets by allowing enterprises to pay taxes in kind and by forgiving the debts of enterprises in the agricultural sector.

These are not isolated initiatives. They are part of a comprehensive policy (even if the government does not recognize it) whose essence is to enable an elite to retain control over valuable properties and to continue to manage enterprises, regardless of their level of efficiency, while the state picks up the tab. This is what has been happening in Russia during the past five months.

A Word of Advice

In conclusion, I would draw a number of lessons from the Russian experience:

- If the socialist economy no longer functions, the government should try to disinflate as rapidly as possible. A delayed disinflation will be much more painful.
- If the government is confronted with delayed disinflation, it should cut budget deficits radically.
- The illusion of being able to finance the deficit out of a short-term portfolio should be abandoned.
- Consideration should be given to the vulnerability of the exchange rate regime to changes in commodity prices.
- It should be understood that hardening the budget constraint is important not only for raising budget revenues but also for allowing market mechanisms to work and thus for increasing the efficiency of the economy.

Time to Rethink Privatization in Transition Economies?   7

John Nellis

Privatization Wins the Day

Privatization appears to have swept the field and won the day.[1] More than 100 countries on every continent have privatized some or most of their state-owned companies in every sector of infrastructure, manufacturing, and services. An estimated 75,000 medium and large firms worldwide, including many in Central and Eastern Europe (CEE) and in the Baltics, Russia, and other countries of the former Soviet Union (BRO), have been divested, along with hundreds of thousands of small business units. Proceeds generated from these efforts are estimated at more than $735 billion (Privatisation International, 1998).[2] Every country (including Cambodia, China, India, Laos, Russia, and Vietnam) that still retains a significant number of publicly owned firms is privatizing some or most of its firms (except Cuba and the Democratic People's Republic of Korea).

One telling measure of privatization's success is that the process has not been reversed: To date, only a small number of privatized firms have been renationalized, and where this happened (for example, in Chile and the Czech Republic a state-owned or state-dominated bank converted bad debt to equity), the instrument has usually been indirect and the period of renewed state ownership temporary.

What have been the operational results of this massive shift of ownership? Megginson and Netter (1998), in summing up their recent ex-

This chapter was first published by the International Finance Corporation as Discussion Paper No. 38. The author thanks Itzhak Goldberg and Simeon Djankov for a number of key suggestions and ideas. Valuable comments were also received from Igor Artemiev, Anders Åslund, Nick Barr, Harry Broadman, Constantjin Claessans, Simon Commander, Francois Ettori, Roman Frydman, Oleh Havrylyshyn, Gregory Jedrzejczak, Homi Kharas, Donal McGettigan, David Phillips, Robert Myers, Thomas O'Brien, Brian Pinto, and Lou Thompson. Remaining errors are the author's.

[1]In this chapter, privatization means the transfer of a majority of ownership equity from state to private hand.

[2]Proceeds, however, are a partial and imperfect measure of privatization's magnitude and importance, because thousands of firms have been privatized through voucher or give-away schemes.

tensive survey of the empirical record on the financial and operating
results of privatization efforts worldwide, state:

> The evidence is now conclusive that privately-owned firms outperform
> SOEs [state-owned enterprises] . . . empirical evidence clearly shows that
> privatization significantly (often dramatically) improves the operating
> and financial performance of divested firms. (From the Abstract)

Much of the positive privatization experience reviewed in Megginson
and Netter is drawn from Organization for Economic Cooperation and
Development (OECD) countries. Although privatization started in in-
dustrialized market economies, it spread widely, and recent assessments of the results in non-OECD settings are also generally positive.
For example, Boubakri and Cosset (1998) review the before- and -after
performances of 79 privatized firms in 21 developing countries—mostly
middle income, but including Bangladesh, Jamaica, Nigeria, Pakistan,
and the Philippines. They conclude that on average the firms in their
sample significantly increased their profitability, operating efficiency,
capital investment spending, output, and employment and showed a
decline in leverage and an increase in dividends. Havrylyshyn and
McGettigan (2000), in their survey of the literature on privatization in
the transition economies of CEE and former Soviet Union, found that
private owners generally outperformed state-owned firms.

The multicountry surveys are supported by the positive findings of
a growing number of country case studies. For example, a review by
Kattab (1998) of the postprivatization performance of 28 divested
firms in Egypt reveals increased sales (71 percent of the sample), increased earnings (68 percent), increased average salary per worker (96
percent), and a decline in both short- and long-term debt (82 percent).[3]
A 1997 study by La Porta and Lopez-de-Silanes[4] of 218 cases of privatization in Mexico found, on average, a 24 percentage point increase
in the ratio of operating income to sales. The study documents increases in profitability and output and substantial declines in unit
costs and employment levels (although the blue-collar workers who
retained their jobs received large salary increases). Seven of the 10
large loss-making manufacturing firms privatized in Bangladesh returned to profitability, showing increases in output, sales, capacity utilization and labor productivity, and declining unit costs (Dowlah,
1996). Much more along these lines could be presented. The fact is that

---

[3]Kattab provides no information on how this set of firms was selected for study from the 91
privatized firms in the country.
[4]A summary of their longer article also appears in World Bank (1997).

almost every rigorous study comparing pre- and postprivatization operation indicates, on average, sizable performance improvement.[5]

Or Does It?

And yet, despite the ubiquity of divestiture,[6] despite the assessment by investment bankers that privatization's success has been indisputable,[7] and despite the large and growing evidence from a variety of settings showing that privatization tends to improve firm-level performance, doubts remain and are growing. Indeed, suspicions and concerns about privatization, driven under by the liberalizing pressures of the 1980s and early 1990s, are resurfacing to a point of revisionism. These doubts are reflected

- in the concerns of observers dissatisfied with the analytical rigor of the theory and the empirical studies supporting privatization;
- in the arguments of opponents of privatization, who believe that privatization is not the right social solution, at least not for all firms or in all economies;
- by fears that although privatization, even if beneficial for shareholders and the selling state, has not proven beneficial for society as a whole, or at least for significant groups of the poor and powerless actors in society; and
- by the concerns of many whose previous acceptance of divestiture has been shaken by recent events in Russia and some of the other transition economies.

This study reviews the accomplishments and shortcomings of privatization in transition economies—where the scope and pace of privatization have been larger than elsewhere and expectations great, and where significant problems have surfaced. The study looks into where performance in transition economies has been unsatisfactory and why and discusses what governments, and those who assist them, should do about turning this experience around. The study's principal findings are as follows:

- Privatization generally proved its worth in the CEE and Baltic states.

---

[5]Other studies showing positive results from privatization include Galal and others (1995), Shaikh and others (1996), and Newbery and Pollitt (1997). Articles demonstrating the superior efficiency performance of private versus public firms include Majumdar (1998) and Dewenter and Malatesta (1998).

[6]Megginson and Netter (1998, p. 5) note that privatization moved "from novelty to global orthodoxy in the space of two decades."

[7]See Morse (1998). Richard Morse is Global Head of Industry at Dresdner Kleinwort Benson.

- However, too much was expected and promised of privatization in institutionally weak transition economies, particularly in countries of the former Soviet Union.
- For seemingly excellent reasons, the emphasis was usually on massive, speedy transactions with substantial ownership stakes awarded to "insider" stakeholders. The reasoning was that the links between the enterprises and the state needed to be cut quickly to create a mass of private property owners, and the only way to do this was by offering substantial ownership stakes to workers and managers in the firms being privatized. If these powerful insiders were not rewarded, and quickly, they would block indefinitely the privatization—and transition—process.
- In the transition states closest to Western markets, there is some evidence that this approach has been successful.
- But the farther east the country, the more evident is the neglect of the supporting institutional frameworks required to promote financial discipline, competition, and freedom (and promotion) of entry of new businesses.
- And in those instances, the speedy, massive, insider-oriented forms of privatization have generally failed to lead to the restructuring needed to enable firms to survive and thrive in competitive market operations.

Despite the severity of this indictment, there is little reason to think that had these firms remained in public ownership, their restructuring performance would have been better. The fact is that states that botch privatization also botch public ownership of enterprises. Overall, privatization has delivered remarkably well in many settings, especially when contrasted to a realistic set of alternatives instead of some theoretical ideal.

Thus, although this study agrees that the methods of privatization have to be altered and improved, and that much more attention needs to be paid to supporting institutions, it argues against renationalization or a search for other ways to make state ownership efficient and effective. *The key unanswered question is how to go about correcting and improving privatization in institutionally weak settings.*

Privatization and Its Detractors

Privatization's detractors base their views on several arguments. A long-standing one is that competition and market structure are as, if not more, important than ownership in determining efficiency outcomes at the firm level. An updated empirical testing of this view

comes from Pankaj Tandon (1995), who, on the basis of a 1994 literature survey, argues:

> There are many cases where privatization has not led to efficiency im-
> provement; these are generally associated with situations where the de-
> gree of competition has remained unchanged before and after privatiza-
> tion. . . . There are of course many cases where privatization appears to
> have "resulted" in efficiency improvement; in most of these cases, how-
> ever, the privatization appears to have been contemporaneous with
> deregulation or other types of competition-enhancing measures (pp.
> 329–30).[8]

Tandon finds most consistent with the evidence the conclusion that
it is the level of competition, not ownership, that best determines efficiency outcomes. He acknowledges that private owners have the right
incentives to promote efficiency, and in line with modern amendments
to neoclassical theory, he believes that government owners are likely to
mismanage principal-agent issues more than private owners. He
nonetheless preaches caution: In a competitive market "there exist
mechanisms that could enable a public enterprise to operate as efficiently . . . as its private cousins. But if a market is monopolized, privatization by itself will not guarantee efficiency" (Tandon, 1995, p. 32).

Tandon's view is that (1) if government owners enhance competitive
forces or use management methods and incentives similar to those
used in the private sector, they should be able to produce efficient behavior and outcomes, and (2) ex post perceived positive results attributed to ownership change may actually be due to increased competition. The implication is that many of the conclusions of the proponents
of privatization may be more ideological than scientific, and insufficiently judicious about alternative ways of achieving objectives without changing ownership and about the possible negative effects of
poor privatization.

"Selection bias" is another methodological criticism of privatization.
The idea is straightforward: Improved performance in privatized
firms does not necessarily show that private owners are better; rather
the improvements may indicate that it is the better firms that are privatized. This criticism has particularly troubled studies of privatization in transition economies—economies characterized by thousands
of transactions, a general tendency to reward insiders (who might

---

[8]Tandon is one of the four authors of the justly celebrated *Welfare Consequences of Selling
Public Enterprises* (Galal and others, 1995), generally regarded as one of the strongest pillars of
the proprivatization argument. He specifically does *not* exclude his previous study from his
conclusions.

have good information on the firm's prospects), and a lack of constraints on insider trading.[9]

In the transition economies the evidence supporting privatization has come from CEE, in particular, from two studies. The first, by Roman Frydman and others (1997), examines performance to mid-1994, and the second, by Gerhard Pohl and others (1997), examines the experience to the end of 1995.[10] A reasonable question is whether the highly positive findings from these relatively early days have been sustained. As shown by the case of the Czech Republic in the next section, the answer may be no.

The evidence shows that the returns to privatization diminish as we move eastward. Some examples:

- A 1998 survey by Djankov and Kreacic of 92 state- and privately owned firms in the Republic of Georgia concluded that it was not private ownership but rather competition and financial discipline that was associated with the restructuring in Georgia—or at least with what restructuring that could be discerned.
- A study of 50 medium and large privatized enterprises in Armenia noted that only three of the set had generated any new investment post-sale. For most of the others, the prognosis was for continuing decline and ultimate bankruptcy (CEPRA, 1997).[11]
- A 1999 study on Mongolia concludes that partially state-owned firms perform better than privatized companies (Anderson, Lee, and Murrell).
- Early surveys in Russia indicated few discernible differences in performance between state- and privately owned firms[12] or modest positive differences in the privatized firms (Estrin and Earle, 1997).
- Barberis and others (1996), one of the few studies of the Russian experience that clearly shows positive restructuring with privatization, dealt with small shops, most of which had been privatized for only a few months when the assessment survey was conducted between June 1992 and August 1993.[13]

---

[9]But Havrylyshyn and McGettigan (2000) review three recent studies that attempt to take selection bias into account, and they still conclude that privatization is associated with better performance.

[10]We return to these studies later in this chapter.

[11]The firms in the sample had been privatized for slightly more than one year.

[12]". . . ownership changes are generally rather weakly associated with most indicators of performance, including sales, wages and employment," Commander, Fan, and Schaffer (1996, p. 8). See also Chapter 7 in the same volume by Earle, Estrin, and Leshchenko (1996). The data in this study run to mid-1994.

[13]The authors are aware of the limitations of their data set and did their best to focus on short-term, quickly visible restructuring measures.

- Djankov (1998b), in examining enterprise survey data from 1997 and 1998 for 960 privatized manufacturing companies in Georgia, Kazakhstan, Kyrgyz Republic, Moldova, Russia, and Ukraine, found that most restructuring had occurred in the small number of firms in which foreigners had acquired significant ownership. Managerial owners had a mixed performance record, and both outside local investors and worker-owners seemed to have produced little restructuring.

In other words, the most likely forms of private ownership were those least likely to promote active restructuring. Even in Central Europe, Poland's experience, which is one of comparatively slow and cautious privatization,[14] combined with robust and sustained growth, has cast doubt on the necessity of privatization as a key element in the process of transition.[15]

The Rise and Fall of Russia

Russia's privatization experience has come in for particular criticism. The voucher-led mass privatization program of 1992–94 transferred ownership of more than 15,000 firms, primarily to insiders. At the end of the exercise, managers and workers combined controlled about two-thirds of the shares in the average privatized firm. The program's designers had tried to avoid insider dominance, but the financial mechanisms that might have prevented this outcome were swept away by the near hyperinflation prevailing at the time. Still, the mass privatization program had taken place without major claim of fraud, and by fall 1994, hopes were modestly high that

- financial discipline and perceived self-interest would start to force secondary trading in the insider-dominated companies and introduce outside ownership; and
- transparent and sound but nonvoucher methods would be used to privatize the half, or more, of industries still in state hands.

Several factors combined to prevent the proper unfolding of this process. First, insiders in the newly privatized firms generally feared loss of control. For most workers the case was one of "better the devil we know" (the existing management) than a cost-cutting, perhaps job-slashing, outsider. In turn, many of the old managers-turned-owners found it easier to lobby the state for assistance than to set the firm on

---

[14]Through 1996, about half of the Polish 1989 state-enterprise sector remained in government hands, including many of the largest firms (see Blaszczyk, 1996).

[15]The issue is examined in Pinto and van Wijnbergen (1995). Hungary eschewed vouchers and mass privatization methods, but did divest the bulk of state-owned assets.

the path to competitive performance. Second, the financial and physical condition of many of the firms were too unattractive for outsider investors. Third, the institutional underpinnings were weak and safeguards—thus incentives—inadequate for transparent secondary trading, thus further discouraging outsiders. Fourth, the various Russian governments failed to put in place the required set of supporting policies and institutions that might have channeled enterprise activity to productive ends (such as a hard budget constraint, reasonable taxes and services, and mechanisms to permit and encourage new business entrants). Fifth, institutionalized property rights (indeed, a consensus on the economic rules of exchange) were generally absent. For the firms transferred in the mass privatization program, this mixture blocked the taking of the essential second step to opening the ownership of privatized firms to external investors and owners who would bring needed capital, market access, managerial know-how, and a bottom-line mentality to privatized companies (Nellis, 1994, p. 2).[16]

And worse was to come: A donor-led effort to persuade the Russian government to sell at least a few large firms by transparent, credible case-by-case methods expended considerable effort but led nowhere. Much of the second wave of privatization, which took place after 1994 (for cash and investment promises), in particular the "loans-for-shares" scheme, turned into fraudulent shambles—a situation pointed out by the strongest supporters of, and contributors to, the first mass phase of Russian privatization. The second phase

> was non-transparent . . . involved clear conflicts of interest . . . created collusion . . . involved a non-level playing field, excluding foreign investors and banks not favored by the government. In two years the Russian privatization program has moved from the outstanding accomplishments of the MPP to the point where the program is now widely regarded as collusive and corrupt, failing to meet any of its stated objectives (Lieberman and Veimetra, 1996, p. 738).

Others go further, arguing that the entire Russian privatization program, including the voucher-led mass effort, has been the principal cause of the country's economic decline. They argue that the program emphasized swift ownership change before (or instead of) the building of market-supported institutions. And without these supportive underpinnings (a basic capital market framework, minimal shareholder information and protection systems, enforceable contracts, a modicum level of capacity and probity in the supervision of the public sector)

---

[16]See also Blasi and others (1997, p. 122), which concludes that the needed postprivatization restructuring of Russian firms proved far more complex than was anticipated.

and without breaking up the huge monopolistic or oligopolistic producers in order to stimulate internal competition, the voucher program left the mass of new shareholders powerless to counteract the manipulations of the well-placed managers and their supporters in the financial community. Thus, a program that was supposed to distribute ownership and launch enterprises on a positive restructuring path became instead a transfer of productive resources from the state to a fortunate few, who—unconstrained by tradition, effective laws, or countervailing powers—stripped the assets from the firms instead of taking actions to renew growth and create jobs—actions that might have justified such a transfer.

Over time, the lack of turnaround, the continuing steep fall in output, the concentration of wealth, the demise of probity, the resistance to standard case-by-case methods, the deepening malaise, and the increasingly common anecdotes that only state-owned firms have resisted criminalization,[17] combined to persuade many presumably predisposed observers to reject not only the notorious loans-for-shares scheme, but almost all of the Russian privatization approach. Thus Kenneth Arrow[18] calls Russian privatization "a predictable economic disaster," arguing that it should have been easy to foresee poor outcomes, given Russia's institutional weakness and high inflation in 1992–95. Jeffrey Sachs[19] says he now favors Russia renationalizing the natural resource firms wrongly privatized earlier. Simon Commander (1998) argues that Russian insider privatization has sanctioned a low investment–low productivity equilibrium, and as such has contributed greatly to Russia's fiscal impasse. Many Russian economists and a few Western colleagues have concluded that the entire privatization approach in Russia was wrong, that it should have been preceded (not accompanied) by institution building, and that the proper way forward is to strengthen the structures of the state.[20] These critics, in particular, stress the need to recreate or reinforce mechanisms to supervise and assist state-owned firms. One suggestion is to use a state-owned

---

[17]A *Washington Post* (1999, p. A16) story on the criminal takeover of coal mines in the Kuzbass Basin region of Russia asserts: "The most productive mines are still largely state-owned, and regional government officials serve on the boards of directors."

[18]Author's notes of Arrow's presentation at a World Bank seminar on What Went Wrong in Russia? Washington, D.C., October 26, 1998.

[19]Author's notes of Sach's presentation by videoconference to the World Bank Institute's Core Course on Privatization, Washington, D.C., November 2, 1998. Sachs is much more critical of the loans-for-shares scheme than of the Mass Privatization Program (MPP).

[20]Three vocal critics of the Russian privatization approach are Nekipelov Alexandr, Stanislav Menshikov, and Oleg Bogomolov; Western economists associated with a "move more slowly; concentrate on institutions in advance of ownership change" include Michael Intriligator, Lance Taylor, Marshall Pomer, Kenneth Arrow, and Dorothy Rosenberg.

holding company, which supposedly would manage assets rationally and prepare firms for a smooth transition to competitive market operations (Alexandr, 1998). The views on privatization are so negative that a fair number of members of the federal legislature (the Duma) have urged that the huge tax arrears owed to the federal government by privatized firms be transformed into equity, which would effect a massive renationalization of industrial assets.

Difficulties in the Czech Republic

The limited expectations of privatization were perhaps reasonable in Russia, given the unfavorable factors against it: the length and intensity of the nonmarket approach, the unfavorable economic and structural conditions existing at the moment transition was launched, and the magnitude of the parallel political and institutional collapse. But in the Czech Republic, conditions and history made it reasonable not only to hope but to claim that the dramatic mass privatization program of 1992–95 would fully and permanently cut the links between the state and the divested enterprises and set the privatized firms on the road to unassisted competition in both domestic and foreign markets.

First signs were very encouraging. By 1995, Czech privatizers had divested more than 1,800 firms in two waves of exchanges for vouchers, sold a group of high-potential firms to strategic investors, and transferred to previous owners or municipalities a mass of other assets.[21] By 1996, then Prime Minister Vaclav Klaus was able to claim that transition had more or less been completed and that henceforth the Czech Republic should be viewed as an ordinary European country undergoing ordinary economic and political problems. All indicators appeared to confirm this view: The Czech Republic was enjoying comparatively low inflation, low unemployment, rapid rise in the private sector's share of GDP, high rates of investment and export growth to countries in the European Union, and a resumption of GDP growth starting in 1993 and peaking at 6.4 percent in 1995.

But at the end of 1995, the Czech GDP growth rate fell, and it fell again in 1996 and 1997 when it reached 1 percent. In 1998 results were starkly negative, with an annual GDP contraction of about 2 percent;

---

[21]However, as of the end of 1998, much remained to be privatized in the Czech Republic: majority or controlling stakes in three of the four major banks, parts or all of infrastructure firms, a number of large industrial concerns. Taken together, the state retained 40 large firms classed as "strategic," and had minority stakes in more than 325 nonstrategic commercial and industrial concerns. Tellingly, the Czech state still retains significant ownership interest in 9 of the 10 largest firms in the country.

projected growth in 1999 was zero or slightly positive. Thus the Czech economy was officially in recession—in contrast to 4–5 percent expansion in neighboring countries.

Many reasons account for the economic slide, including a mini-recession in Germany (now the Czech Republic's largest trading partner) and some financial mismanagement at the end of 1995 and early 1996. Nonetheless, an increasingly large amount of the blame is being placed on the way privatization was carried out.

A 1998 OECD report states the argument: The Czech voucher approach to privatization produced ownership structures that impeded efficient corporate governance and restructuring. The crux of the problem was that insufficiently regulated privatization investment funds ended up owning large or controlling stakes in many firms privatized by vouchers, as citizens diversified risk by investing their coupon points in these funds. But most of the large funds were owned by the major domestic banks—banks in which the Czech state retained a controlling or even majority stake. The results, say the critics, were predictable:

- Investment funds tended to overlook poor performance in firms, because pulling the plug would force the fund's bank owners to write down the resources lent to these firms.
- The state-influenced, weakly managed, and inexperienced banks tended to extend credit to high-risk, privatized firms with poor potential (whether or not they were owned by subsidiary funds), and to continually roll over credits rather than push firms into bankruptcy.
- The bankruptcy framework itself was weak and the process lengthy, further reducing financial market discipline.
- The lack of prudential regulation and enforcement mechanisms in the capital markets opened the door to a variety of highly dubious, and some overtly illegal, actions that enriched fund managers at the expense of minority shareholders and harmed the health of the firm, for example, by allowing fund managers to load firms with debt, then lift the cash and vanish, leaving the firm saddled with debts it had not used for restructuring.

Because of these experiences, many have concluded that the Czech firms privatized through vouchers did not sufficiently restructure where investment funds had the controlling stakes.[22] And although

---

[22]Weiss and Nikitin (1997, p. 21) looked at financial performance in a set of Czech firms. They concluded that while "ownership concentration in hands other than funds has a major (and positive) effect on performance," there is "no evidence of a positive effect of ownership shares by funds on the performance of operating companies." Pavel Mertlik (Minister of Economy in the Social Democrat government that came to power in 1998) argued much the same point (see Mertlik, 1998, pp. 103–22).

the proximate and most visible determinants of inadequate restructuring lie in the glaring weaknesses of the capital and financial markets, the voucher privatization method is viewed as the underlying cause. The emphasis of the method on speed, neglect of institutional issues, such as the weak legal and regulatory framework, and atomization of ownership helped to undermine its success. David Ellerman (1998) is the most outspoken critic of the Czech scheme. He argues that the negative outcomes were predictable given the separation of ownership from control. Moreover, the funds themselves lacked stable ownership, and the broader economy provided few institutional mechanisms to instill decent corporate governance in either the funds or the firms. The natural result was a "two-sided grab-fest by fund managers and enterprise managers" accompanied by "drift, stagnation and decapitalization of the privatized industrial sector . . . ." (Ellerman, 1998, p. 11).[23]

Other Transition Economies

Similar concerns have been raised in some of the other transition economies. Many officials and observers, particularly in the smaller and more geographically isolated transition countries, cautiously agree to privatization in general but argue against rapid and mass privatization. Those from Albania, Mongolia, and countries of the former Soviet Union are particularly skeptical, for the following reasons. First, they see few positive outcomes from privatization in Russia. And since they consider their industrial assets and business environments to be similar to those in Russia, they believe they cannot avoid the same problems.

Second, they fear that the countries lack the administrative and legal mechanisms needed to transform rapacious grasping into tolerable and productive attempts at acquisition. Third, many aspects of the economies of countries that were once part of the former Soviet Union are still under the influence of Russian supply, transport, energy, and sometimes criminal networks. Fourth, some of the countries that tried mass privatization schemes, such as Albania, Kazakhstan, Mongolia, and Moldova, concluded that they gained little from this effort. They found that dispersing ownership among the inexperienced population has not improved governance of firm managers. Too often, firm

---

[23]Pistor and Spicer (1997) were also critical, concluding that funds generally have been unable to enhance the value of their holdings because of the import of "the initial design problems in mass privatization—asymmetric information and imperfect property rights . . ." (from the Summary).

managers remained unchanged, failed to restructure their firms, and remained largely unaccountable for their actions. Leaders in Uzbekistan, for example, are increasingly convinced of the correctness of their neighbor's policies of general gradualism and of their opposition to handing over firms to owners lacking in financial strength and expertise. These experiences are claimed to justify, to necessitate, a slower, more cautious, more evolutionary, and more government-led path to ownership transfer.[24]

In light of all this, it is not surprising that in some post-Soviet countries—especially those in which the political transition entailed less of a break with the past than in Russia and where the inherited state structure maintained some cohesion and effectiveness—a Chinese-style approach to enterprise reform and ownership change is considered the proper model to follow.[25] The overall Chinese record of high and sustained growth, largely without a shift to formal private ownership, poses a stark contrast to the generally poorer transition performance elsewhere. Moreover, the approach is the subject of encouraging comments from a number of Western economists. For example, Joseph Stiglitz (1998) states that the Chinese experience shows that an economy might achieve more effective growth by focusing first on competition, leaving privatization until later. Thomas Rawski (1997), whose overall conclusion is that economists overstate the importance of ownership, states:

> The generally negative evaluation of state enterprise performance is overdone . . . China's state industry has increased output, productivity, and exports . . . the upper tier of state firms is not far removed from international market standards . . . . The main source of SOE financial problems lies in their history, not their ownership . . . . (Without politically imposed financial burdens) SOE profitability may equal or exceed the financial performance of China's highly touted collective factories . . . the productivity performance of state industry may match or surpass the accomplishments of the collective sector . . . (p. 14).

The attack on privatization could be expanded in several ways: for example, by noting the insufficiency of analytical work on the macroeconomic and fiscal impact of privatization; by pointing out that the "fiscal space" justification for privatization (that is, governments

---

[24]It has to be pointed out, however, that many proponents of this line are benefiting from the substantial rents produced by a system of heavy government involvement in the economy.

[25]For an assessment of the various approaches on enterprise performance and reform in use and under consideration by the Chinese, see Broadman (1995). For a discussion of the competing and hotly debated interpretations of the results of Chinese reforms short of privatization, see Sachs and Woo (1997), especially pp. 18–31, "The SOE Sector Under Reform."

should cease pouring resources into inefficient and badly managed state-owned firms; instead, they should sell them and concentrate resources and action on those socially needed activities that only governments can and should undertake) states a hope, not a known reality. However, very little is known in emerging markets or the transition economies about how the proceeds of privatization are actually applied.[26] And given the nature of the political and administrative systems in many of these settings, doubts are warranted about transition governments' abilities to collect and allocate wisely the sums generated through privatization.

Political Economy Aspects of the Question

What are the political economy aspects of privatization—the issue of who in transition society wins and loses from transactions? As noted, a good part of the criticism of privatization in Russia and the Czech Republic stems from the widespread perception that reform in general and privatization in particular have yielded benefits to the very few at the expense of many—for example, the Czech workers in Ellerman's (1998) "decapitalized and stagnant" privatized firms; and the voucher investors in the two countries who were led to believe their investments would yield an income stream and a capital gain, neither of which materialized for most.

To date, no study of transition countries has examined these issues in the rigorous manner pioneered by Galal and colleagues' 1994 study, *Welfare Consequences of Selling Public Enterprises*, which studied the gains and losses of sellers, buyers, workers, consumers, and competitors. Indeed, very little empirical work of any sort has yet appeared on the question of privatization's effects on income distribution in transition settings (or elsewhere). Analysts have begun to produce some oblique and tantalizing hints about the relation between privatization and incomes. For example, Garner and Terrell (1998) looked at movements in income distribution in the Czech Republic and Slovakia through 1993. They concluded that income inequality had risen much less than was claimed in the World Bank's 1996 *World Development Report*. They also predicted more inequality in these countries as the returns from asset distribution are realized.

Newell and Socha (1998) looked at the related issue of privatization's impact on wage distribution in Poland. They concluded that

---

[26]Since this writing, Davis and others (2000) have conducted a study to examine the macroeconomic and systemic fiscal impacts of privatization, among other issues.

private sector workers typically earned less than their state-sector counterparts after privatization, and the gap was widening; but they also noted that after controlling for experience, tenure, and workplace size, their research showed a small positive private sector premium. Not much can be made of these beginnings, and more work is needed on the subject.[27]

A common allegation is that women in transition countries bear a higher percentage of the costs of privatization than do men. In one of the only studies to examine this issue, Sewall (1997) argues that privatization in Hungary was triply costly to women, because women formed a disproportionately higher percentage of those laid off by new owners, privatization often involved the closing of the firm's social services—canteens, clinics, day-care centers—so crucial to female participation in the workforce, and women formed almost the entire workforce in these social service units. Although Sewall's study is one in a single country, the findings can reasonably be expected to apply to many other transition countries.

Privatization is often assumed to inevitably and automatically result in increased unemployment; but the relationship between employment and privatization in transition countries is not straightforward. For example, the Czech Republic privatized rapidly but maintained a low unemployment rate (a remarkable 3 percent) through 1997. The low rate was at first taken as a sign of the Czech reformers' success but was later revealed as too good, as an indication that the needed level of corporate restructuring was not taking place in the privatized firms. The recent steep rise in Czech unemployment (7 percent and climbing at the end of 1998) came about even as the pace of privatization had slowed to almost a halt. Something of the same phenomenon has taken place in Russia: that is, mass and rapid privatization, but a relatively small increase in the official unemployment rate. (Although masses of people are officially employed, they are working part time, or not at all, but are kept on the books, or are not being paid.)

In Poland and Hungary, in contrast, privatization started and progressed much more slowly, and neither country followed a "mass" approach. Yet official unemployment grew rapidly in both countries, reaching 16.7 percent in Poland in 1993–94 (down to 9.6 percent in 1998), and 14.1 percent in Hungary in 1993 (falling to 10.8 at the end of 1996). The conclusion must be that employment levels are as much a function of the scope and pace of overall economic restructuring as they are of ownership.

---

[27]The Europe and Central Asia region of the World Bank is commissioning a study on this topic.

A Summation of the Critique

The perception of many citizens, analysts, and some leaders in transition settings—especially those in the BRO countries—as well some knowledgeable external observers, is close to the following:

In far too many privatization transactions and in far too many transition countries, mass and rapid privatization has turned over mediocre assets to large numbers of people who have neither the skills nor the financial resources to run them well. Most high-quality assets have in one way or another (sometimes by "spontaneous privatization" that preceded official schemes, sometimes by manipulation of the voucher schemes, and perhaps most often in the nonvoucher second phase or in secondary trading) gone to the resourceful, agile, and politically well-connected few. In many instances where ordinary citizens managed to obtain and hold minority blocks of shares in the high-quality firms, the shareholders have been induced to turn over their shares to others at modest prices, or they have seen, without warning or explanation, the value of their minority shares fall to nothing.

These occurrences are particularly prevalent in countries where the post-transition state structures are weak and fractured. This allows significant parts of government to become captured by groups whose major objective is to use the state to legitimatize or mask their acquisition of wealth. (Poor outcomes also can occur when strong governments fail to create a modicum of prudential regulation for financial and capital markets.) The international financial institutions must bear some of the responsibility for the poor outcomes, since they often insisted on the primacy of economic policy (or they followed uncritically the lead of intensely committed reformers). They requested and required transition governments to privatize rapidly and extensively, assuming that private ownership by itself would provide sufficient incentives to shareholders to monitor managerial behavior and push firms to good performance. Competitive policies and institutional safeguards could follow at a later date. The immediate need was to create a basic constituency of property owners. The key assumption was that to build capitalism, one needed capitalists, lots of them, and fast.

But capitalism requires much more than private property. It functions because of the widespread acceptance and enforcement of fundamental rules and safeguards that make the outcomes of economic exchange secure, predictable, and of reasonably widespread benefit. Where such rules and safeguards, such institutions, are absent, not only fairness and equity suffer, but performance of firms suffer as well, because in an institutional vacuum the chances are high that no one in a privatized firm is interested in maintaining the long-run health of the assets.

Too many supervising state officials become interested mainly in extracting rents and selling licenses, permissions, and protection to the firm, rather than enforcing policy. Even when the state retains a significant minority share of the firm and representation on the firm's board of directors (as is common in many transition countries), the representatives are often looking more for perks, payoffs, and protection of bureaucratic interests than ways to boost shareholder value. Faced with voiceless shareholders and a rapacious or ineffective state that makes believing in the sanctity of property rights difficult (and inflicts punishing tax and interest rates), the manager of a firm may conclude that promoting shareholder value is impossible or not worthwhile. The easier course of action is to lobby the state for assistance or to strip assets and walk away. The former can often be arranged with the collusion and blessing of supposedly supervisory government officials or private bankers or fund managers. Workers, shareholders or not, are caught in the maelstrom, searching for stability and safety, and hoping only to keep their jobs. The other mechanisms of corporate governance—financial and capital markets, the economic and financial press, the insolvency/bankruptcy regimes—are too weak or embryonic to provide countermeasures.

In such circumstances, privatization is more likely to lead to stagnation and decapitalization than to improved financial results and enhanced efficiency.

Can the Problems Be Corrected?

This conclusion is a substantial indictment of privatization, sufficient to establish that at least in some institutionally weak settings the promise of privatization has remained unfulfilled and mistakes have been made. But is the evidence sufficient to condemn the concept? The answer is no.

The Defense

The first counterpoint to the arguments against privatization is the large volume of rigorous studies cited earlier. These studies, conducted in a wide variety of sectoral, geographical, and income settings, show that firms tend to perform much better after privatization than before, as measured by a number of financial and operational efficiency indices at the firm level. A smaller amount of evidence—mainly from several middle- and high-income economies—also show welfare improvements from privatization.

The question is whether we can expect similar positive results in transition settings. Country conditions matter. Several studies indicate that the lower a country's income, the less dramatic or speedy will be the results of privatization and the more likely that the process could go wrong.[28] As noted earlier, countries in CEE—closer geographically, historically, and culturally to Western commercial traditions and markets—have generally privatized more swiftly and with much better results than their more Eastern counterparts. (A more optimistic interpretation would be that the positive results of privatization are taking much longer to show in most of the countries of the former Soviet Union than in the CEE or Baltic states.) Important differences—not only in location and history, but also in institutional density and capacity and adherence to the rule of law—distinguish these countries from those of the former Soviet Union. These factors affect the type of privatization policies and approaches chosen and the ways in which the choices are implemented and the financial and economic outcomes obtained.[29] But these caveats do not contradict the main point: The mass of empirical evidence indicates that privatization, when correctly conducted, produces positive benefits. For transition countries, the question is not *whether to privatize* but *how to privatize better*.

This conclusion is not accepted by all. Given the difficulties already elaborated, and drawing on the general criticism of Tandon (1995), many argue that the best course of action for transition economies, especially in the former Soviet Union, is to further postpone privatization until competitive forces and an enabling institutional framework are in place. And, as noted, some analysts call for the renationalization of some of the firms already divested, with the intention of managing them in the public interest, through greater state involvement. The more liberal of these critics add that some or all of the renationalized firms could be sold again in the future, when firm and market conditions have improved and investors are offering better prices. Response to this line of reasoning is threefold.

In some transition settings, privatization produces clear benefits

The first and easy point to make is that a return to statism would be blatantly nonsensical in the CEE and Baltic states. In those regions, the

---

[28]See, for example, Boubakri and Cosset (1998).

[29]This has long been recognized. Kikeri, Nellis, and Shirley (1992) concluded that the two key factors determining privatization outcomes were the nature of the market into which the firm was being divested—competitive or noncompetitive—and country conditions. The latter refers to a country's overall macroeconomic policy framework and capacity to regulate. "In unfavorable country settings, where the existing private sector is small, capital markets are thin, and the interest of external investors is limited, the sale of enterprises even in competitive sectors may be more difficult"(pp. 4–5).

trials of the Czech approach notwithstanding, evidence strongly suggests that privatized firms generally and significantly outperform state-owned companies. Two studies (Frydman and others, 1997, and Pohl and others, 1997) presented strong evidence of the superior performance of privatized firms, particularly in the Czech Republic, Hungary, and Poland. Looking at a variety of performance indicators to the end of 1995, Pohl and his colleagues (1997) found that in 6,300 firms in seven countries privatization was the key to restructuring, because divested firms registered much higher rates of productivity growth, investment, and positive operating cash flows than the state-owned enterprises in the sample. The study also concluded that all forms and methods of privatization (except those that gave ownership to workers) produced the same positive results, a disputed issue to which we shall return.

In this study, the highest percentage of strongly performing privatized firms are found in the maligned Czech Republic. Pohl[30] states that an updating of the database shows this still to be the case at the end of 1997 (although performance by Hungarian firms was by then about as good as that of the Czechs).

Frydman and colleagues (1997) reviewed the effects of privatization on corporate performance in a sample of 188 Czech, Hungarian, and Polish firms (half privatized, half state-owned) covering the years 1990 through 1994. The authors found that private ownership in their sample (except for cases where workers became owners) significantly improved the key aspects of corporate performance, particularly revenue generation. Moreover, the privatized firms laid off relatively few employees in the early days of transition and increased employment more than state firms did. Indeed, the authors argue that "privatization is the dominant employment strategy in transition"(p. 30). The study[31] also found no selection bias present. Rather, it found just the opposite: Where insiders had obtained the better firms, they had tended to manage them badly, whereas outsiders had tended to get below-average firms but had turned them around, as measured by later revenue performance.

Papp and others (1998) reviewed Hungary's privatization efforts and found that they were far from faultless. They had failed to increase significantly either income to the seller or competitive forces (but Hungary has also earned more than $8 billion from privatization sales,

---

[30]Communication from Gerhard Pohl, August 1998.

[31]The methodological rigor of this study is exemplary, but the sample size is small, the firms are medium size (perhaps larger firms are more difficult to turn around?), and the data somewhat dated.

more than any other transition country in CEE and the former Soviet Union). Still, the overall conclusion of Papp and his coauthors was as follows:

> Privatization has led to better asset management and corporate gover-
> nance; to greater efficiency in production, restructuring and moderniza-
> tion of older enterprises; to the production of new and improved prod-
> ucts; and to a greater export orientation (p. 339).

Simonetti, Rojec, and Rems (1999) looked at the relationship between financial and operating performance and ownership form in
Slovenia. Because of the Yugoslav heritage of the "social capital" concept, ownership is a particularly tangled issue in Slovenia. The authors
examined six ownership categories: private firms (but not privatized),
foreign-owned firms, firms whose majority shares were sold to insiders, firms whose majority shares were sold to external buyers, nonprivatized (socially owned) firms, and state firms (mainly public utilities). The authors' sample of 1,902 firms represents about three-fourths
of Slovenia's industrial assets, sales, and employment during 1994–96.
The result is that, although few in number, foreign-owned firms are
doing the best, averaging a respectable 5.4 percent return on equity
during this period, compared with 3.9 for private firms, –0.03 for internally privatized firms, 1.2 for externally privatized firms, –4.6 for
nonprivatized firms, and –0.60 for the state firms. When we add profit
margin:

> Foreign and private companies remain much better than companies from
> other ownership categories, followed by internal and external companies
> with positive figures, while non-privatized and state companies are
> pretty much under water (Simonetti, Rojec, and Rems, 1999, p. 2).

Although the performance of the Slovenian privatized firms is
hardly outstanding, they are doing much better than the nonprivatized companies from the same sectors. The latter are the poorest performers by almost every measure. This last is an important point: *The
standard against which privatized firms should be measured is the performance of the nonprivatized sector from which the privatized firms were
drawn, and not some theoretical ideal.*

Djankov and Pohl (1998), who examined the performance of large
privatized firms in Slovakia, found generally improved performance,
even though most of the firms had been turned over to the old managers (the very insiders whose ownership so often was hypothesized
to account for poor performance elsewhere).

Much indirect evidence suggests that liberalizing reforms, in general, and privatization, in particular, produce good results. Estonia

privatized the bulk of its enterprises quickly, mostly to external investors, and in a minority of cases it used vouchers, but always to divest a minority of shares (see Nellis, 1996). The country returned to positive GDP growth rapidly and sustained it. Estonia is the only transition country to register double-digit growth rates and continued to grow at a high rate despite the world and Russian crises. Haltiwanger and Vodopevic (1998), analyzing the effects of Estonian reform on labor, found that in the early days following the separation from the Soviet Union, layoffs increased dramatically, but later in transition, hires and job creation surged. The layoffs tended to take place in large manufacturing and state-owned firms, whereas job creation took place in smaller, service-oriented private companies. "These results suggest that Estonia's liberal and radical reforms enabled huge worker and job reallocations without producing massive unemployment" (from the Abstract). Much of the job creation came about in new entry firms, but the privatized companies contributed to the growth as well. Thus, a fair amount of evidence suggests that privatization in the CEE and Baltic states works and that the portrait of privatization drawn earlier is overly negative and critical, at least in this part of the transition world.

Renationalization is unlikely to work

The second part of the response is that renationalization would be a desperate measure and highly likely to fail, particularly in those countries of the former Soviet Union where it is most likely to be espoused. At first glance, the idea of renationalization certainly has appeal: Select some or all of the most egregiously misprivatized firms and put them back in the portfolio of the state; then sell them again, but this time do it correctly. Correctly, presumably, would mean the following:

- Sell the enterprises in an open, transparent manner, with valuation procedures that conform to international standards of practice.
- Involve internationally recognized professional financial and transaction advisers; fully disclose all relevant information to all bidders, with no restrictions on the number or nationality of these bidders.
- After the sale, pose no restrictions on the buyer to maintain the same line of business, the same number of employees, and so on.

But only a few transition governments outside CEE (or even within) can reasonably be expected to undertake this process and handle it well. Only a few have the capacity to prevent the assets stripping in state-owned companies or the technical and political capability and willingness to divest firms according to this set of procedures. As

Shirley (1999) has shown, the irony is that countries with the administrative skills and political capacity to run state-owned firms effectively and efficiently are usually the same countries that can privatize well. Conversely, the forces and conditions that lead governments to botch privatization are the same that prevent decent management of state-owned enterprises. Shirley's point is significant—not only with regard to renationalization but also in response to the concerns of Tandon and Stiglitz that competition more so than ownership determines outcome efficiency. Her point is that few governments have the luxury of choosing between enhancing competition or changing ownership. Her findings reveal that it is a mistake "to think of privatization as totally distinct from reform of enterprises under continued state ownership. Rather the two demand similar, politically costly reforms and tend to succeed or fail together" (p. 28).[32]

Shirley's recommended course of action for countries clearly not ready for major reform (a category that includes some if not many of the countries of the former Soviet Union) is to build the foundation for reform:

> by reducing fiscal deficits to increase pressures for SOE reform by making the burden of SOE deficits explicit; easing trade restrictions to strengthen exporters who can become a constituency for SOE reform when SOE inefficiencies harm their ability to compete in global markets; removing barriers to entry since new entrants can also be a voice for reform; eliminating regulatory and policy obstacles to new job creation (such as restrictions on firing or taxes or subsidies that encourage employers to substitute capital for labor) and uncoupling SOE jobs and social services such as education or health care to encourage labor mobility (p. 30).

These steps might be sufficient to launch reform in a mixed economy in which state-owned enterprises account for a fifth or less of GDP. But these measures are unlikely to turn the tide in institutionally weak transition economies, except perhaps in the very long run. In the latter, the problem is not revealing the costs and inefficiencies of the state enterprises, but rather establishing the basic rules to enable any form of ownership to be efficient. Moreover, in transition countries the remaining state-owned enterprises are only part of the problem; the equal or greater question is what to do about misprivatized firms—a question the Shirley measures would only obliquely address. Djankov (1998a and b) provides evidence suggesting that many transition governments will find restructuring firms under state

---

[32]Shirley made related points in her earlier work (see Shirley, 1998).

ownership difficult. In this case study, Djankov examines Romanian efforts to isolate a set of large, financially troubled companies in order to determine what is required for their recovery and sale or closure. Djankov presents data showing that none of the intentions of the isolation program were fulfilled. Moreover, the program may have delayed restructuring by not imposing hardened budget constraints on loss-making enterprises. He concludes that transition governments should "privatize rapidly, and not attempt to restructure enterprises prior to privatization" (p. 10).

The conclusion: Renationalization is not the alternative; rather, governments must find ways to privatize correctly and to set and enforce performance standards on those already privatized. The critical question, of course, is how.

What's wrong with caution?

The third part of the response is much more intricate. Even if one accepts the notion that renationalization is unlikely to work, one could still make an argument against further rapid privatization. The reasoning is that in institutionally weak and politically fractured transition countries, long removed from or never fully integrated into the Western commercial tradition, governments should halt privatization of the remaining portfolio (majority or minority stakes) and shift their efforts to (1) strengthening market-supporting institutions (mainly public but some private as well), with the goal of channeling present "wild east" commercial activity into socially productive and acceptable modes, and (2) imposing discipline on and competition in the remaining public enterprises, accompanied or followed by staged, incremental shifts in ownership patterns, in a more or less evolutionary, Chinese-style manner.[33]

Once again, the idea has a prima facie appeal and one that other governments, such as Vietnam, have tried to follow, with some early success.[34] But again, the solution assumes the existence of a desired end state at which it is aiming—an effective state mechanism and institutional framework.

---

[33]In essence, this is the approach long recommended by Intriligator and others (1995, pp. 10–11); see also my response in the same issue (Nellis, 1995).

[34]At least for a time. But even before the East Asia crisis, investor enthusiasm for Vietnam was waning, for reasons of both policy and interfering practices. Moreover, Vietnam has not experimented as broadly or boldly as China with ownership models. At the end of 1998 fewer than 50 small and medium-size firms had been "equitized," the Vietnamese term for divesting ownership to firm insiders. (See Amin and Webster, 1998.)

The paradox is that those countries that had largely rejected the communist state and political systems but that possessed little or nothing of a capitalist past to anchor them are having considerable trouble moving in an orderly manner to the market system. And ironically, the once planned Asian economies that have avoided political transition but have maintained enough administrative competence and political legitimacy to allow them to discipline the most blatant forms of theft and corruption have so far best combined the move to market principles and tactics with sustained growth, but without formal privatization. By this reasoning the Soviet Union might have successfully adopted such an evolutionary strategy in, say, the 1960s or early 1970s, but by the time the attempt was made by Gorbachev in the late 1980s, state power and legitimacy had sunk so low that the attempt failed.[35]

A second and powerful part of the explanation for the inapplicability of the Chinese approach is that China's economy was structurally very different from that of Russia and other countries of the former Soviet Union. China embarked on its form of transition at a time when agriculture accounted for more than 70 percent of GDP, and industry only 15 percent; the corresponding figures in Russia were 13 and 42 percent (World Bank, 1996). The courage and vision of Chinese policymakers who launched and sustained the liberalizing reforms should be acknowledged. But we must also recognize that shifting resources from agriculture to nontraditional forms of industry was a different, more manageable task than restructuring an industrial base that produced almost nothing for private needs. It is thus not surprising that attempts in the CEE or BRO to find a slower and less painful move to the market without much privatization have also proven ineffective: for example, in Ukraine, Romania, Bulgaria (prior to the 1997 elections), and Belarus.[36] During the long periods of nonprivatization in these countries, many state-owned enterprises had their assets stripped; when privatization eventually comes, there will probably be little left to transfer.

The overall assessment appears bleak: Privatize incorrectly and the result will not be increased production, job creation, and increased incomes, but rather stagnation and decapitalization. But keeping enterprises in the hands of a weak and venal state is likely to lead to a

---

[35]This reasoning is similar to that found in Sachs and Woo (1994, pp. 102–45).

[36]With its regulated prices and minimal privatization of medium and large firms, Belarus is an anomaly both in terms of policy and outcomes so far. Outside observers argue that Belarus's relative stability in terms of output and job maintenance is fragile, heavily dependent on the volatile Russian market, and thus potentially unsustainable. The fact remains that at the moment the unemployment rate in Belarus is lower and the wage arrears much less than in Russia or Ukraine.

similar end. In both instances the evident long-term solution is to build the administrative and policymaking and enforcing capacities of the government. And to this end there are questions that need satisfactory and operationally viable answers, for example: What precisely must governments do in this regard to produce a public service with the public interest in mind, and how precisely do they go about doing it? What is the role of external assistance in this process, and how long will it take to effect reasonable progress? Can anything be done in the shorter term? Several transition governments have tried to compensate for managerial deficiencies by contracting out much or all of the privatization process to agents and advisers. For example, at the beginning of its privatization program the government of Estonia relied heavily on German technical assistance from the *Treuhandanstalt*, obtaining not simply expertise but an entire approach, which was applied with great success. The Bulgarian Privatization Agency has turned over to privatization agents and transaction advisers (PATAs) much of the responsibility for the sale of about 30 large firms and has pooled batches of smaller firms and contracted the sale of these firms to private actors;[37] results are starting to flow in.

The government of Uzbekistan has resolved to privatize 30 of its largest firms, delegating major responsibility to international financial advisers in every step of the process. Romanian officials have expressed an intent to follow a similar procedure for more than 200 of the largest firms remaining in state hands. These efforts go beyond the common tactic of employing experienced consultants to assist a national privatization agency; they turn over significant decision making power to the agents employed in order to circumvent the constraining political process and to find technical solutions to perceived political and institutional difficulties.

But it is neither possible nor desirable to eliminate entirely the role of the sovereign. Worldwide experience has shown that it is imperative that representatives of the body politic ultimately approve and ratify, and be seen to ratify, the privatization recommendations of technical advisers and agents. If this is not done, there will be no political counterweight to offset the claims and allegations of opponents.

Technicians and politicians often differ on what constitutes an appropriate or acceptable transaction. In good circumstances, such as in Estonia, a spirit of compromise prevails. For example, German advisers strongly opposed the use of vouchers because they considered them harmful to corporate governance and revenue generation, whereas the

---

[37]See p. 9 of Alexieva and others (1998) for a description of the approach.

political authorities needed a mechanism to garner public support for a contentious program. Both sides eventually agreed on a scheme whereby a minority of shares (and only in some firms) was exchanged for vouchers, after a core investor had taken a controlling majority stake. In Russia, on the other hand, an effort to construct a case-by-case privatization program, with intensive use of private sector financial advisers, has not produced the anticipated results, because Russian authorities have been reluctant to turn over to the agents anything other than accounting and valuation exercises. The Bulgarian PATA program has produced some results and promises more, but not without significant strains and disputes between the agents and the supervising government officials over the extent of the agents' decision making powers. It took four years of difficult negotiations for the various Polish governments to put together their mass privatization program, which in effect hands over to private agents (organized in National Investment Funds) the task of taking some 500 larger firms to market—but it is now producing good results. The point is that contracting out is an option worth considering, but it is far from a generalized or speedy solution. And as always the effectiveness of the effort depends heavily on the existence of a modicum of governmental will and capacity.

- Based on the experience with privatization in Poland, Romania, Russia, and Uzbekistan, Itzhak Goldberg argues for what he terms "reprivatization."[38] According to Goldberg, the principal obstacle to progressive restructuring in privatized firms in Russia and elsewhere is the excessive concentration of ownership in the hands of insiders who lack the means and incentives to lead the firms forward.[39] Accepting the futility of renationalization, Goldberg argues instead for increasing the capital in privatized firms, and then diluting the stake of insiders by selling the resulting shares to external investors. His list of steps (in addition to the capital increase) required to bring about this opening to real owners includes strengthening mechanisms that allow owners to select managers, improving labor mobility, strengthening disclosure and audit, and strengthening the rights of shareholders.

---

[38]This phrase and notion, and many of the ideas in the following paragraphs, were provided by Itzhak Goldberg, of the World Bank, in several written communications in December 1998 and January 1999.

[39]In contrast to the view of Pohl and others (1997) that all forms of privatization, to insiders or outsiders alike (other than to workers alone), result in positive outcomes, Goldberg's is the increasingly accepted view. See Frydman and others (1997). See also Aghion and Blanchard (1998, p. 88), who state "outsider ownership is a necessary, although not a sufficient condition for deep restructuring and there is little evidence of strategic restructuring in firms without outsider ownership . . . ."

To the question, How can new shares be issued without the cooperation of existing owners? the answer is that the Russian government, for one, could easily bring about a capital increase in many firms. As noted, most privatized firms are heavily in arrears on their tax payments. Moreover, government has retained a minority stake in the majority of privatized firms. A conversion of tax debt to equity would provide the government with a substantial set of shares to sell. In many cases the addition to capital, when added to the retained shares, would be large enough to provide a purchaser with a controlling stake.

This proposal is both a long-term and a partial solution (in the sense that only some firms will attract core investors). Moreover, the political and institutional deficiencies elaborated above deeply affect the likelihood that a government would undertake such corrective measures or that it would succeed in implementing them even if it made a sincere effort to do so. The suggestion is that the reforming elements in the transition governments, and the international assistance community (the international financial institutions, the European Community, the bilateral donors) abandon speed as a priority and shift their efforts to a necessarily slower and less dramatic form of case-by-case or tender privatization. This approach would aim at creating, from the bottom up, the climate in which monied, core, competent investors could take over the currently stagnant, decapitalized firms.

Overall, despite the many and evident obstacles hindering good privatization policy and practice, there seems to be no alternative, especially in institutionally weak transition countries, to a continuation of efforts to privatize. These new efforts may differ considerably from those of the recent past; and they may need to be less ambitious and accept a slower pace of implementation. But they need to continue.

Conclusion

So the answer is: Yes, it is time to rethink privatization, at least in those transition settings where history, geography, and politics have so readily channeled seemingly laudable economic policy into suboptimal outcomes. In Russia and elsewhere too much was promised of privatization, both by reformers who seemed at first to view ownership change as a sufficient condition to bring about a new liberal order and (less forgivably) by external advisers and aid providers, whose hopes for fast and relatively simple solutions may have clouded their judgment on whether the necessary supporting systems for privatization were in place, or how long it would take to put them in place and what was likely to happen in their absence.

But the admission of error should not be overdone. The fact remains that

- Privatization is the right course of action when it can be carried out correctly. Recall that in a number of CEE countries the policy is an undoubted success, far superior to letting the firms remain in state hands.

- In most countries and sectors around the world privatization yields great benefits at the firm level; it was not immediately obvious that some transition countries would differ from some of the low- to middle-income, institutionally weak, nontransition settings in which privatization has been successful. Early transition evidence showed a strong correlation between liberalization and stabilization and a return to growth.[40] And it was thought privatization was an integral part of this reform package. The problems of the approach emerged later, in corrupt second-phase sales for cash, in the lack of restructuring in insider-dominated firms, in the unregulated actions of investment funds, and so on. Many critics voiced concerns about vouchers, but few anticipated how badly some of the post-voucher transactions would be conducted.

- Those who say they had predicted the problem all along offer no viable alternative. For most transition countries, the alternative to privatization is not likely to be some Chinese-style combination of macroeconomic reform and unclear property rights. Because of the large differences in the political systems and starting conditions of these countries, such an approach would result in asset stripping and further stagnation under weak state supervision rather than high economic growth.

- Complaints from inside the countries are more justified but must be examined carefully. Doubtless, many transition government officials opposed to privatization are expressing sincere convictions, based on the assessment that the policy is not working or is proving too costly. But just as clearly, some officials are benefiting greatly from the continued state involvement in firms, and in the close relation between government and business that provides many opportunities for rent seeking. Thus the assertions of these officials on the superiority of continued state involvement are suspect.

- One must continually ask, What was and is the alternative to privatization? It is *not* clear that Russia would be better off today had

---

[40]See World Bank (1996), which presents the evidence for these points in the Introduction and in Chapters 1 and 3.

it avoided mass privatization in 1992–94. Several other institutionally weak transition economies that eschewed, delayed, or approached privatization more cautiously have little to show for it: Belarus, Bulgaria, Romania, and Ukraine, for example (although in no case is privatization or its absence the whole of the explanation).

- The radical reformers in then Czechoslovakia, Poland, Russia, and elsewhere insisted at the outset that speedy privatization was essential to create a constituency for transition to the market, to prevent further asset stripping, to sever the links between the enterprises and the state; and, most dramatically, to prevent the communists from returning.[41] In retrospect, it appears that more time was available than was thought. The return of communism in its traditional format was not a realistic possibility (though the failure of reform may be increasing the prospect). It might have been possible to approach privatization in a more deliberate manner; the results might have been less insider ownership and domination, less resistance to external investors, more protection for minority shareholders, and so on. But recall again that countries that tried a slow approach have not made a go of it.

Armenian officials vigorously argue that despite the problems of their privatized firms, the absence of external purchasers, plus the need for speed, gave them no choice but to proceed with voucher privatization. Although they would prefer that a higher percentage of the privatized firms were turning around, they argue that even very weak private owners are better than state ownership. In state hands these firms today would be making strong claims on scarce public resources, threatening the whole of the hard-won reform program. The same argument could be made in other countries.

So, in sum:

- Privatization remains the generally preferred course of action, but its short-term economic effectiveness and social acceptability depend on the existence of the institutional underpinnings of capitalism. Where these are present, privatization should and can go forward.
- If these underpinnings are missing but the government is effectively addressing their construction or reinforcement, it might be better to delay privatization until this effort is bearing fruit: Hungary and Poland are cases in point.

---

[41]The most tightly reasoned argument along these lines is found in the writings of three economists deeply involved in the Russian privatization program: Maxim Boycko, Andrei Shleifer, and Robert Vishny. See in particular Boycko, Shleifer, and Vishny (1995).

• The heart of the matter is in cases where government is unwilling or incapable of creating the supportive underpinnings. The evident long-term course of action here is to support measures enhancing will and capacity (assuming one knows what they are). Nonetheless, the reasonable short-term course of action is to push ahead with case-by-case and tender privatization along the lines espoused by Goldberg, in cooperation with the international assistance community, in hopes of producing success stories that will lead by example.

Bibliography

Aghion, Philippe, and Olivier Blanchard, 1998, "On Privatization Methods in Eastern Europe and Their implications," *Economics of Transition*, Vol. 6 (No. 1), p. 88.

Alexandr, Nekipelov, 1998, "On the Nature of Russian Economic Catastrophe and Possible Approaches to Dealing with It," unpublished paper presented at the Second Boston Seminar on Economic Globalization, October, pp. 16–17.

Alexieva, N., J. Nellis, T. O'Brien, and Lada Stoyanova, 1998, "A Review of Bulgarian Privatisation," paper for the seminar on Bulgaria—Enterprise Privatization: Progress and Issues, Paris, OECD.

Amin, Reza, and Leila Webster, 1998, "Equitization of State Enterprises in Vietnam: A Progress Report," Mekong Project Development Facility, Hanoi, Vietnam.

Anderson, James, H. Young Lee, and Peter Murrell, 1999, "Do Competition and Ownership Affect Enterprise Efficiency in the Absence of Market Institutions? Evidence after Privatization in Mongolia," Working Paper, Department of Economics and IRIS Center (College Park: University of Maryland).

Barberis, Nicholas, Maxim Boycko, Andrei Shleifer, Natalia Tsukanova, 1996, "How Does Privatization Work? Evidence from Russian Shops," *Journal of Political Economy*, Vol. 104 (No. 4), pp. 764–90.

Blasi, Joseph, Maya Kroumova, and Douglas Kruse, 1997, *Kremlin Capitalism: Privatizing the Russian Economy* (Ithaca: Cornell University Press).

Blaszczyk, Barbara, 1996, "Privatization and Ownership Transformation in Poland," in *Privatization in Post-communist Countries*, 2 Volumes, ed. by B. Blaszczyk and Richard Woodward (Warsaw: Center for Social and Economic Research).

Boubakri, Narjess, and Jean-Claude Cosset, 1998, "The Financial and Operating Performance of Newly Privatized Firms: Evidence from Developing Countries," *Journal of Finance*, Vol. 53 (June), pp. 1081–110.

Boubakri, Thesia, 1998, "A Gini Decomposition Analysis of Inequality in the Czech and Slovak Republics During the Transition," *Economics of Transition*, Vol. 6 (No. 1), p. 41.

Boycko, Maxim, Andrei Shleifer, and Robert Vishny, 1995, *Privatizing Russia* (Cambridge: MIT Press).

Broadman, Harry, 1995, *Meeting the Challenge of Chinese Enterprise Reform*, World Bank Discussion Paper No. 283 (Washington: World Bank).

Center for Economic Policy Research and Analysis (CEPRA), 1997, "Mass Privatization of Enterprises in the Republic of Armenia: An Early Assessment" (unpublished, Washington: U.S. Agency for International Development).

Commander, Simon, 1998, "Russia: What Is To Be Done?" *EDI Forum*, Vol. 3 (No. 2), pp. 7–8.

———, Qimiao Fan, and Mark Schaffer, eds., 1996, *Enterprise Restructuring and Economic Policy in Russia*, EDI Development Series (Washington: World Bank).

Davis, Jeffrey, Rolando Ossowski, Thomas Richardson, and Steven Barnett, 2000, *Fiscal and Macroeconomic Impact of Privatization*, IMF Occasional Paper No. 194 (Washington: International Monetary Fund).

Dewenter, Kathryn, and Paul Malatesta, 1998, "State-Owned and Privately-Owned Firms: An Empirical Analysis of Profitability, Leverage, and Labor Intensity," Working Paper (Seattle: University of Washington).

Djankov, Simeon, 1998a, "Enterprise Isolation Programs in Transition Economies," Policy Research Working Paper No. 1952 (Washington: World Bank).

———, 1998b, "Ownership Structure and Enterprise Restructuring in Six Newly Independent States" (unpublished, Washington: World Bank), pp. 2–3.

———, and Gerhard Pohl, 1998, "The Restructuring of Large Firms in the Slovak Republic," *Economics of Transition*, Vol. 6 (No. 1), pp. 67–85.

Djankov, Simeon, and Vladimir Kreacic, 1998, "Restructuring of Manufacturing Enterprises in Georgia: Four Case Studies and a Survey" (unpublished, Washington: World Bank).

Dowlah, C.A.F., 1996, "Privatization Experience in Bangladesh, 1991–1996" (unpublished, Washington: World Bank).

Earle, John, Saul Estrin, and Larisa Leshchenko, 1996, "Ownership Structures, Patterns of Control, and Enterprise Behavior in Russia," in *Enterprise Restructuring and Economic Policy in Russia*, ed. by Simon Commander, Qimiao Fan, and Mark Schaffer (Washington: World Bank).

Ellerman, David, 1998, "Voucher Privatization and Investment Funds: An Institutional Analysis," *World Bank Working Paper No. 1924* (Washington: World Bank).

Estrin, Saul, and John Earle, 1997, "After Voucher Privatization: The Structure of Corporate Ownership on Russian Manufacturing Industry," Center for Economic Policy and Research Discussion Paper No. 1736 (London: CEPR).

Frydman, Roman, Cheryl W. Gray, Marek Hessel, and Andrzej Rapaczynski, 1999, "The Limits of Discipline: Ownership and Hard Budget Constraints in the Transition Economies," Transition Economics Series No. 5 (Vienna: Institute of Advanced Studies).

————, and others, 1997, *Private Ownership and Corporate Performance: Some Lessons from Transition Economies*, World Bank Policy Research Working Paper No. 1830 (Washington, World Bank).

Galal, Ahmed, and others, 1995, *Welfare Consequences of Selling Public Enterprises* (Washington: Oxford University Press).

Garner, Thesia, and Katherine Terrell, 1998, "A Gini Decomposition Analysis of Inequality in the Czech and Slovak Republics During the Transition," *Economics of Transition*, Vol. 6 (No. 1), p. 41.

Haltiwanger, John, and Milan Vodopevic, 1998, "Gross Worker and Job Flows in a Transition Economy: An Analysis of Estonia," paper presented at the World Bank seminar on Poverty, Household Economics, and Rural Development (unpublished, Washington: World Bank).

Havrylyshyn, Oleh, and Donal McGettigan, 2000, "Privatization in Transition Countries," *Post Soviet Affairs*, Vol. 16, No. 3.

Intriligator, Michael, Robert McIntyre, Marshall Pomer, Dorothy Rosenberg, and Lance Taylor, 1995, "Checklist for Action in the Russian Economy," *Transition*, Vol. 6 (September–October), pp. 10–11.

Kattab, Mokhtar 1998, "Constraints of Privatization in the Egyptian Experience," paper delivered at the conference on Public-Private Partnerships in the Middle East and North Africa Region, Marrakech, September.

Kikeri, Sunita, John Nellis, and Mary Shirley, eds., 1992, *Privatization: The Lessons of Experience* (Washington: World Bank).

La Porta, Rafael, and Florencio Lopez-de-Silanes, 1997, "The Benefits of Privatization: Evidence from Mexico," National Bureau of Economic Research Working Paper No. 6215 (Cambridge, Massachusetts: NBER).

Lieberman, Ira, and Rogi Veimetra, 1996, "The Rush for State Shares in the 'Klondyke' of Wild East Capitalism: Loans-for-Shares Transactions in Russia," *The George Washington Journal of International Law and Economics* Vol. 29 (No. 3), p. 738.

Majumdar, Sumit, 1998, "Assessing Comparative Efficiency of the State-owned, Mixed, and Private Sectors in Indian Industry," *Public Choice*, Vol. 96 (July), pp. 1–24.

Megginson, William L., and Jeff Netter, 1998, "From State to Market: A Survey of Empirical Studies on Privatization," paper presented to the Global Equity Markets Conference (unpublished, Paris), December.

Mertlik, Pavel, 1998, "Czech Privatization: From Public Ownership to Public Ownership in Five Years?" in *Privatization in Post-Communist Countries*, Vol. 1, ed. by B. Blaszczyk and Richard Woodward (Warsaw: Center for Social and Economic Research).

Morse, Richard, 1998, "The Paradox of Privatisation," *Privatisation International*, No. 123 (December), p. 6.

Nellis, John, 1994, "Introduction," in *Russia: Creating Private Enterprises and Efficient Markets*, ed. by Ira Lieberman and John Nellis (Washington: World Bank).

———, 1995, "The Dangers of *Dirigisme*," *Transition*, Vol. 6, (September–October), pp. 11–13.

———, 1996, "Finding Real Owners: Lessons from Estonia's Privatization Program," *Viewpoint* No. 66 (Washington: World Bank).

Newbery, David, and Michael G. Pollitt, 1997, "The Restructuring and Privatization of the U.K. Electricity Supply—Was It Worth It?" in *The Private Sector in Infrastructure: Strategy, Regulation, and Risk* (Washington: World Bank).

Newell, Andrew, and Mieczyslaw Socha, 1998, "Wage Distribution in Poland: The Roles of Privatization and International Trade, 1992–96," *Economics of Transition*, Vol. 6 (No.1), p. 47.

Organization for Economic Cooperation and Development (OECD), 1998, *Czech Republic* (Paris: OECD).

Papp, Anita, Millard Long, Mihaly Kopanyi, and Peter Mihalyi, 1998, "Privatization: Restructuring Property Rights in Hungary," in *Public Finance Reform During the Transition: The Experience of Hungary*, ed. by Lajos Bokros and Jean-Jacques Dethier (Washington: World Bank).

Pinto, Brian, and Sweder van Wijnbergen, 1995, "Ownership and Corporate Control in Poland: Why State Firms Defied the Odds," CEPR Discussion Paper No. 1273 (London: Centre for Economic Policy Research).

Pistor, Katharina, and Andrew Spicer, 1997, "Investment Funds in Mass Privatization: Lessons from Russia and the Czech Republic," *Viewpoint*, No. 110 (Washington: World Bank).

Pohl, Gerhard, Robert E. Anderson, Stijn Claessens, and Simeon Djankov, 1997, *Privatization and Restructuring in Central and Eastern Europe-Evidence and Policy Options*, World Bank Technical Paper No. 368 (Washington: World Bank).

Privatisation International, 1998, No. 123 (December), p. 4.

Rawski, Thomas, 1997, "China and the Idea of Economic Reform," paper prepared for the Symposium on China's Gradualism Reconsidered (unpublished, Yokohama, Japan).

Sachs, Jeffrey, and Wing Thye Woo, 1994, "Structural Factors in the Economic Reforms of China, Eastern Europe and the Former Soviet Union, *Economic Policy*, Vol. 9 (April), pp. 102–45.

————, 1997, "Understanding China's Economic Performance," HIID Development Discussion Paper No. 575 (Cambridge, Massachusetts: Harvard University), pp. 18–31.

Sewall, Rebecca, 1997, "Gender Impact of Privatization," paper delivered to the World Bank Group on NGO Dialogue on Privatization, October 21–22 (unpublished, Washington: World Bank).

Shaikh, Hafeez, and others, 1996, *Argentina Privatization Program: A Review of Five Cases* (Washington: World Bank).

Shirley, Mary, 1998, "Why Performance Contracts for State-Owned Enterprises Haven't Worked," *Viewpoint,* No. 150 (Washington: World Bank).

————, 1999, "Bureaucrats in Business: The Roles of Privatization Versus Corporatization in State-Owned Enterprise Reform," *World Development*, Vol. 27 (January), 115–36.

Simonetti, Marko, Matija Rojec, and Marko Rems, 1999, "Enterprise Sector Restructuring and EU Accession of Slovenia" (unpublished, Washington: World Bank).

Stiglitz, Joseph, 1998, "Knowledge for Development: Economic Science, Economic Policy and Economic Advice," paper given at the Annual Bank Conference on Development Economics (Washington: World Bank).

Tandon, Pankaj, 1995, "Welfare Effects of Privatization: Some Evidence from Mexico," *Boston University International Law Journal*, Vol. 13 (No. 2), pp. 329–30.

Weiss, A., and G. Nikitin, 1997, "Performance of Czech Companies by Ownership Structure" (unpublished, Boston: Massachusetts: Boston University).

World Bank, 1996, "From Plan to Market," in *World Development Report* (New York: Oxford University Press).

World Bank, 1997, *Viewpoint*, No. 117 (Washington: World Bank).

Banking Sector Reform in Central and Eastern Europe   8

Lajos Bokros

The history of the last 10 years of banking sector reform and re-structuring in Central and Eastern Europe (CEE) is a fascinating story, because in most of these countries, what existed before the political transformation could not be called a banking sector at all. Rather it was a mechanism for redistributing funds according to the central plan or, in those countries where central planning had diminished in impor-tance by the time of the political transformation, according to some other mechanism. In either case, there was nothing resembling true fi-nancial intermediation because there was no risk management in the system, nor were the banks themselves making responsible, indepen-dent decisions about resource allocation or to attract the savings of households and other financial actors.

The Pillars of an Effective Banking Sector

The three most important pillars of prudent and efficient banking are competition, good corporate governance, and effective prudential regulation and supervision (Figure 1). The optimal situation is to have all three. But a country that has only two of the three is still better off than if it had none, which is, unfortunately, the case in most of CEE. Even in those countries considered the most developed, only two of these pillars are in place today. Prudential regulation and, first and foremost, supervision and the implementation of regulation are very weak in all the transition countries.

In Hungary, which is regarded as one of the leading reformers, the government was obliged last December to recapitalize Postabank, one of the few remaining partly state-owned banks, with a capital infusion of almost $700 million, or more than 1 percent of Hungary's GDP. This happened because, among other reasons, the regulatory and supervi-sory authorities were unable to identify the bank's problems in time. Management had engaged in serious abuses, and losses had accumu-lated over a very long period. Political corruption was also involved. Of course, similar examples could be cited in many other transition countries.

Figure 1. Pillars of an Effective Banking Sector

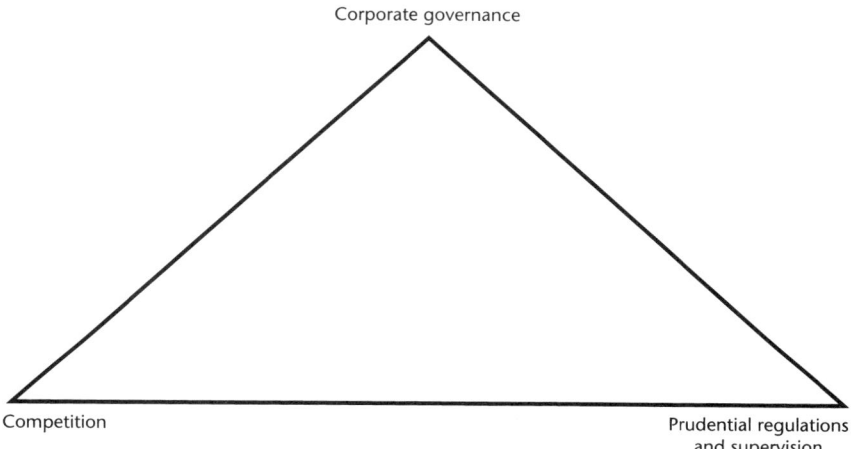

Corporate governance

Competition

Prudential regulations
and supervision

Ten Key Factors in Banking Sector Restructuring

The three pillars listed in Figure 1 can be thought of as the goals toward which countries in CEE and the former Soviet Union are striving in the reform of their banking sectors. Table 1 lists 10 factors that will determine the pace and degree of success in moving toward these goals. It is important to analyze each of these factors because a wide variety of development patterns can be seen across the region. Indeed, it is difficult to pinpoint any generalized pattern that all countries have followed. It is also hard to say unequivocally which countries' banking sectors are more developed than the others, precisely because progress depends on so many factors and dimensions. All banking sectors in the region have structural and institutional weaknesses, as evidenced by the continued recurrence of situations in which the viability of the banking sector is questioned. Therefore we have to be very careful, for even in the region's most advanced countries the banking sector requires careful attention all the time. The problem is not something that one can fix once and for all and then sit back and relax. Rather, the dynamics of financial sector development are so unpredictable and so fast-paced in most of these countries that the authorities are always at least two steps behind.

Initial Conditions

The first factor to be taken into account is the initial condition of the two-tier banking sector, which was tailored differently in different countries. In this regard we can speak of two alternative models: the

Table 1. Ten Key Factors in Banking Sector Restructuring

1. Initial conditions: the two-tier system
   The competitive model
   The segmented model
      Sectoral segmentation
      Regional segmentation

2. Liberalization
   Entry and exit
   Regulation of banking activities
      Interest rate regulation
      Regulation of the client base
      Regulation of products and services offered

3. Development of new, private commercial banks

4. Rehabilitation of existing banks

5. Privatization
   To foreign strategic investors
   To domestic investors

6. Corporate governance

7. Regulation and supervision

8. International liberalization

9. The enabling environment

10. Linkages between bank and nonbank financial institutions

competitive model and the *segmented* model. By a competitive model, I mean one in which there were no restrictions of entry into any kind of financial services and products, and therefore no administrative limitation on banks seeking to enter each other's business. This allowed a competitive environment to be created from within.

In countries adopting the segmented model, this was not the case, because the two-tier system was tailored in such a way that either sectoral or regional monopolies were carved out of the one-tier banking system at that time; this was later, of course, relaxed. But even today, in some countries, some banks find themselves in difficulty because they have been obligated to focus their lending in certain sectors, leaving them unable to spread their risk across a wide swath of the economy.

There are also examples of regional segmentation, especially in the case of the former Yugoslav republics, where a two-tier banking system did exist, at least formally, well before the political transformation. In terms of competitiveness and efficiency, this system was no better than any of the monolithic, formally one-tier banking sectors in place elsewhere. And even today, these systems have some drawbacks that put them at a relative disadvantage.

Liberalization

The second important factor is the ongoing liberalization of the banking sector, and in this regard, the importance of entry and exit regulations cannot be overemphasized. What we are seeing in terms of financial sector development—and precisely the same thing is happening in the real sector as well—is not the privatization of the existing banks. Rather the appearance of new players in the market is driving the sector's development and creating the bulk of new, more efficient products and services. Therefore, not only the regulation of entry—but also the regulation of exit—is proving to be a critical ingredient in putting together a more or less efficient and competitive banking sector.

In some countries, regulation of banking activities at first included limits on the interest rates that at least some banks could charge. Banks were also restricted in the client base they could serve, reflecting the sectoral segmentation already noted, and in the range of products and services they could offer. All this was later eliminated in most countries, but the legacy of these restrictions remains important today.

Development of New, Private Commercial Banks

The third factor that is shaping the future of the banking sector has been the development of new, private commercial banks. Here one needs to distinguish between domestic and foreign banking, because serious restrictions on foreign entry apply even today. In some countries, the newly established domestic commercial banks have taken over the role of the former state-owned banks and developed in a very energetic way. In other countries, however, their role has been and remains marginal.

It is difficult to say which of these paths was the right one to follow, because in most countries in the region the development of small domestic commercial banks has a very bad track record. Regulation of entry was very liberal, and this proved to be a double-edged sword. Some private entrepreneurs who were allowed to establish banks used them to finance nothing else but their own connected businesses, and in so doing they grossly abused their public responsibility. And in many countries, at the end of the day this was a recipe for disaster.

Rehabilitation of Existing Banks

Having compiled this more or less dismal record, governments in all countries—at least once, if not repeatedly—have decided to rehabilitate some of the banks. Of course, bank rehabilitation and recapitalization have proved to be a time-consuming, painful, politically controversial, and costly exercise. Unfortunately, these government-orchestrated rehabilitations turned out not to be a very efficient vehicle for recreating efficient, sound, and competitive banking, even in the countries considered the strongest performers. Many governments have spent a fortune on rehabilitating banks yet have little to show for their efforts.

Hungary, for example, has spent the equivalent of roughly 10 percent of its GDP over the course of at least three attempts at rehabilitation, restructuring, and consolidation. Nevertheless, this rehabilitation was not itself the key to success in the end; rather it was the subsequent, rather quick privatization of those banks that had been rehabilitated.

Privatization

Indeed, the important lesson from our experience with bank restructuring is that *privatization* is the crucial issue. This may seem paradoxical: if these countries have a dubious track record at developing new, private commercial banks that are safe and sound, how can privatization be the ultimate solution? Does that not once again put shaky owners in the driver's seat, where they can run their banks into the ground just as they did before?

Therefore privatization must be accompanied with some strong qualifications. Many different approaches to privatization have been tried, and not all have proved successful. And radical as it may sound, the important common factor in the bulk of the banking privatizations—the successful ones, at least—has been the involvement of foreign strategic investors. This is what has contributed the most to the development of safe and sound, competitive, and prudent banking in the region.

But here another qualification is in order: not all foreign banks are safe and sound, either. One has to be very careful in privatizing banks even when foreign participation is allowed. At issue here is the cultural dimension of banking: prudent banking is something that was not part of the culture of the CEE countries or of the former Soviet Union. What privatization needs to achieve, therefore, is not only the recapitalization of banks, and not only their greater operational efficiency. One must also make sure that prudent behavior will be the norm and will be the most important factor considered when assessing bank management.

Corporate Governance

That, in turn, depends on the quality of corporate governance. In any privatization, the important question is whether the transaction will contribute to an improvement of corporate governance or not. If it does, then privatization is a blessing. If instead it contributes to a deterioration of corporate governance, privatization should be avoided, or at least postponed until it can be done right.

John Nellis's paper (in this volume) rehearses the agonizing discussions about real sector privatization in the transition. Nellis concludes that, for the real sector, the "how" of privatization matters as much as, if not more than, the fact of privatization itself. But this is even more important in banking, because in running a bank, bank managers are not just playing with the bank owners' money, they are playing with other people's money—with depositors' money—as well. Therefore, the principal issue in corporate governance and privatization is how to protect the interests of the depositors.

Russia today presents the best available example of the potential for conflict between the interests of the depositors and the interests of shareholders. Almost all of the big Russian banks and most of the smaller ones have lost sums exceeding several times their capital. They have huge holes in their balance sheets. Yet many of the shareholders seem unconcerned about this insolvency because they can easily walk away, set up a new bank, and leave all the losses to the depositors and to other stakeholders.

In short, when trying to understand the real level of security and soundness achieved in the banking system, as well as the challenges of cyclical vulnerability, it is crucial to highlight the interlinkages among government-orchestrated rehabilitation, the method of privatization, and the resulting improvement or lack thereof in corporate governance.

Regulation and Supervision

Bank regulation and supervision are not a straightforward matter; no transition country in Europe or Central Asia has yet achieved anything close to perfect regulation and supervision thus far. We have learned the lessons of the first decade of transition the hard way, and there is a lesson here for both the International Monetary Fund and the World Bank. We have to spend much more time improving the legal and institutional structures of regulation and supervision as part of the enabling environment. In all of these countries there is a systemic risk of still more banking crises, and indeed in some of these countries the next crisis is already in the making. Therefore, we have to devote much more time and effort toward helping those countries that have a genuine desire to strengthen their banking structures.

International Liberalization

International liberalization of the financial sector is an important issue as well. The opening of the sector to foreign entry has contributed to the varied development of the financial sector in most of the transition countries. There is no uniform pattern that all countries have followed in the last decade, but a few lessons have been learned. To the extent one wants to strengthen competition, one has to liberalize almost immediately the establishment of subsidiaries and joint ventures of foreign banks. But at the same time one has to be very careful, because if financial liberalization goes ahead without a proper restructuring of the whole macro- and microeconomy, it can contribute to vulnerability and exacerbate the difficulties. The history of many countries shows how difficult it is to calibrate the proper level of international liberalization at any single point of time without putting the whole economy into a dangerous position.

In this respect again, sequencing is very important, and a gradual approach is probably better. One can start by liberalizing foreign direct investment and from there move almost immediately to liberalize portfolio equity investment. If instead liberalization begins by allowing short-term institutional money to flow into speculative areas, problems will arise. Unfortunately, the Russian government securities market was nothing but a short-term speculative arena, which ultimately came to a bad end. Financial liberalization was used simply as a means of postponing real reform because it created the illusion that everything was already in place and that the government could go ahead without undertaking any serious public finance reforms.

The Enabling Environment

Another important factor is the enabling environment. It is possible for the financial sector to be too much in the limelight. As a consequence of the crises in East Asia, Russia, and Brazil, we tend to look almost exclusively at macrofinancial parameters and banking sector issues. Yet this may lead us to disregard the interlinkages between real sector development and financial sector development.

The quite uneven development of the financial sector in many transition countries is to a large extent explained by the fact that the development of the real sector is very uneven as well. To put it bluntly, in some countries banks can find virtually no good clients. Even the best banks, under the best circumstances and with the best corporate governance structures, cannot find enough profitable business out there. Therefore, it is only natural for them to go after short-term speculative instruments and try to generate a relatively high level of profit in foreign exchange dealings, in trading government securities, and even in investment banking. Yet all this is just another way of deteriorating their risk profile. In many transition countries supply-side adjustment has not reached the stage where sustainable growth can be achieved in the long run, and thus the problems of the financial sector, including banking, are nothing more than a mirror image of the way the real sector is developing.

In this respect, two issues may prove to be more important in most transition countries than privatization. The first is the organic, de novo development of small- and medium-size businesses, and the second is the role of foreign direct and portfolio investment. In some countries, privatization was successful only because it was well coordinated with these two lines of development.

Needless to say, in many countries the fact that banking is very much in the limelight has led to important political impediments. Banking is a very easily abused sector. The interlinkages between influential political groups—the oligarchs and politicians on the one hand and the banking sector on the other—is so intimate, again even in the most developed environments, that one has to be careful when looking at the real dynamics.

Linkages Between Banks and Nonbank Financial Institutions

Last, but not least, it is important to highlight the interlinkages between bank and nonbank institutions in the financial sector. Insurance, contractual savings institutions, stock exchanges, and all kinds of investment vehicles are becoming increasingly widespread. But banking remains the core of the financial sector in all transition countries, with all the blessings and shortcomings that stem from that fact.

It remains to be seen how this situation will change in the second phase of transition. Here, again, a certain kind of sequencing is called for. There is no way to have a healthy financial sector without a healthy banking sector. In this respect, it is also true that banking is the core of financial sector development.

Conclusion

The experience of banking reform in the past decade suggests three main lessons. First, all countries, no matter their level of development or their initial conditions, must aim at establishing the same three pillars of an effective banking sector: competition, good corporate governance, and solid prudential regulation. Second, banking reform is a long, incremental process that is far from complete, even in the most advanced transition economies. Third, weak banks are seldom transformed by rehabilitation, which is both costly and rarely effective. Rather, the solution to weak banks lies in privatization built on good governance and strong bank management. Just as the best inoculation against banking problems is to avoid politically motivated lending, so too the best antidote to problem banks is to avoid rescuing them artificially.

Challenges for the Next Decade of Transition 9

Nicholas Stern

The scale and speed of economic change in Central and Eastern Europe and the former Soviet Union have been remarkable: markets now operate through much of the region, and most national income is generated by the private sector. The new democratic systems have shown remarkable resilience in the face of economic and other crises. However, in much of the region the functioning of markets and the institutions necessary to support them are deeply flawed, for reasons having to do not only with the legacy of the old systems, but also with events during the transition process itself and choices made early in that process. The commitment of governments to reform is being tested by the severe social costs of adjustment as well as by the resistance of vested interests, both old and new.

Indeed, the challenges go deeper than the resolve of governments, for many of the problems facing the region and its transition lie in the functioning of the state itself. The fundamental questions are not only that special favorite of economists, what the state should do, but also, and in many ways more troubling, how the state can be changed. This chapter briefly reviews the last decade from the perspective of these basic questions and then turns to some of the specific challenges of the coming years.

The Experience of the First 10 Years

The European Bank for Reconstruction and Development (EBRD) assesses the progress of transition each year in its annual *Transition Report*. Viewed as a whole, the region has made very rapid progress, but that progress has varied strikingly across the different dimensions of transition and from country to country. Over the 1990s the majority of transition economies advanced strongly in price and trade liberaliza-

Although this paper draws on the EBRD's *1998 Transition Report* and on a recent review of the EBRD's strategic orientation by its management and board, the responsibility for the views expressed is the author's own. The author is very grateful for the help and guidance of Vanessa Glasmacher, Christian Mumssen, and Martin Raiser.

tion, as well as in small- and large-scale privatization. The private sector share of GDP exceeds 50 percent in 19 of the 26 countries in which the EBRD operates. On the other hand, progress has been much slower on the more difficult institutional reforms, such as the creation of sound financial systems and securities markets, enterprise restructuring, corporate governance, and effective and market-oriented legal systems.

Transition has also advanced much more slowly in the countries of the Commonwealth of Independent States (CIS) than in the western part of the region, although there is sharp variation both within the CIS and within Central and Eastern Europe. These differences are due in part to initial conditions—economic structures, history, geography, endowments, culture, and levels of indebtedness—which varied dramatically across countries. However, they are also due to the fact that different countries have followed different reform paths. It is therefore crucial to distinguish carefully among countries; generalizations can be misleading.

The first decade of transition has shown that economic reforms can show their returns fairly quickly. In the more advanced reformers in Central Europe and the Baltics, output growth resumed much earlier than elsewhere, and macroeconomic stability has largely been maintained in the face of recent turmoil in emerging markets generally. In these countries, deep restructuring in the enterprise sector has begun, often driven by strategic foreign investors. As competitiveness has grown, trade has been reoriented toward western markets. Reflecting these achievements, five transition countries have been invited to start accession negotiations with the European Union. Renewed commitment to reform is also beginning to bear fruit in countries such as Bulgaria, where reforms had previously been more hesitant.

The slower and less committed reforms in the CIS have been accompanied by much more volatile economic performance. For geographical reasons, but also reflecting the structural legacies of Soviet industrialization, the countries of the CIS remain more dependent on trade with each other. Several have also been disrupted by internal and external military conflict and face the task of reconstruction as well as structural adjustment. The social strains of the transition have also been much more severe in those countries that pursued reforms less aggressively. These are perhaps reflected most strikingly in age-specific mortality rates and life expectancy, which, for example, fell by six years for males in Russia in the early 1990s. It is now lower than that for males in India.

The lessons of recent years, however, go beyond the returns to strong and committed reforms. It is surely now clear, as it should have been from the outset, that the transition is a long haul, not a quick fix. Decisions made early in the process can have profound and long-lasting effects, since vested interests can be established very quickly but dislodged only with difficulty. It has also become clear that the political transition and the economic transition are intricately intertwined and that political support for reform is vital for their success.

The Russian crisis of 1998 embodies all these lessons. Before the crisis, Russia had developed into an economy of striking contrasts. Banks traded sophisticated financial derivatives but were virtually unable to attract ordinary household deposits. Trading on the stock market reached volumes of over $100 million per day, but shareholders were often unable to exercise their most basic rights. Vast financial-industrial groups were created to promote synergies between banks and large-scale enterprises, while an ever-increasing number of firms resorted to barter to stay afloat. The self-styled oligarchs in command of these groups amassed substantial fortunes, but left their workers and the state with a mushrooming backlog of wage and tax arrears. The crisis shows the dangers of early liberalization of short-term capital flows at a time when fiscal discipline is weak and the financial sector is not regulated effectively. The large inflows of foreign capital partly reflected a misjudgment by investors in search of quick profits, who did not think sufficiently carefully about the depth of the underlying structural problems. At the same time, this misjudgment softened the budget constraint of the state and weakened an already fragile resolve to face fiscal challenges and begin tackling the structural imbalances.

However, perhaps the most important lesson from the Russian crisis and the first decade of transition has been that free trade and private ownership will not by themselves bring well-functioning markets, and that market-supporting institutions are fundamental. Russia had developed markets and private ownership no less rapidly than many of the more advanced transition economies had. But the incentives for private actors were distorted through inadequate regulation, corruption, and weakness in the rule of law. Ultimately, it became more attractive to lobby the government for favors and to manipulate the system than to undertake serious restructuring. The roots of the crisis in Russia are discussed in detail in the EBRD's *1998 Transition Report*. Its lessons apply in varying degrees across all the other transition countries and may be summarized in a single sentence: Markets, if they are to function well, need a state with the strength to regulate responsibly, tax effectively, and provide its people with basic services, including the rule of law. This much should have been obvious to us all. What is much less obvious is how such a state can be constructed when the basic foundations have been corroded.

Challenges for the Next Decade

This brief review of the first decade of transition has highlighted the importance of strong, market-supporting institutions. The depth and difficulty of building the institutional basis of a market economy were perhaps misjudged by many at the outset of transition, and this led to overoptimistic assessments of the stresses that would accompany the process and of the time it would take. Although there are many possible approaches, and each country must find its own way, the broad characteristics that sound market institutions should embody are relatively uncontroversial. Again, the deeper challenge is to find ways to build them.

The task of building these institutions is of such magnitude and complexity that it will inevitably take time. Although some rules, procedures, and organizations can and should be set in place rather quickly, the capacity of institutions to build practices and shape behavior can be developed only over the long term. Moreover, institutional change in transition requires the state to change itself and to take on new roles, as a regulator, as an impartial arbiter, and sometimes as an active partner facilitating economic restructuring. A second major reason why the transition will be long and difficult is the scale of the industrial legacy—physical, organizational, environmental, and behavioral—left by the old regime. The problems of adjustment are such, and on such a scale, that they cannot be shaped only by the Darwinian forces of competition, hard budget constraints, and bankruptcy law.

Reform of the enterprise sector will be at the heart of the next phase of transition. It will involve both the entry and growth of new private firms and the restructuring of privatized and state-owned companies. Public and private institutions need significant reform to provide a sound investment climate and improved corporate governance, to facilitate investment and entry, and to establish an effective mechanism for the exit of unprofitable firms. The Russian crisis, analyzed in the EBRD's *1998 Transition Report*, tells a cautionary tale on how shortcomings in enterprise reform can result in dramatic economic instability. Russia's financial crisis was rooted in a fiscal crisis, which in turn was rooted in a structural crisis of the enterprise sector.

Evidence from across the region indicates that reform of the enterprise sector has been patchy and inconsistent. A few countries have been successful in stimulating growth of new private enterprises. In Poland, for instance, new private firms have driven most of the country's substantial economic growth over the last decade. In Hungary, the substantial inflow of foreign direct investment has contributed to a vibrant and dynamic economy that has attracted high-technology and research and development activities for both new and existing enterprises. However, most other countries have seen far less entry of new firms, and the "old" enterprise sector has often been slow to adapt to the new market realities.

The most obvious sign of the slow pace of restructuring is the persistence of unprofitable enterprises. From the Czech Republic to Russia, a significant number of firms, especially large ones, are losing money and falling in arrears to their suppliers, banks, and the tax authorities. Their survival is often sanctioned by weak payments discipline and weak creditor rights, combined with ineffective bankruptcy procedures. In Russia and other CIS countries, weak payments discipline has been reinforced by barter, IOUs, arrears, and myriad other arrangements, which reduce the transparency and credibility of enterprises. The state itself, particularly in Russia and Ukraine, has played a significant role here. Publicly owned utilities are prominent in the whole barter and arrears network, effectively undermining the tight credit policies associated with the tough monetary policies that had such an effect in bringing down inflation between 1994 and 1998. These problems have not only eroded the efficiency of the enterprise sector still further, but have also weakened the banking sector and tax collection.

It would be wrong, however, to blame the persistence of these soft budget constraints on a few poor decisions or bad legislation. The real question is why the relevant laws—often styled after Western models—are not applied effectively in practice. Weak institutional capacity of the courts, or, more broadly speaking, low credibility of public institutions, is certainly part of the story. Yet to understand the root causes behind the persistence of unprofitable firms, one needs to examine the role of the state in the transition process.

The state has often been unwilling to accept the significant employment implications associated with the exit or transformation of large firms. In Russia, in particular, the sheer scale of the necessary closure of firms, with their domination of local employment and social services (especially housing), has made the immediate imposition of hard budget constraints politically infeasible. Furthermore, vested interests and the often incestuous relationships between enterprises and the state, involving oligarchs old and new, have often inhibited taking a tough stand toward money-losing enterprises. The insider relationships and vested interests formed near the beginning of the transition are now very difficult to break up.

The economic and social dislocations associated with the sweeping economic changes of a successful transition process require both a vibrant new private sector, to reemploy displaced workers, and an effective social safety net. In the CIS, neither exists today. New economic opportunities are limited by high barriers to entry and growth, such as bureaucratic interference, corruption, and crime, or by lack of access to bank credit. Fiscal constraints and the weak institutional capacity of the state reduce the scope for managing exit through targeted subsidies or social packages.

Given these economic, political, and institutional constraints, restructuring is a formidable challenge for most transition countries. In this context, the international financial institutions (IFIs) can play an important role in fostering change. Since its establishment in 1991, the EBRD has promoted the transition through projects that are financially sound and aimed at enhancing the market orientation of companies and institutions. The EBRD's management and board have reviewed the experience of the early years of the transition and the EBRD's strategic orientation set in 1994. As a result of this exercise, the EBRD is reemphasizing its commitment to three important pillars of transition that are at the heart of the enterprise reform process. They are to promote a sound investment climate, to facilitate the growth of a vigorous small and medium-size enterprise sector, and to support the difficult process of enterprise restructuring.

These three pillars of enterprise reform require close coordination and collaboration among governments, the IFIs, foreign investors, and domestic institutions. Important as it is to accentuate the differences among countries, enterprise reform remains a key challenge in most. As already discussed, the problem is not so much agreeing on what types of institutions would be desirable, but agreeing on how these institutions can be built, given the huge obstacles. As already mentioned, it will be essential in all these areas to develop a state with the strength to regulate responsibly, tax effectively, and provide its people with basic services. In what follows, I lay out some key elements of a strategy for change that would support enterprise reform in particular and the functioning of markets and the state in general.

First, creating new opportunities for workers depends crucially on the *growth of the new private sector*. For this to happen, new entrepreneurs must be able to develop without hindrance from corruption and crime and with the support of sound bank lending practices. Although there is no simple way to eradicate corruption, the effort must be made, and it must entail a reduction of bureaucratic discretion by simplifying laws and regulations. The state thus has a fundamental role to play. The IFIs can help foster new private sector initiatives by channelling finance to enterprises either directly or through local intermediaries, and by providing technical assistance in building the institutions that can foster a more positive investment climate. Small and medium-size enterprises will be the largest source of alternative employment and will lay the foundation for the development of entrepreneurship and future growth. They also provide a sense of participation, a basis for political stability, and a commitment among the population to the market economy. Providing the proper environment and adequate finance for the growth of these enterprises must be a top priority for the next phase of transition.

Second, the downsizing and restructuring of large enterprises will generally require a *reallocation and realignment of ownership and control*. Foreign strategic investors are often ideal partners in that they both provide crucial skills and seek out profitable opportunities. Given the macroeconomic and political risks in the region, international institutions like the EBRD can play an important role in providing comfort and cofinancing to potential investors, domestic or foreign. They can at the same time provide some reassurance to governments and to companies in the region about the behavior of investors. Generating a spirit of *mutual partnership and trust* is crucial, and an IFI, if it conducts itself well and shows long-term commitment, can be a fundamental part of the process.

Third, the ability of enterprises to raise *working capital and investment finance* depends both on an *effectively regulated and supervised financial sector* and on the *business practices of enterprises* themselves. Financial sectors across the region will have to be strengthened in order to promote public confidence in financial institutions, an orientation toward the real sector, and an efficient allocation of credit. However, only firms with sound corporate governance standards can attract debt and equity finance. Those enterprises have to respect creditor and shareholder rights, pay their taxes, and adhere to high standards of transparency. IFIs must therefore work to support the development of sound business practices in the local banking sector as well as in the enterprise sector. In this, the state, markets, and IFIs can work together to promote and support the incentives and corporate governance that will encourage enterprises to make the tough decisions necessary for restructuring.

Fourth, new owners in charge of restructuring old companies or parts of such companies cannot and should not take over all *labor and social obligations*. Governments and IFIs must work together on a coherent strategy to find ways of cushioning the social impact of transition. The fiscal consequences will be challenging, but surely less costly than attempting, as at present, to avoid restructuring through countless implicit subsidies that allow nonviable enterprises to avoid radical change or exit.

Fifth, it is essential to promote a market orientation, payments discipline, and effective bankruptcy procedures. This requires a fundamental reorientation of the role of the state. The state must redefine itself as an *effective regulator and provider of market-supporting institutions*. Indeed, as I have emphasized, one of the key lessons from the whole transition process so far is that a market economy requires a sound and effective state. Of special importance in the transition economies is the phasing out of implicit support of unrestructured enterprises through tolerance of nonpayment and through barriers to entry for potential competitors. The primary responsibility for rebuilding the state and shaping the transition lies with the country itself. However, a key challenge for IFIs is to find ways to support this process more deeply and to avoid the ritual proposing of simplistic or formulaic prescriptions.

Sixth and finally, none of these initiatives can succeed without *macroeconomic stability internally and the growth of market opportunities externally*. Transition economies have been grappling with the ripple effects from crises in other emerging markets. More likely than not, contagion will continue to affect the transition economies and pose recurring threats to their hard-won gains from economic stabilization. Experience has shown that those countries that are able to make deep and lasting progress in the difficult institutional reforms outlined above have a better chance of weathering the effects of turmoil in global markets.

But it is not enough for the international community to draw attention to the benefits of reform. It must also work to provide an international environment that is stable, growing, and open. The transition economies have been encouraged to open their own markets, and many—indeed, most—have done so. It is now the responsibility of the more advanced market economies to open their markets still further and take careful account of the implications of their own economic policies for the growth and stability of the region. They also must realize that the restructuring of "old" industries in the transition economies may have implications for sensitive sectors in the European Union and other advanced market economies.

Progress in fundamental enterprise reform and restructuring will require close attention to all six of these issues. This is not to say that unless one does everything, nothing will happen. But the process will move more quickly, more effectively, and less painfully if there is movement on all fronts simultaneously. Governments in the transition countries themselves must take the lead and provide the overall framework. However, the work of the IFIs can assist them in this task. Different IFIs have comparative advantages in different areas. Cooperation among and long-term commitment from central and local governments and the different IFIs will be vital.

In conclusion, the first decade of transition has been one of both real achievement and profound strain. Political freedoms and economic choices have expanded enormously. Market economies exist, and growth has returned in much of the region. A successful transition is of fundamental importance not only to the prosperity and stability of the region itself, but also to the rest of Europe and the world. But we have all come to understand that the transition will be neither brief nor straightforward, particularly in the CIS. The international community, particularly the IFIs, must therefore show a spirit of constructive partnership and of long-term commitment in the difficult years ahead.

Institutions and the Underground Economy 10

Simon Johnson and Daniel Kaufmann

What went wrong with transition in the former Soviet Union? Instead of following more or less the Eastern European path of sustained reform, we see countries such as Russia and Ukraine failing to make progress or even falling back. In both countries, as in most other former Soviet countries, there is continued macroeconomic instability, limited restructuring of privatized firms, and slow development of new firms.

In both Russia and Ukraine a leading symptom of the problem with transition is that many firms exist largely underground, hiding their activity from the authorities. This diversion into unofficial activity undermines the tax base and makes it hard for the state to provide important public services, such as an efficient legal system. In the case of Russia and Ukraine, the large underground economy also makes it harder for the government to balance its budget.

What has driven so many firms underground? The most important problem appears to be not high marginal corporate or personal income tax rates but rather high levels of regulation, bureaucratic discretion, and corruption. There is also evidence that these countries have experienced a downward spiral, in which firms leaving the official sector have reduced state revenue, forcing a reduction in publicly provided services, which in turn has further reduced the incentive to register in the official sector.[1] Most of the former Soviet Union countries have thus ended up in a "bad" equilibrium, with low tax revenue, a large unofficial economy, and low quality of publicly provided services.[2]

The authors thank Eric Friedman, John McMillan, Andrei Shleifer, Christopher Woodruff, and Pablo Zoido-Lobaton for letting them draw on their joint work. Parts of this research have been supported by the World Bank, the European Bank for Reconstruction and Development, and the National Council for Soviet and East European Research. Simon Johnson also gratefully acknowledges support from the MIT Entrepreneurship Center. The views expressed here are those of the authors only.

[1]Loayza (1996) reports similar findings for Latin America. In his model unregistered firms use but do not pay for public services, thus leading to congestion costs for public goods such as roads, and slower growth.

[2]A Western manager, who decided against locating a plant in Russia, illustrates the logic behind the decision to go underground. Recounting the pressures he would have faced in Russia, he explained: "It doesn't matter who it is: fire inspector, zoning committee member, mayor

This situation stands in striking contrast with that in Central and Eastern Europe (CEE), especially Poland. Poland is not perfect by any means, but its unofficial economy remains small and may actually have fallen relative to GDP during the reform period. Before 1989 Poland had earned a reputation for being extremely corrupt (Clark and Wildavsky, 1990). Yet to a remarkable degree, Poland has managed to reduce corruption through three measures. First, elections have installed new political leaders at both the national and the local level. Almost everyone who runs a significant level of government in Poland was not in power under communism. Second, the Mazowiecki government moved quickly, in 1989–90, to eliminate important lobbying organizations that existed under communism. Third, workers' councils fired the managers of large state enterprises at the very beginning of transition. Particularly when seen in comparison with other transition economies such as Russia and Ukraine, Poland's experience shows that the principal need is to reduce the scope for capricious action by government officials, including by changing those officials.[3]

This chapter summarizes our main findings from three strands of research on the unofficial economy that have tested this idea and explored its implications. First, we report aggregate evidence on the size of the underground economy in CEE and the countries of the former Soviet Union since 1989. The underground economy has shrunk or remained about the same size in CEE during the transition, at the same time that it has grown dramatically in many of the countries of the former Soviet Union. Most of the divergence in the size of the unofficial economy can be attributed to greater levels of corruption in the latter set of countries. Tax rates are either quite similar across these countries or, in some cases, actually lower in the countries of the former Soviet Union than in CEE.

Second, we report estimates of the size of the underground economy based on firm-level surveys in five countries: Poland, Romania, Russia, the Slovak Republic, and Ukraine. This work confirms that there is a large difference in the size of the unofficial economy between CEE

---

for that region, anybody can come and shut you down in five minutes. The fire guy could come, find fire hazards, and demand $50,000 into his overseas account. They know that if you shut down production for a few days, you're going to lose a lot more" (Wilson, 1996). Faced with this hostile environment, foreign firms may choose not to invest in Russia. However, for local entrepreneurs seeking to avoid the same risks, the usual course is to go underground (Kaufmann, 1997).

[3]For transition economies this idea was developed in Kaufmann (1994 and 1997), Kaufmann and Kaliberda (1996), Shleifer (1997), Frye and Shleifer (1997), Kaufmann and Siegelbaum (1997), and Johnson, Kaufmann, and Shleifer (1997). Important previous work dealing with these issues includes de Soto (1989) and Shleifer and Vishny (1993 and 1994). Most recently this view has been tested and developed further by Havrylyshyn and Wolf (this volume).

and the countries of the former Soviet Union. It also confirms that regulation and corruption, rather than official tax rates, lie behind the much larger underground economy in Russia and Ukraine. This work also provides a great deal of detail about the magnitude of bribes being paid for certain services and emphasizes the importance of payments made to tax officials and other government inspectors.

Third, we summarize evidence and analysis on regulation and the size of the unofficial economy from a comparative sample of 69 countries. Our analysis reveals no positive correlation between direct or indirect tax rates and the size of the unofficial economy. In contrast, more regulation, greater corruption, and a weaker legal environment are all associated with a larger unofficial economy, even (in most cases) when we control for income per capita. Russia and Ukraine now resemble developing countries at similar income levels. They have high levels of corruption and a large unofficial economy. In contrast, Poland and, to a lesser extent, other countries in CEE have made impressive progress in bringing economic activity back into the official sector.

Aggregate Data on the Size of the Underground Economy, Corruption, and the Legal Environment

This section, which reports our main results for both CEE and the countries of the former Soviet Union on the size of the underground economy, on the extent of corruption, and on the effectiveness of legal institutions, draws heavily on Johnson, Kaufmann, and Shleifer (1997). Data on the unofficial economy are available only through 1995.

Size of the Unofficial Economy

Table 1 shows estimates of the share of the unofficial economy in GDP using the methodology presented in Johnson, Kaufmann, and Shleifer (1997), which is based on electricity consumption. The data reveal two divergent development paths. The average (unweighted) share of the unofficial economy in the CEE countries starts at 16.6 percent of GDP in 1989, peaks at 21.3 percent in 1992, and falls to 19.0 percent by 1995. In contrast, the average share in the countries of the former Soviet Union starts at 12.0 percent and rises to 36.2 percent in 1994 before dropping to 34.4 percent in 1995. Even more striking is the contrast between Poland and Romania on the one hand, where the unofficial economy's share fell from 1989 to 1995 by about 3 percentage points of GDP, and Russia and Ukraine on the other, where the unofficial share rose 29.6 and 36.9 percentage points, respectively, over the same period.

Table 1. Share of the Unofficial Economy in CEE and the Countries of the Former Soviet Union

| Country | Share of the Unofficial Economy (in percent of GDP) | | | | | | | GDP (Index, 1989 = 100) | | | |
| | | | | | | | | 1994 | | 1995 | |
	1989	1990	1991	1992	1993	1994	1995	Official	Total	Official	Total
Eastern Europe											
Bulgaria	22.8	25.1	23.9	25.0	29.9	29.1	36.2	72.3	78.7	73.7	89.2
Czech Rep.	6.0	6.7	12.9	16.9	16.9	17.6	11.3	81.0	92.4	84.3	89.3
Hungary	27.0	28.0	32.9	30.6	28.5	27.7	29.0	83.4	84.3	84.7	87.1
Poland	15.7	19.6	23.5	19.7	18.5	15.2	12.6	92.0	91.4	98.3	94.9
Romania	22.3	13.7	15.7	18.0	16.4	17.4	19.1	72.7	68.4	77.7	74.7
Slovak Rep.	6.0	7.7	15.1	17.6	16.2	14.6	5.8	77.9	85.8	83.1	82.9
Former Soviet Union											
Azerbaijan	12.0	21.9	22.7	39.2	51.2	58.0	60.6	30.1	71.5	31.4	70.1
Belarus	12.0	15.4	16.6	13.2	11.0	18.9	19.3	62.5	67.8	56.1	61.2
Estonia	12.0	19.9	26.2	25.4	24.1	25.1	11.8	67.1	78.8	69.1	68.9
Georgia	12.0	24.9	36.0	52.3	61.0	63.5	62.6	15.6	37.6	16.0	37.6
Kazakhstan	12.0	17.0	19.7	24.9	27.2	34.1	34.3	51.0	68.2	46.5	62.3
Latvia	12.0	12.8	19.0	34.3	31.0	34.2	35.3	48.1	64.3	47.3	62.3
Lithuania	12.0	11.3	21.8	39.2	31.7	28.7	21.6	43.9	54.1	45.1	50.6
Moldova	12.0	18.1	27.1	37.3	34.0	39.7	35.7	41.7	60.9	43.0	58.8
Russia	12.0	14.7	23.5	32.8	36.7	40.3	41.6	51.3	75.5	49.1	74.0
Ukraine	12.0	16.3	25.6	33.6	38.0	45.7	48.9	44.2	71.6	39.0	67.0
Uzbekistan	12.0	11.4	7.8	11.7	10.1	9.5	6.5	85.0	82.6	84.0	79.0

Source: Johnson, Kaufmann, and Shleifer (1997).

Corruption and Legal Institutions

The rest of this section summarizes our empirical results from regressing the share of the unofficial economy in 1995 on measures of corruption and the legal environment. Our proxy for corruption is the *Wall Street Journal*'s index of "crime and corruption." A one-point improvement in this index (which ranges from 1 to 10) is associated with a fall in the share of the unofficial economy by 3.4, to 4.7 percentage points of GDP.

We use four measures of the legal environment. The first two are the result of evaluations by two different panels for the *Wall Street Journal*, the first on "legal safeguards for investment," and the second more generally on the "rule of law." The third measure, constructed by the European Bank for Reconstruction and Development (EBRD, 1995, p. 103, and 1996, p. 14) evaluates countries in terms of the de jure extensiveness of their legal systems in protecting investment. The fourth measure, also from the EBRD (1995, p. 103, and 1996, p. 14), assesses the de facto effectiveness of legal systems in protecting investment.

A negative relationship is found between the supply of law and order to the official economy and the relative size of the unofficial economy. CEE and the Baltics score significantly higher on the rule-of-law measure than do the countries of the Commonwealth of Independent States (CIS, which is the countries of the former Soviet Union minus the Baltics). In the *Wall Street Journal*'s measure of the rule of law, only one CEE country, Bulgaria, has a lower score than the CIS country with the highest score, Moldova, and the difference is very small. The lowest legal safeguards score among the non-CIS countries is that of Romania, at 5.6, and the highest in the CIS is that of Moldova, at 4.3.

Controlling for the initial share of the unofficial economy, a one-point improvement in the index of legal safeguards (which also ranges from 1 to 10) is associated with a 5.1-percentage-point fall in the share of the unofficial economy. A change in the rule-of-law index has only a slightly smaller effect. The EBRD's (1997) legal effectiveness and extensiveness indices have effects of similar magnitude, although precise comparisons are difficult because their values range only from 1 to 5. This evidence supports the theoretical prediction that the unofficial economy is larger where the official sector's public goods are poorer, and particularly where the rule of law is weaker.

To summarize, across CEE and the countries of the former Soviet Union, liberalization, privatization, fairer taxation, and fewer regulations are all associated with a smaller unofficial economy. Better provision of public goods to the official economy is associated with a relatively larger official economy. Public finance mechanisms also appear to be at work: countries with less distortionary tax and regulatory systems collect more tax revenue and provide more public goods to their official economies.[4] However, posted tax rates do not appear to be an important explanatory variable. Corporate tax rates are actually lower in Russia and Ukraine than in much of CEE. The problem appears to lie with the more general burden imposed by government officials.

Detailed Evidence from Five Countries

To understand this issue in more detail, we turn to our firm-level data in Poland, Romania, Russia, the Slovak Republic, and Ukraine. This section draws heavily on Johnson, McMillan, and Woodruff (1998, 1999a, and 1999b).

The Extent of Reform

Three independent sources measure the extent of reform: the EBRD, the *Wall Street Journal*, and the Heritage Foundation.[5] Reform is usually considered to have three dimensions: stabilization, which primarily considers the rate of inflation; liberalization, meaning the extent of restrictions on economic activity; and privatization (World Bank, 1996). However, recent analysis indicates the potential importance of the legal environment in explaining outcomes in transition economies (Johnson, Kaufmann, and Shleifer, 1997; Havrylyshyn and Wolf, this volume), so we include these measures as well. We also report the available country-level measures of reform of the banking system and securities markets.

The five countries in our sample had markedly different inflation experiences during the 1990s. Since 1990, inflation in Poland and the

---

[4]Appendix 4 in Johnson, Kaufmann, and Shleifer (1997) shows the available numbers on general government spending as a percentage of both official and total GDP. There is a marked difference between the CEE and the CIS countries. General government spending in Poland was 48.8 percent of GDP in 1989, 39.8 percent in 1990, and 47.5 percent in 1994 (EBRD, 1996, p. 201); in the Czech Republic it was 60.1 percent in 1990 and 50 percent in 1994 (EBRD, 1996, p. 191); and in Hungary it was 53.5 percent in 1990 and 56.1 percent in 1995. In contrast, Russian government spending fell from 60.5 percent of official GDP in 1992 to 31.9 percent in 1995. For the latest available year, general government spending as a share of total GDP was about 40 percent for Poland (1994) and under 20 percent for Russia (1995). A large decline in general government spending as a percentage of GDP has occurred in the CIS countries, but not in CEE or in the Baltics.

[5]The World Bank indices (World Bank, 1996) give results similar to those of the EBRD, but their content is harder to interpret, so we prefer to leave them out. See Johnson, Kaufmann, and Shleifer (1997) for a more detailed discussion of indices of reform, including those of the World Bank, the IMF, Freedom House, and Transparency International.

Slovak Republic has not exceeded 60 percent and has fallen fairly steadily. In comparison, inflation in Romania peaked at nearly 300 percent in 1993, and the government has struggled to bring it under control. Both Russia and Ukraine experienced hyperinflations, with peaks in average annual inflation of 2,500 percent in 1992 for Russia and over 10,000 percent in 1993 for Ukraine. In terms of cumulative inflation from 1990 or 1991 to 1997, the five countries therefore differ dramatically.[6] However, by 1996 inflation in all five countries was under control: at 19 percent in Poland, 57 percent in Romania, 22 percent in Russia, 5 percent in the Slovak Republic, and 40 percent in Ukraine (EBRD, 1997, p. 118). It remains essentially under control until today, although there is still strong inflationary potential in Romania, Russia, and Ukraine. On this dimension, policy and outcomes have definitely converged in the five countries.

The initial focus of economic reform in these countries was on the liberalization of prices, and the EBRD's index (EBRD, 1997, p. 14) indicates that by 1996 all five countries had the same level of price liberalization. Again, all five have converged in this dimension of reform.[7] The EBRD's index of "trade and foreign exchange system" reform, which measures the liberalization of current account transactions, shows Poland at the highest level (4+), followed closely by Romania, Russia, and the Slovak Republic (at 4), with Ukraine lagging behind (at 3; EBRD, 1997, p. 15).[8] Given that a score of 4 represents almost complete liberalization, all the countries except Ukraine can be considered to have achieved a high degree of liberalization.

The EBRD (1997, p. 14) offers two measures of privatization: "large-scale privatization," meaning large firms, usually in manufacturing, and "small-scale privatization," meaning small firms, primarily shops. On the first measure, in 1996–97 the Slovak Republic led the group with a score of 4 (primarily the result of privatization organized while still part of Czechoslovakia), while Poland and Russia scored 3+,

---

[6]Åslund, Boone, and Johnson (1996) argue that cumulative inflation is highly correlated with rent seeking. This would suggest that the extent of corruption and other forms of preying on private business should be highest in Ukraine and Russia, followed by Romania.

[7]All five countries scored 3 on this index, which denotes "substantial progress on price liberalization: state procurement at non-market prices largely phased out."

[8]A 4+ denotes "standards and performance norms of advanced industrial economies: removal of most tariff barriers; membership in WTO." A 4 denotes "removal of all quantitative and administrative import and export restrictions (apart from agriculture) and all significant export tariffs; insignificant direct involvement in exports and imports by ministries and state-owned trading companies; no major non-uniformity of customs duties for non-agricultural goods and services; full current account convertibility." A 3 denotes "removal of almost all quantitative and administrative import and export restrictions; almost full current account convertibility."

Romania was at 3–, and Ukraine was at 2+.[9] In terms of small-scale privatization, Poland and the Slovak Republic scored 4+, Russia scored 4, Ukraine scored 3+, and Romania scored 3.[10] In this case it seems that Poland, Russia, and the Slovak Republic can claim almost complete reform in terms of privatization, with Romania and Ukraine lagging only slightly behind. Again, there is not much variation between countries.

Three organizations offer measures of these countries' legal environments for business. The EBRD's (1997, p. 17) measure of the legal system's effectiveness attempts to capture how commercial laws are being enforced and administered. The data are from a survey of lawyers in the region. According to this index, there were significant differences among the countries: Poland scored 4+; Romania, Russia, and the Slovak Republic scored 3; and Ukraine scored 2.[11]

The *Wall Street Journal*'s panel of investment professionals rates the countries according to their attractiveness as a place to do business over the coming year. The ratings are on a scale of 1 to 10, with 10 being the best (*Central European Economic Review*, 1997–98).[12] At the end of 1997, their overall ratings placed Poland in the lead with 7.8, followed by Russia at 6.0, the Slovak Republic at 5.8, Romania at 5.7, and Ukraine at 3.9. Two subindices, measuring the rule of law and corruption, particularly address the legal environment. On the rule-of-law measure, Poland scored 9.0, Romania 6.4, the Slovak Republic 6.2, Russia 5.4, and Ukraine 3.9. On the corruption subindex, Poland scored 8.2, the Slovak Republic 5.7, Romania 5.4, Russia 3.7, and Ukraine 2.1.

The Heritage Foundation's Index of Economic Freedom is also the result of evaluation by outside experts (Johnson, Holmes, and Kirkpatrick, 1998). This index is a simple average of a country's scores

---

[9]A score of 4 denotes "more than 50 percent of state-owned enterprise and farm assets in private ownership and significant progress on corporate governance of these enterprises." A 3 denotes "more than 25 percent of large-scale enterprise assets in private hands or in the process of being privatized (with the process having reached a stage at which the state has effectively ceded its ownership rights), but possibly with major unresolved issues regarding corporate governance." A 2 denotes "comprehensive scheme almost ready for implementation; some sales completed."

[10]A 4+ denotes "standards and performance typical of advanced industrial economies: no state ownership of small enterprises; effective tradability of land." A 4 denotes "complete privatization of small companies with tradable ownership rights." A 3 denotes "nearly comprehensive programme implemented."

[11]The EBRD's explanations for these scores are rather long and should be consulted by the reader (EBRD, 1997, p. 19). To summarize, a score of 4+ denotes clear commercial laws that are supported by an effective court system; 3 indicates that the commercial laws are clear but not fully supported by the court system; and 2 indicates that "commercial legal rules are generally unclear and sometimes contradictory."

[12]See the discussion in Johnson, Kaufmann, and Shleifer (1997) for details of how this panel operates and its results in previous years. It appears to give consistent and reasonable results over time.

on 10 specific indexes.[13] A lower score on the overall index means the economy is "more free" or offers a more favorable environment for private business. The 1998 index basically measures the environment as it existed in 1997. In the overall index, the Slovak Republic did best, with a score of 3.05, Poland scored 3.15, Romania 3.3, Russia 3.45, and Ukraine was last again with 3.8. On the taxation index, Poland and Russia scored 3.5, the Slovak Republic 4.5, Ukraine 4, and Romania 5.[14] On the property rights index, Poland was ahead with a score of 2, the Slovak Republic and Russia each scored 3, and Romania and Ukraine scored 4.[15] Finally, on the regulation index, Poland and the Slovak Republic each scored 3, and Russia, Romania, and Ukraine all scored 4.[16]

The picture from these measures of legal and regulatory environment is therefore fairly consistent. Poland is usually the best performer, followed closely by the Slovak Republic. Ukraine consistently scores the lowest. Russia and Romania occupy intermediate positions, with Romania having a slight advantage in terms of corruption and rule of law.[17]

Finally, the EBRD offers two measures of financial system reform: "banking reform and interest rate liberalization," and "securities markets and nonbank financial institutions." On the first measure, Poland scores a 3, Romania and the Slovak Republic both score 3–, Russia scores 2+, and Ukraine scores 2.[18] On the securities markets index, Poland scores 3+, Russia scores 3, the Slovak Republic scores 2+, and Romania and Ukraine both score 2.[19]

---

[13]The specific indexes cover trade, taxation, government intervention, monetary policy, foreign investment, banking, wages and prices, property rights, regulation, and the black market. See Johnson, Holmes, and Kirkpatrick (1998, pp. 35–51) for a detailed description of each measure.

[14]The taxation index is an average of a country's score on separate income tax and corporate tax grading scales. On both scales a 3 denotes moderate taxes, a 4 high taxes, and a 5 very high taxes (Johnson, Holmes, and Kirkpatrick, 1998, pp. 40–41)

[15]This index measures the protection of private property by the government and judicial system. A 2 denotes "very high" protection, a 3 "high" protection, a 4 "low" protection, and a 5 "very low" protection (Johnson, Holmes, and Kirkpatrick, 1998, p. 47).

[16]This index measures "how easy or difficult it is to open and operate a business" (Johnson, Holmes, and Kirkpatrick 1998, p. 49). A 3 denotes a moderate level of regulation, and a 4 denotes a high level of regulation.

[17]The more detailed analysis in Johnson, Kaufmann, and Shleifer (1997) shows basically the same relative rankings across all the available measures of legal reform. The largest difference is consistently between CEE and the countries of the former Soviet Union.

[18]A 3 denotes "substantial progress in establishment of bank solvency and of a framework for prudential supervision and regulation; full interest rate liberalization with little preferential access to cheap refinancing; significant lending to private enterprises and significant presence of private banks." A 2 denotes "significant liberalization of interest rates and credit allocation; limited use of directed credit or interest rate ceilings."

[19]A 3 denotes "substantial issuance of securities by private enterprises; establishment of independent share registries, secure clearance and settlement procedures, and some protection

Size of the Unofficial Economy

In their comprehensive survey, Schneider and Enste (1998) use our estimates of the unofficial economy but express reservations about the electricity consumption methodology. However, alternative estimates by other authors seem to confirm our findings.

In 1997–98 we carried out detailed firm-level surveys to obtain independent information on the size of the unofficial sector in Poland, Romania, Russia, the Slovak Republic, and Ukraine. This evidence indicates that the size of the unofficial economy is roughly the same as estimated using the electricity consumption methodology. For Ukraine we found the same result from microsurvey work in the mid-1990s and from the electricity consumption method (Kaufmann and Kaliberda, 1996; Kaufmann, 1997). We also find that interactions with the government are much more costly in the countries of the former Soviet Union, primarily because of the need to pay bribes.[20]

Taxation and Corruption

Firms are understandably reluctant to reveal the level of their payments to the government, even when the payments are official. We therefore phrased questions about these payments in terms of payments made by "firms in your industry."

Tax rates are high in all five countries, but the taxes supposed to be paid by firms (corporate and social security tax rates) in Russia and Ukraine are generally not higher, and in some instances may be lower, than in Poland, Romania, and the Slovak Republic. The picture for personal tax rates is mixed, with Ukraine and Romania having the highest tax rates, followed by the Slovak Republic and Russia, and then Poland. Overall, however, we can conclude that the posted tax rates that firms are supposed to pay are, if anything, higher in the CEE countries of our sample than in Russia and Ukraine.

However, our survey indicates that the effective or perceived tax rates are almost twice as high in Russia and Ukraine as in the other three countries. Managers of start-ups report higher tax rates than do managers of privatized firms in all the countries.[21] Other payments to

---

of minority shareholders; emergence of non-bank financial institutions (e.g., investment funds, private insurance and pension funds, leasing companies) and associated regulatory framework." A 2 denotes "formation of securities exchanges, market-makers and brokers; some trading in government paper and/or securities; rudimentary legal and regulatory framework for the issuance and trading of securities."

[20]See Frye and Shleifer (1997) for further evidence that Poland's regulatory environment is more supportive of business activity than Russia's.

[21]Given that taxes are levied on corporate income, this result is consistent with the fact that start-ups are more profitable.

the government are also higher in Russia and Ukraine than in other countries. Lower response rates in Russia and Ukraine probably indicate that some firms who pay bribes preferred not to say anything about it.

Where tax rates and bribes are high, one might expect firms to underreport sales, wages, and other data. Our respondents were asked, "It is thought that many firms in your industry, in order to survive and grow, may need to misreport their operational and financial results. Please estimate the degree of underreporting by firms in your area of activity." The estimated underreporting of sales is highest in Ukraine (41.2 percent), followed by Russia (28.9 percent), the Slovak Republic (7.4 percent), Romania (5.7 percent), and Poland (5.4 percent). In Russia and Ukraine, managers of privatized firms said that such firms underreport sales to a greater extent than managers of start-ups do, whereas the opposite was true in the other three countries. The results for underreporting of salaries are quite similar.

We asked the top manager in each firm to estimate the fraction of his or her time devoted to various activities. Managers in Russia and Ukraine say they spend, respectively, a fifth and a quarter of their time dealing with the government, much more than their counterparts in the other three countries. Managers of start-ups spend more time dealing with the government than do managers of privatized firms in Russia, the Slovak Republic, and Ukraine.

There are other significant costs of doing business. Our respondents were asked the total cost, official plus unofficial charges in dollars, of various services.[22] Unofficial payments are uniformly a low part of total cost in Poland, Romania, and the Slovak Republic. The highest share of unofficial payments is for initial enterprise registration in Romania, where it stands at just over 25 percent. There is also a significant share of unofficial payment in the cost of a fire or sanitary inspector's visit in Romania and the Slovak Republic (about 25 percent of the total), but the total cost is still low.

In contrast, in Russia and Ukraine the unofficial payment ranges from 64 percent (for a telephone line in Russia) to 100 percent (for a tax inspector's visit in Russia). These unofficial payments are also large in absolute terms. For example, in Ukraine the average official payment is $464 for a telephone, $526 for initial enterprise registration, and $236 for a visit from the tax inspector. The absolute level of payments in Russia is slightly lower than in Ukraine, but still far above the level of CEE.

---

[22]Again, in an attempt to elicit honest answers, they were asked not what they themselves pay but what they believe typical charges are for firms in their industry.

It appears that taxation and the time cost of dealing with the government are significant burdens on private firms, and particularly on start-ups in Russia and Ukraine. The problem lies not with high posted tax rates, but rather with the way in which the tax system is administered: large bribes to tax inspectors in Russia and Ukraine are typical. However, our surveys also show very high unofficial payments for all kinds of government-related services in Russia and Ukraine. We also find evidence that firms in the countries of the former Soviet Union hide a significant proportion of their activities.

Worldwide Evidence

This section, which examines the extent to which our hypotheses hold in a wider sample of countries, is based on Johnson, Kaufmann, and Zoido-Lobaton (1998) and Friedman and others (2000).

Size of the Unofficial Economy

Comparable data on the unofficial economy are available for 69 countries: 8 in Asia, 4 in Africa, 4 in the Middle East, 15 in Latin America, 20 in industrial countries (in Europe, North America, and Australia), and 18 in CEE and the countries of the former Soviet Union (Schneider and Enste, 1998). To what extent can we explain variation in the size of the unofficial economy using the same variables as in our analysis above?

Measures of Institutions

Nine indices from six different organizations measure some aspect of corruption.[23] The relationship between the share of the unofficial economy and corruption is strong and consistent across these nine measures. All nine suggest that the unofficial economy is a larger share of the total in countries with more corruption. It would be useful to suggest that a few other rule-of-law variables, including property rights, do work out as well. In contrast, there is no significant relationship between official tax rates and the size of the unofficial economy.

Every available measure of regulation is significantly correlated with the share of the unofficial economy, and the sign of the relationship is

---

[23]Each index of corruption has its own strengths and weaknesses. Generally they are based on perceptions and subject to various errors. We therefore use the full range of indices that are available and are confident only about results that are robust across indices.

unambiguous: more regulation is correlated with a larger unofficial economy. For six out of our nine measures, the correlation is significant even once we control for income per capita (in logarithms). This is strong evidence that, across countries, more regulation is associated with more unofficial activity.

A weaker legal environment is strongly correlated with a larger share of the unofficial economy in GDP. All five of our legal environment measures are significant in the basic regressions using the ordinary least-squares method, and three of these remain significant when we control for the logarithm of GDP per capita. The results for shareholder rights are much weaker: two out of three measures are significant, although only at the 10 percent level.

We have information on eight measures of tax rates from three independent sources. In summary, higher tax rates are generally correlated with a lower share of the unofficial economy. This is true whether we use tax rates directly or use an index representing the effective tax burden. However, in almost all cases this relationship ceases to be significant when we control for income per capita.

The interpretation is that richer countries have both higher tax rates and a smaller unofficial economy. Across the countries in our sample, the incentive to go underground to dodge higher tax rates is outweighed by the benefits of remaining in the official economy when tax rates are higher. This is probably because, at least for this set of countries, higher tax rates generate revenue that provides productivity-enhancing public goods and a strong legal environment.

Reassessing Reform in Poland

Our cross-country results show that less corrupt countries have a smaller unofficial economy, and their governments have an easier time obtaining revenue and providing the public services that encourage firms to stay in the official sector. One reaction to this finding may be to argue that countries' legal environments are determined by their history and are not easily amenable to change. We find this argument unconvincing, and we address it here by asking, Was it inevitable that Poland would become relatively uncorrupt in the 1990s?

By all accounts, Poland was very corrupt before 1989. Bribery was rampant throughout society. Payments to various government officials were needed to obtain access to basic necessities, to import goods, and to obtain housing. Corruption appears to have worsened during the 1980s (Clark and Wildavsky, 1990). In particular, spontaneous privatization, in which the *nomenklatura* (the communist elite) obtained property rights, began in 1988 and reached a peak in 1989. This process was very similar to what was seen in the Soviet Union in 1989–92 (Johnson and Kroll, 1991).

A very important part of Poland's political changes, beginning with the roundtable discussion in the spring of 1989, was the opening up of government to new people. Beginning with Solidarity's electoral success in June 1989, and continuing through the formation of the Mazowiecki government in September and into the new local elections in May 1990, great emphasis was placed on improving transparency and replacing the existing political leaders. Important lobby groups, like the coal industry association, were effectively dismantled (Johnson and Kowalska, 1994). In addition, workers' councils forced existing management out of many large state enterprises. This did not usually lead to impressive restructuring, but it did prevent these managers from obtaining property rights in the enterprises (Johnson and Loveman, 1995).

This is not to argue that macroeconomic stabilization and balancing the budget were not important. In fact, there is strong evidence for the countries of the former Soviet Union that the printing of money transferred vast resources into the hands of the old elite and worsened corruption (Åslund, Boone, and Johnson, 1996). More generally, however, Poland not only created conditions for private sector growth, but also created the incentive for private business to remain in the official economy and to pay taxes. Polish tax rates have not been low, but the tax system has been administered in a reasonable and relatively fair way. Poland has succeeded because corruption has been controlled through institutional reform.

Conclusion

What drives entrepreneurs and large businesses underground? One school of thought identifies high statutory tax rates as the main culprit. Our findings, on the other hand, suggest that the institutions that govern the economy are to blame. Overregulation, corruption, and a weak legal system bear primary responsibility for driving businesses underground. Enterprise managers may be willing to be taxed fairly, but they are unwilling to put up with the constant threat of arbitrary, extortionate demands.

We find that, when faced with onerous regulations, high levels of corruption, and a weak legal system, businesses tend to hide their activities underground. Consequently, tax revenues fall, and the quality of public administration declines accordingly, further reducing the firm's incentives to remain in the official economy. Poor institutions are also associated with a smaller share of tax revenue in GDP. Compared with other countries, Poland's success in bringing firms into the official sector is unusual; the growing unofficial sectors in Russia and Ukraine represent a common malaise.

The problem in Russia and Ukraine, as in many of the most troubled countries of the world, is not that official tax rates are too high, but rather that an ineffective and corrupt government administration drives firms underground. Eliminating corruption requires administrative reform, greater transparency, changes in institutional incentives, and, above all, the political will to remove corrupt officials.

We would emphasize the need for three specific forms of institutional reform in the former Soviet Union. First, there needs to be tax reform, including a great deal of tax simplification. An improvement in the transparency of tax administration is also a priority. Second, fundamental change is needed in the way the civil service is run, again with an increase in transparency. Third, the judiciary needs to become more independent. Alternative dispute resolution mechanisms should also be promoted.[24]

Bibliography

Åslund, Anders, Peter Boone, and Simon Johnson, 1996, "How to Stabilize: Lessons from Post-Communist Countries," *Brookings Papers on Economic Activity*, 2, pp. 217–313, Brookings Institution.

Central European Economic Review, 1997–98, "Welcome to the World," Vol. 6 (December–January), pp. 15–21.

Clark, John, and Aaron Wildavsky, 1990, *The Moral Collapse of Communism* (San Francisco: Institute for Contemporary Studies).

de Soto, Hernando, 1989, *The Other Path: The Invisible Revolution in the Third World*, translated by June Abbott (New York: Harper and Row).

European Bank for Reconstruction and Development (EBRD), 1995, *Transition Report 1995* (London).

———, 1996, *Transition Report 1996* (London).

———, 1997, *Transition Report 1997* (London).

Friedman, Eric, Simon Johnson, Daniel Kaufmann, and Pablo Zoido-Lobaton, 2000, "Dodging the Grabbing Hand," *Journal of Public Economics*, Vol. 76 (June), pp. 459–93.

---

[24]See Johnson, McMillan, and Woodruff (1999a) for evidence that such mechanisms are already functioning even in the countries of the former Soviet Union.

Frye, Timothy, and Andrei Shleifer, 1997, "The Invisible Hand and the Grabbing Hand," *American Economic Review, Papers and Proceedings,* Vol. 87, No. 2, pp. 354–58.

Johnson, Bryan T., Kim R. Holmes, and Melanie Kirkpatrick, 1997, *1997 Index of Economic Freedom* (Washington and New York: Heritage Foundation and Wall Street Journal).

———, 1998, *1998 Index of Economic Freedom* (Washington and New York: Heritage Foundation and Wall Street Journal).

———, 1999, *1999 Index of Economic Freedom* (Washington and New York: Heritage Foundation and Wall Street Journal).

Johnson, Simon, and Marzena Kowalska, 1994, "Poland: The Political Economy of Shock Therapy," in *Voting for Reform,* ed. by Stephan Haggard and Steven B. Webb (New York: Oxford University Press).

Johnson, Simon, and Heidi Kroll, 1991, "Managerial Strategies for Spontaneous Privatization," *Soviet Economy,* Vol. 7, No. 4, pp. 281–316.

Johnson, Simon, and Gary Loveman, 1995, *Starting Over in Eastern Europe: Entrepreneurship and Economic Renewal* (Cambridge, Massachusetts: Harvard Business School Press).

Johnson, Simon, Daniel Kaufmann, and Andrei Shleifer, 1997, "The Unofficial Economy in Transition," *Brookings Papers on Economic Activity, 2,* pp. 159–239, Brookings Institution.

Johnson, Simon, Daniel Kaufmann, and Pablo Zoido-Lobaton, 1998, "Regulatory Discretion and the Unofficial Economy," *American Economic Review,* Vol. 88, No. 2, pp. 387–92.

Johnson, Simon, John McMillan, and Christopher Woodruff, 1998, "Job Creation in the Private Sector: Poland, Romania, Slovakia, and Ukraine Compared" (unpublished; Cambridge, Massachusetts: MIT Press).

———, 1999a, "Contract Enforcement in Transition," Centre for Economic Policy Research Discussion Paper Series No. 2081 (London: CEPR).

———, 1999b, "Why Do Firms Hide? Bribes and Unofficial Activity After Communism," Centre for Economic Policy Research Discussion Paper Series No. 2105 (London: CEPR).

Kaufmann, Daniel, 1994, "Market Liberalization by Stealth—Curse or Blessing in Disguise?" in *Trade in the New Independent States,* ed. by Constantine Michalopoulis and David G. Tarr (Washington: World Bank).

———, 1997, "The Missing Pillar of a Growth Strategy for Ukraine: Reforms for Private Sector Development," in *Ukraine: Accelerating the Transition to Market,* ed. by Peter K. Cornelius and Patrick Lenain (Washington: International Monetary Fund).

————, and Aleksander Kaliberda, 1996, "Integrating the Unofficial Economy into the Dynamics of Post-Socialist Economies: A Framework for Analysis and Evidence," in *Economic Transition in Russia and the New States of Eurasia*, ed. by Bartlomiej Kaminski (Armonk, New York: M.E. Sharpe).

Kaufmann, Daniel, and Paul Siegelbaum, 1997, "Privatization and Corruption in Transition Economies," *Journal of International Affairs*, Vol. 50, No. 2, pp. 419–58.

Loayza, Norman V., 1996, "The Economics of the Informal Sector: A Simple Model and Some Empirical Evidence from Latin America," *Carnegie-Rochester Conference Series on Public Policy*, Vol. 45, pp. 129–62.

Schneider, Friedrich, and Dominik Enste, 1998, "Increasing Shadow Economies All Over the World: Fiction or Reality?" (unpublished; University of Linz, Austria).

Shleifer, Andrei, 1997, "Joseph Schumpeter Lecture: Government in Transition," *European Economic Review*, Vol. 41, No. 3–5, pp. 385–410.

————, and Robert Vishny, 1993, "Corruption," *Quarterly Journal of Economics*, Vol. 108, No., 3, pp. 599–617.

————, "Politicians and Firms," 1994, *Quarterly Journal of Economics*, Vol. 109, No. 4, pp. 995–1025.

Wilson, Drew, 1996, "Acer Computer in Russia" (unpublished case study; Durham, North Carolina: Fuqua School of Business, Duke University).

World Bank, 1996, *World Development Report 1996: From Plan to Market* (New York: Oxford University Press).

Transition and the Changing Role of Government 11

Vito Tanzi and George Tsibouris

Over the past decade, many socialist countries with centrally planned economies have embarked on a process of change aimed at transforming them into market economies. If this process proves successful, it will in time provide these countries with the institutions necessary for private markets to operate successfully and with a government whose role is complementary rather than hostile to a market economy.

Although much has been written about the economic changes that must take place for these countries to become market economies, much less has been written about the changes that will occur in the role and function of the state in the economy. In the "shock therapy" approach to transition advocated by various economists, including Jeffrey Sachs, the main elements of the transition during the early phase are assumed to be price liberalization, macroeconomic stabilization, and privatization. Although the advocates of shock therapy were not explicit about it, they conveyed the impression that these elements would be sufficient to take these economies from where they were to where, at the time, their policymakers indicated that they wanted to go, that is, to become market economies.

In an interesting paper, Andrei Shleifer (1996) pointed out that although price liberalization eliminates government control over prices, and stabilization imposes a harder budget constraint on the government, and privatization deprives it of direct control over firms, these changes may be sufficient to destroy a centrally planned economy but not to change it into a market economy. For that to occur, many other, deeper changes have to take place. And to be sure, the proponents of shock therapy were silent about the role that the government should play in the new economic world.[1]

To function well, market economies need governments that are efficient at establishing and enforcing essential rules of the game (say, on competition), at promoting widely shared social objectives, at raising needed revenue to finance public sector activities, at spending pro-

---

[1]The papers in Bokros and Dethier (1998) give a feel for what deep reform means.

ductively the revenue thus raised, at bringing needed corrections to and controls over the working of the private sector, at enforcing contracts and protecting property, at producing public goods, and so on. Without the constable at the street corner, the private sector game can become very rough.

To perform these tasks, governments need well-developed institutions run by competent persons who are guided by correct incentives. In other words, the objectives of those running the institutions must not diverge from the objectives of the institutions, which must in turn be consistent with the public interest. Such institutions do not arise by magic. They need to be created and, once created, continually reformed. In industrial countries the creation of these institutions took centuries, and in some cases they are still being developed and improved. In transition economies their creation has had to be compressed into a much shorter time span and pursued under much less favorable circumstances. Given that some of the skills these institutions need were not easily available domestically, errors were inevitable. To perform its useful and essential functions, the government need not be large, as measured by taxes collected and money spent, but it does need to be efficient, especially in its regulatory role. Inefficient governments often cause major problems, especially when their sphere of action is broad and their powers are extensive.

When the needed public institutions do not exist, or when the incentives facing those who run these institutions are perverse, the government can easily become an impediment to economic activity, because it ends up being controlled for private gain. That is what normally happens with corruption (Tanzi, 1998). Corruption is the effective privatization of some parts of the government apparatus for the benefit of certain special interest groups or individuals. Social objectives then become difficult to achieve, and some actions of the government acquire a predatory nature. Governments cease to be market-friendly and become instead an impediment to the proper working of the market. In this context, and as a commentary on the limitations of the shock therapy approach, it should be noted that governments have many ways, besides price controls, ownership of enterprises, and macroeconomic imbalances, of influencing economic activities.

To set the stage for the discussion that follows, we outline some of the essential characteristics of the economic environment that prevailed at the beginning of the transition. At that time, the share of GDP derived from private sector activities was very small in all of the transition countries. It was less than 1 percent in such countries as Czechoslovakia and Russia and reached a high of almost 20 percent in Poland. By contrast, it was about 80 percent in the United States (see Saving,

1998). Economic production in the transition economies was over-whelmingly in the public sector, because few productive assets could be privately owned and few private activities were allowed—the government was everywhere.

Prices and genuine economic profits played a small role in the allocation of resources, which was determined by political decisions made within the planning office. In market economies political decisions have a major influence on the use of public resources but much less in the economy at large. In the environment that prevailed under central planning, it made little sense to speak of "public finance," because the existence of public finance presupposes that of private finance.

These countries, moreover, did not need market-type tax systems to raise public revenue, because the government could simply appropriate any share of total, and mostly public, production for its own needs. As the owner of almost everything, the government would decide how it wanted to divide and use total output. Taxes were, in effect, mostly transfers from some activities to others. Thus there was little need for the tax administrations found in market economies. The function of these administrators was mostly to ensure that funds were transferred to the government account and that they were accounted for. More surprising is the fact that there was no budget office or budget law and no treasury.[2] In this environment there could be no well-defined or fixed rules of law to which individuals or enterprises could appeal if they disagreed with the actions of the government.

Transition cannot be assumed to be complete at the point when prices have been liberalized, state enterprises have been privatized, and the macroeconomy has been broadly stabilized. It requires a far deeper transformation of the economy, institutions, and processes. Shock therapy deals with the easy or superficial part of the transition. A mature transition requires that most prices be liberalized and that many public enterprises be not only privatized, but privatized in a process that is seen as transparent and as fair as possible. Furthermore, not only the ownership of enterprises but especially their management must be freed from political interference. In this environment profitability becomes the guiding criterion for most investment decisions. Those activities deemed socially desirable are financed by the government and not by enterprises, public or private. The government needs to perform well its basic or core functions in the economy, and it should withdraw from, or drastically reduce its role in, many

---

[2]Budgetary allocations to various functions and programs were made through the central plan, and the treasury function, especially in its cash allocation role, was performed by a department of the single state bank, called the monobank.

secondary or less basic activities. This is especially important with respect to its regulatory function.

Economies, like traffic, need some regulations. Like those that regulate traffic, the rules that regulate the economy must be few, must be clear, and must leave little scope to interpretation or discretion by either the citizens or the bureaucrats who enforce the rules. Whereas the guiding principle under central planning was that nothing was permitted unless explicitly authorized, the guiding principle in a market economy should be that everything is permitted unless expressly forbidden. Adherence to this principle would eliminate a substantial portion of unnecessary governmental interference in the economy and would reduce corruption.

In the fiscal domain, which includes public revenue collection and public spending, a successful process of transition requires the creation of necessary and well-functioning fiscal institutions and of reasonable and affordable expenditure programs. Spending programs should include the provision of basic safety nets against fundamental risks such as becoming unemployed or old or ill. These safety nets and expenditure programs must be similar to some of those common in market economies rather than those inherited from the past. The yoke of past commitments must be minimized. This is particularly important in the area of pensions and employment. A market economy cannot guarantee a job for everyone; therefore, social provisions for unemployment are necessary. The pension commitments made by the government must be consistent with the new fiscal reality. Also, in an environment where real GDP is shrinking, as it has in many of these countries, budgeting becomes extremely difficult. It is especially in this environment that the government must focus on essential social needs and reduce its commitments to realistic levels. This requires major reforms.

When the transition economies reach their final destination, their governments will have spending programs that can be financed from public revenue, generated without creating an excessive burden on the private sector.[3] Because public expenditures are financed primarily by tax revenue, and a country's level of taxation, other things being equal, depends on its economic development and on the sophistication of its tax systems and tax administrations, this revenue constraint must be kept in mind when determining the programmed level of public spending. Once spending plans are made, they may be difficult to

---

[3]For example, some economists have argued that, in countries with defined benefit pension systems, high pension commitments required high payroll taxes, and high payroll taxes discouraged employment or forced enterprises to go underground to evade taxes, thus reducing public revenue. The empirical relevance of this observation is not clear.

change, especially in a downward direction. This is especially relevant for expenditures, such as pensions, health benefits, and public employment, that involve long-term commitments.

Tax revenues in developing countries are generally about half as large as a percentage of GDP as those of industrial countries. In terms of income per capita and economic structure, most of the economies in transition are, by and large, much closer to developing countries than to the industrial countries. Thus one would expect to see, over time, a tendency for the share of taxes in GDP to fall toward the 15 to 25 percent range prevailing in the richer developing countries, even though in some transition economies the ratio of taxes to GDP might still be much higher today. This points to the need for countries to be realistic in the expenditure programs to which their governments commit themselves.[4]

Finally, because the desirable role of the government emerges not just from economic considerations but also from the interplay of political and economic forces, the views of the executive branch of government must broadly match those of the legislative branch if a coherent definition of that role is to result. This outcome, of course, is influenced by the political process by which legislators are chosen and the executive branch of government is created. If the executive and legislative branches are miles apart in their views of what the government should do, as has been the case in Russia and in some other countries, it is unlikely that an optimal government role or rational policies can emerge.

In a similar vein, clear rules must establish the fiscal responsibilities of the subnational and the national governments, because the role of government cannot be defined only in terms of the national government.[5] These rules cannot be allowed to become too flexible, and they must be precise enough to indicate when one level of government is overstepping its limits. In several transition countries the fiscal arrangements between national and subnational governments are vague, and the activities of local governments have been largely uncontrolled. In some countries, despite the importance of subnational governments in the fiscal area, a kind of iceberg mentality has developed in which all the attention has gone to the visible part (the national government) while the role and activities of the subnational

---

[4]There is no question that in some transition economies, such as Hungary, the level of public expenditure is much too high (see Bokros and Dethier, 1998).

[5]Obviously the assignment of revenue must bear a clear relationship to the assignment of expenditure. Subnational governments must be given adequate resources to meet their commitments, and their budgets cannot be soft.

governments have been largely ignored. In Russia, for example, so much attention has been paid to the difficulties of the national government in raising revenue that a widespread perception has developed that Russian taxes are low and that the solution to Russia's fiscal problem is an increase in tax revenue. Rather, what is needed is a rationalization of total spending or a reallocation of tax revenue between national and subnational governments.[6]

Progress Toward General Reforms

How far along has the process of transition come? Focusing only on the shock therapy aspect of the transition gives the impression that much progress has been made (see EBRD, 1998). Indeed, in some countries and in some areas, this is the case. But in other countries and in other areas, transition still has a long way to go. In some countries one gets the impression that the old system is largely gone but that a new system is far from coming into existence. A kind of institutional vacuum has thus developed.

The private sector share in GDP, which was almost insignificant 10 years ago, has risen dramatically in many countries, to 70 percent or more in countries like Albania, Czech Republic, Estonia, Hungary, Lithuania, Russia, and Slovak Republic. Only in Belarus, Tajikistan, and Turkmenistan does it remain at 30 percent or lower. Although impressive, these percentages refer to privatization of ownership and not necessarily of management. In many countries either the same managers are running the enterprises as were running them 10 years ago, or the managers continue to behave as if the enterprises were still state owned.

One intriguing aspect of the privatization experience is the low correlation between what has happened to state ownership and the fiscal proceeds from privatization. As already mentioned, the state owned almost everything before the transition, and "everything" probably meant a multiple of GDP in total value.[7] Yet the fiscal revenue that the government realized from the sale of its assets was minuscule (Table 1). Privatization proceeds in transition economies were, in fact, much smaller than those in many developing or developed market economies (with the notable exception of Kazakhstan, where privatization centered around the primary sector).

---

[6]At 28 percent of GDP, tax revenue in Russia is not very low. General public revenue is even higher. As large sectors of the economy are not taxed, however, the fully taxed sector of the economy is likely to experience particularly high tax burdens.

[7]In fact, given that resources were not used productively, the total wealth-GDP ratio is likely to have been particularly high.

Table 1. Proceeds from Privatization in 25 Transition Economies
(In percent of GDP)

Economy	1987	1988	1989	1990	1991	1992	1993	1994	1995	1996	1997	1998
Average for all countries[1]	...	...	...	...	...	0.4	0.6	0.5	0.7	0.8	1.1	1.0
BRO												
Armenia	...	...	...	...	...	...	...	0	0	0	0	...
Azerbaijan	...	...	...	...	...	...	...	...	...	...	...	...
Belarus	...	...	...	...	...	0.1	0.3	0.3	0	0.1	...	...
Estonia	...	...	...	...	...	...	...	...	...	...	...	...
Georgia	...	...	...	...	...	...	...	...	0.1	0.3	0.2	0.5
Kazakhstan	...	...	...	...	...	...	4.5	1.7	3.1	3.8	3.1	...
Kyrgyz Rep.	...	...	...	...	...	0	0	0	0	0.5	0.1	0.2
Latvia	...	...	...	...	...	...	0.1	0.3	0.4	0.3	1.3	1.0
Lithuania	...	...	...	...	...	0.8	0.9	0.4	0.2	0.1	0.3	5.3
Moldova	...	...	...	...	...	...	...	0.4	0.3	0.4	2.4	0.8
Russia	...	...	...	...	...	0.5	0.4	0.8	0.2	1.1	...	...
Tajikistan	...	...	...	...	...	0.7	0.2	0.3	0.5	0.2	0.6	0.5
Turkmenistan	...	...	...	...	...	...	...	...	...	...	...	...
Ukraine	...	...	...	...	...	...	0.1	0.2	0.1	0.2	0.1	0.4
Uzbekistan	...	...	...	...	...	...	0.2	0.7	0.8	0.8	0.5	...
Average	...	...	...	...	...	0.5	0.7	0.5	0.5	0.6	0.8	1.2
Central and Eastern Europe												
Albania	0	0	0	0	0	1.0	0.7	1.2	0.1	0.2	0.3	0.2
Bulgaria	0	0	0	0	0	0	0	0	0	0	3.2	0.9
Croatia	...	...	...	...	...	...	...	0.4	0.8	1.2	1.3	1.7
Czech Rep.	...	...	...	...	...	0	0.7	1.6	1.1	0.2	0.4	0.4
Hungary	...	...	...	0	0.1	0.8	0.4	0.8	3.1	3.9	3.1	0.4
Macedonia, FYR	...	...	...	...	...	...	...	...	...	...	...	1.2
Poland	...	...	...	0	0.2	0.4	0.8	0.3	0.3	0.5	1.5	...
Romania	...	...	...	...	...	...	...	...	...	...	1.0	1.0
Slovak Rep.	...	...	...	...	...	0	0	0.2	...	...	...	...
Slovenia	...	0	0	0	0	0	0	0	0.4	0.4	0.5	0
Average	0	0	0	0	0.1	0.3	0.4	0.5	0.8	0.9	1.4	0.7

Source: Data provided by the national authorities and Fund staff estimates.
Note: BRO = Baltics, Russia, and other former Soviet Union countries; . . . = no data.
[1]Averages are unweighted.

There are several reasons for this outcome, but the results are the same. A small group of individuals used their positions or their connections to amass enormous wealth. Privatization was in effect a fire sale to which only a privileged few were invited. In Russia, for example, it was reported that assets valued at $50 billion to $60 billion were bought for $1.5 billion. Schleifer (1996) has raised the question of whether a society where individuals have become so rich by essentially raiding the public treasury would be inclined to pass laws that protect private property. In these circumstances, privatization, which must be a fundamental step toward a market economy, becomes itself an obstacle to the enforcement of a fundamental prerequisite for a market economy, namely, the protection of private property.

Privatization of enterprises to the *nomenklatura* (communist elite) and other similar developments have dramatically changed the income distribution of the transition countries. Before the transition these countries had some of the most equitable income distributions in the world, an achievement of which the leaders of these countries were very proud. As Table 2 shows, the Gini coefficients for the period 1987–88 were in the low 20s in most centrally planned economies, which was very good by international standards. By the mid-1990s, however, the Ginis had increased sharply, and in the Kyrgyz Republic, Russia, and Ukraine they had reached values seen only in a small group of developing countries. These coefficients have probably increased further more recently. What is worse is that this increase in inequality occurred not because those who had moved up in the income distribution had created wealth, but because wealth had been raided from the government, at times with the implicit connivance of the government.[8]

Countries where income differences had been sharply compressed in the past found themselves, within a few years, with some of the richest men and women in the world living a life of conspicuous consumption. Some of these newly rich individuals also acquired substantial political power. It is easy to guess the reaction of the populations of these countries toward the economic changes that allowed this to happen. In such an environment, many of the measures necessary to make a market economy vibrant and efficient will be seen by the majority of the population as measures taken to protect the ill-gotten wealth of the new rich. It should therefore be no surprise if such measures do not encounter an easy time in the political process.

In conclusion, it should not be surprising if privatization is not seen as a sign of positive progress toward a market economy. At some point, the governments of these countries will have to take seriously their role in promoting equity. After all, the pursuit of a socially accepted income distribution is one of the fundamental roles of government. It remains to be seen what form this role will take, although it is not likely that it will be one friendly to a market economy.

---

[8]The sharp fall in the incomes of some groups (such as pensioners) also contributed to this deterioration in Gini coefficients.

Table 2. Changes in Income Inequality in 18 Transition Economies

Economy	Gini Coefficient Based on Income per Capita	
	1987–88	1993–95
Slovak Rep.	20	19
Hungary	21	23
Slovenia	22	25
Czech Rep.	19	27[2]
Belarus	23	28[3]
Poland	26	28[4]
Romania	23[1]	29[2]
Latvia	23	31
Uzbekistan	28[1]	33
Kazakhstan	26	33
Bulgaria	23[1]	34
Estonia	23	35[3]
Turkmenistan	26	36
Moldova	24	36
Lithuania	23	37
Ukraine	23	47[2]
Russia	24	48[3]
Kyrgyz Rep.	26	55[3]

Sources: United Nations Development Program (1996); Kolodko (1998).

Note: For most countries, the income category for 1993–95 is disposable income. In 1987–88 it is gross income, since, at that time, personal income taxes were small, as was the difference between net and gross income. Income includes consumption in kind, except for Hungary and Lithuania in 1993–95.

[1] Data are for 1989.
[2] Monthly.
[3] Quarterly.
[4] Semiannually.

Much progress has been made in the liberalization of prices and in some other reforms. Table 3, from EBRD (1998), ranks countries on an index of price liberalization that goes from 1 (little progress) to 4 (much progress). Although some countries (Belarus, Turkmenistan, Uzbekistan) score poorly, most show some progress, and a few (Hungary, Poland) display significant progress. Of course, although a movement from 1 toward 4 is a welcome indication of progress toward complete price liberalization, in a second-best world the removal of one restriction while others remain in place provides no guarantee that efficiency has increased. If the remaining price controls are in large and vital sectors such as energy, they may imply large distortions.

Figure 1, also from EBRD (1998), is a useful visual presentation of the pattern of shock therapy reforms summarized in Table 3. This would lead one to conclude that much has been accomplished, but that there is still a long way to go.

**Table 3. Private Sector Share of GDP and Indexes of Economic Reform in
26 Transition Economies**

| | Enterprises | | | |
Economy	Private sector share of GDP mid-1998[1] (in percent)	Large-scale privatization	Small-scale privatization	Governance and enterprise restructuring
Albania	75	2	4	2
Armenia	60	3	3	2
Azerbaijan	45	2	3	2
Belarus	20	1	2	1
Bosnia and Herzegovina	35	2	2	2–
Bulgaria	50	3	3	2+
Croatia	55	3	4+	3–
Czech Rep.	75	4	4+	3
Estonia	70	4	4+	3
Georgia	60	3+	4	2
Hungary	80	4	4+	3+
Kazakhstan	55	3	4	2
Kyrgyz Rep.	60	3	4	2
Latvia	60	3	4	3–
Lithuania	70	3	4	3–
Macedonia, FYR	55	3	4	2
Moldova	45	3	3+	2
Poland	65	3+	4+	3
Romania	60	3–	3+	2
Russia	70	3+	4	2
Slovak Rep.	75	4	4+	3–
Slovenia	55	3+	4+	3–
Tajikistan	30	2	2+	2–
Turkmenistan	25	2–	2	2–
Ukraine	55	2+	3+	2
Uzbekistan	45	3–	3	2

Source: EBRD, (1998).
Note: Indexes are from 1 (least) to 4 (most reform).
[1]EBRD estimate.

Fiscal Reforms in the Past Decade

The 1990s saw major reforms in most transition economies. Some
were much more successful than others. As a consequence, as Figure 1
shows, countries differ widely in the extent of progress achieved. In
general, the Central and Eastern European countries and the Baltic
countries have made rapid progress, whereas the other countries have
been less successful in establishing fiscal institutions, in controlling fiscal imbalances, and in redefining the role of the state. But even within

Markets and Trade			Financial Institutions	
Price liberalization	Trade and foreign exchange liberalization	Competition policy	Banking reform and interest rate liberalization	Reform of securities, markets, and non-bank financial institutions
3	4	2	2	2–
3	4	2	2+	2
3	3	1	2	2–
2	1	2	1	2
3	2	1	2	1
3	4	2	3–	2
3	4	2	3–	2+
3	4+	3	3	3
3	4	3–	3+	3
3	4	2	2+	1
3+	4+	3	4	3+
3	4	2	2+	2
3	4	2	3–	2
3	4	3–	3–	2+
3	4	2+	3	2+
3	4	1	3	2–
3	4	2	2+	2
3+	4+	3	3+	3+
3	4	2	2+	2
3–	2+	2+	2	2–
3	4+	3	3–	2+
3	4+	2	3	3
3	3–	1	1	1
2	1	1	1	1
3	3–	2	2	2
2	2–	2	2–	2

these broad groups of countries, differentiation is very important. The discussion that follows provides a broad overview of some of these changes.

In the pretransition economies, most tax revenue was obtained from three major sources: turnover taxes, taxes on enterprises, and payroll taxes. Foreign trade taxes also provided some, but never much, revenue. These revenue sources generated very high tax revenues (at times up to 50 percent of GDP) without the need for full-fledged or sophisticated tax administrations. Taxes were not collected on the basis

Figure 1. Average Transition Indicator Score by Region
(Average score)

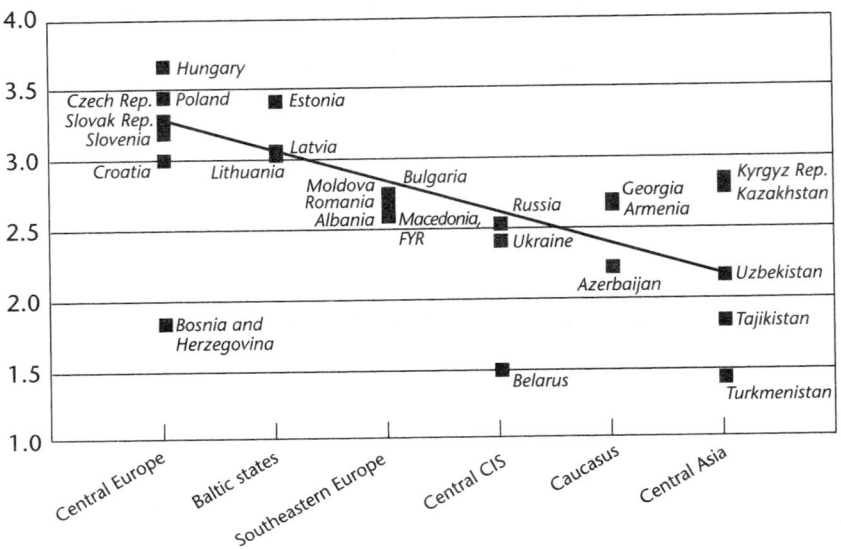

Source: EBRD (1998).

of detailed and codified tax laws that precisely defined tax bases and taxed them at parametric rates while respecting taxpayers' rights. Rather, especially for taxes on enterprises, they were collected largely on the basis of negotiations between the enterprises and government officials. The government was always free to change the rates and, in fact, it did so often (Tanzi, 1994). Turnover tax rates, for example, were not even published and were often changed. In this environment, tax liabilities tended to be soft and negotiable rather than well-defined and rigid obligations. When an enterprise was in difficulty, its taxes were negotiated downward; when the government needed extra revenue, they were negotiated upward. Under central planning, then, taxes, unlike death, were not certain.

Certain characteristics of the centrally planned economies made the collection of these taxes relatively simple. First, the authorities knew, from the central plan, the quantities of goods being produced by the state enterprises. Second, the monobank played an important role in processing payments and in imposing restrictions on how payments were to be settled. Third, the high concentration of economic activities in a few very large enterprises made controls and tax collection much easier. In this environment, most individuals never met a tax inspector and never had contacts with the tax authorities. As most taxes were hidden from those who finally bore them, most people were not even aware that, indirectly, they were paying high taxes. Thus, a "tax consciousness" or a tax culture never developed. This tradition created a hostile attitude toward the payment of explicit taxes brought about by the transition (Kornai, 1997) and has made the imposition of a transparent tax system more difficult.

The impact of the transition on the traditional revenue system was radical and damaging. The process of transition destroyed the plan and thus eliminated the information (good or bad) that the plan had provided on quantities produced and on prices at which output was sold. The government now had to rely on other sources, including taxpayers' declarations, to get this information. As a consequence, the prospect of tax evasion arose. The number of producers, and thus the number of potential taxpayers, increased dramatically with transition, as many new private sector activities came into existence. Tax administrations that had been used to dealing with relatively few, friendly enterprises had to deal with hundreds of thousands or even millions of unfriendly taxpayers. Some of these administrations were hardly prepared for this change and were slow to adapt. The large state enterprises that had provided the bulk of tax revenue began to lose importance, while the new, small, and difficult-to-tax private producers became the most dynamic sector of the economy, where much of the growth originated. These required a lot of close attention on the part of the tax authorities because of their high propensity to evade taxes. At the same time, however, they required protection from unscrupulous tax officials. Tax evasion and corruption on the part of tax officials had hardly existed in the previous system. Restrictions were also removed on methods of payments among enterprises and taxpayers in general that had existed when all payments were channeled through accounts with the monobank. Unfortunately, in the new environment, payments in the form of barter and tax arrears have grown, creating major difficulties for the new tax system. Finally, the transition created income and production in areas such as financial markets that had not existed in the previous system and that often involved foreigners.

All these changes and others not mentioned reveal why the old tax systems could not simply be reformed at the margin. Rather, totally new tax systems, capable of operating in the new environment, were needed. Yet such systems required not only new tax laws but also new fiscal institutions and new skills. Tax laws could be imported or even copied from other countries. The new fiscal institutions, however, had to be created from scratch, in circumstances that were far from ideal. These new institutions (such as tax administrations) needed financial resources (for computers and new staff, for example) and specialized skills (accountants, lawyers, computer specialists, auditors, and others). At the same time, they needed clear strategies and objectives, well-defined legal powers vis-à-vis the taxpayer, and well-defined legal obligations toward those taxpayers. These would establish clear rules of the game, which, like Chinese walls, would separate them from the inevitable pressures—from powerful political figures in the legislative branch, in the executive branch, or in local governments—to reduce the tax liabilities of specific taxpayers or to close their eyes to tax arrears.

All these reforms are necessary to establish a market-oriented system guided by the rule of law. However, they are so demanding in terms of time, resources, skills, technical knowledge, and political capital that only a few transition economies have been able to meet them. Even the leaders of the transition, such as Hungary and Poland, have not yet completed the process of creating new tax systems and tax administrations. Many other countries lacked the financial resources, the specialized skills, or a clear understanding of what needed to be done, or the ability or willingness to insulate the day-to-day administration of the tax system from political interference.

Many countries tried to patch up the old institutions to make them behave like new ones. But as the saying goes, it is difficult to teach old dogs new tricks. Often the poorly paid personnel of these institutions, schooled in the old ways, were themselves the main obstacle to change, and those put in charge of these institutions often had very limited knowledge of how tax administrations work in market economies. The incentives facing them were to maintain the old system. It would have been far better at the outset to create new institutions from scratch.

Many governments have failed to accept or to understand that, in a market economy, a tax system should be a parametric tool with one overwhelming objective, namely, to raise revenue in as efficient and equitable a way as possible. Rather, the tax system came to be seen as a multipurpose tool that should accomplish many things, including keeping failing enterprises in business, sustaining employment by allowing money-losing enterprises to pay wages instead of taxes, and stimulating economic activity. In some ways, the tax system replaced the plan as the key instrument for economic and social policy. Thus, in some of these countries, taxes have continued to be soft or nonparametric, especially for large enterprises, and key ministers have continued to spend much time dealing with individual taxpayers' tax problems rather than reforming the tax system (Tanzi, 1998).[9] This may have sharply increased the tax burden on that part of the economy that could not benefit from this preferential treatment.

Tables 4 and 5 report data on tax revenue and total general government revenue and grants as percentages of GDP since 1992 or, in the case of some Eastern European countries, since the late 1980s. Although Table 4 shows a large fall in tax revenue across most countries since the late 1980s, it also shows the wide range in tax burdens. For example, at the low end of the spectrum, the ratio of taxes to GDP ranged from under 6 percent in Georgia during 1993–95 to about 13 percent of GDP in the Kyrgyz Republic and Tajikistan during 1996–98. At the high end of the spectrum, one finds Slovenia, Czech Republic, Slovak Republic, and Poland with tax burdens exceeding 37 percent of GDP. Hungary and Slovenia have the highest tax rate at over 41 percent. These higher tax ratios are unlikely to be sustainable over the medium or the long run.

Despite the high tax ratios still prevailing in many of these countries, it has not proved possible to completely close the fiscal deficit. In many of these countries, especially the larger ones, public spending has remained very high as a percentage of GDP. One reason is, of course, that many of these countries have experienced falls in their output, which would have required extraordinary cuts in spending to reduce the ratio of spending to GDP. Another reason is that there has not yet been a well-thought-out policy of shrinking the role of the state. The government remains engaged in far too many activities.[10]

Table 6 reports data on general government expenditure and net lending as a percentage of GDP. For 1998 one still finds shares of 41.7 percent in Belarus, 36.7 percent in Ukraine, and about 40 percent in Russia. The Central and Eastern European countries also show very high shares. With such high expenditure rates, it is not surprising that most of these countries are still experiencing large fiscal deficits (Table 7).

Two observations emerge from these tables. First, the data in Table 6 indicate clearly that either governments are budgeting on the basis of past national incomes and have not reacted to the fact that most of these countries are much poorer than they used to be, or they have not recognized that, as market-oriented economies, their capacity to

---

[9]In countries where local governments are important, the personnel of the tax administration have had difficulty determining whether their allegiance is to the national government or to the local governments that often provided them with housing, offices, and so forth. Often, national taxes have received less attention than local taxes.

[10]For example, in many countries the government is still heavily engaged in the provision of housing and continues to subsidize energy consumption. The price of energy in the majority of transition economies remains much lower than in market economies.

Table 4. Tax Revenue in 25 Transition Economies
(In percent of GDP)

Economy	1987	1988	1989	1990	1991	1992	1993	1994	1995	1996	1997	1998
Average for all countries[1]	...	...	...	...	...	28.7	29.2	29.2	26.8	26.8	27.4	27.5
BRO												
Armenia	...	...	...	...	...	20.5	13.1	13.1	12.7	12.9	16.3	16.9
Azerbaijan	...	...	...	...	...	31.1	33.2	16.9	10.4	14.2	17.0	15.0
Belarus	...	...	...	...	...	...	44.4	32.5	23.7	23.9	28.0	27.8
Estonia	...	...	...	...	...	30.8	36.5	38.8	37.8	37.1	37.1	37.1
Georgia	...	...	...	...	...	8.2	2.0	4.6	5.4	10.9	13.0	13.4
Kazakhstan	...	...	...	...	...	21.5	16.7	12.3	11.0	11.3	12.2	16.2
Kyrgyz Rep.	...	...	...	...	...	14.6	14.8	13.6	15.0	13.2	12.5	14.4
Latvia	...	...	...	...	...	...	36.1	36.1	35.1	33.7	34.8	34.3
Lithuania	...	...	...	...	...	30.3	27.8	31.4	31.6	28.8	32.0	32.9
Moldova	...	...	...	...	...	20.8	21.1	26.4	28.8	27.4	29.9	29.0
Russia	...	...	...	...	...	35.9	31.7	30.9	28.3	28.3	29.3	29.2
Tajikistan	...	...	...	...	...	34.2	35.4	53.7	12.8	11.7	13.3	11.7
Turkmenistan	...	...	...	...	...	10.6	13.9	6.2	9.1	13.6	18.6	18.7
Ukraine	...	...	...	...	...	41.6	41.1	39.1	34.8	34.7	35.6	31.8
Uzbekistan	...	...	...	...	...	26.4	28.4	23.3	27.7	32.3	27.7	29.4
Average	...	...	...	...	...	25.1	26.4	25.3	21.6	22.3	23.8	23.9
Central and Eastern Europe												
Albania	46.2	45.3	44.2	42.2	26.7	16.4	18.1	19.1	17.7	15.3	13.5	15.9
Bulgaria	...	48.2	50.0	43.0	37.7	33.1	28.9	31.8	29.3	26.5	26.6	30.6
Croatia	...	...	...	...	14.3	18.5	20.2	26.7	26.9	26.6	26.3	31.0
Czech Rep.	...	...	...	...	...	38.8	41.2	40.3	39.7	38.8	38.0	36.9
Hungary	...	...	...	46.6	47.9	45.6	45.2	42.9	41.9	43.5	42.9	41.2
Macedonia, FYR	...	...	...	...	...	...	...	41.9	38.8	37.9	36.1	34.4
Poland	...	...	...	...	35.4	36.5	39.1	39.6	38.7	38.3	37.5	...
Romania	...	...	...	35.8	36.2	34.2	31.5	28.3	28.9	27.1	28.0	28.2
Slovak Rep.	...	...	...	...	...	39.4	36.5	38.8	42.0	41.1	38.4	37.2
Slovenia	...	...	...	...	...	41.7	42.9	42.6	42.3	41.3	40.4	41.2
Average	46.2	46.8	47.1	41.9	33.0	33.8	33.7	35.2	34.6	33.6	32.8	33.0

Source: Data provided by the national authorities and Fund staff estimates.
Note: BRO = Baltics, Russia, and other former Soviet Union countries; . . . = no data.
[1]Averages are unweighted.

sustain high levels of expenditure will be limited. Some of the Central European transition countries, for example, are trying, imprudently, to maintain expenditure levels typical of rich welfare states. Second, the fiscal deficits shown in Table 7 are measured on a cash basis and do not show fully the pressures exerted on the fiscal authorities when budgeted expenditures far exceed financial resources. As a result, the au-

**Table 5. General Government Revenue and Grants in
25 Transition Economies**

(In percent of GDP)

Economy	1987	1988	1989	1990	1991	1992	1993	1994	1995	1996	1997	1998
Average for all countries[1]	...	...	...	...	...	35.1	34.9	35.4	32.1	31.5	31.6	31.2
BRO												
Armenia	...	...	...	...	...	26.7	28.9	27.7	19.9	17.6	19.7	20.6
Azerbaijan	...	...	...	...	...	51.0	40.5	33.8	17.6	17.6	19.7	17.1
Belarus	...	...	...	...	...	46.0	54.3	47.5	42.7	40.9	31.4	39.0
Estonia	...	...	...	...	...	33.3	38.6	41.3	40.5	39.0	39.6	39.4
Georgia	...	...	...	...	...	10.2	9.7	7.7	10.7	14.2	17.8	16.4
Kazakhstan	...	...	...	...	...	24.5	21.1	18.5	16.9	13.2	13.6	18.2
Kyrgyz Rep.	...	...	...	...	...	16.7	25.1	20.8	16.7	16.6	16.2	18.1
Latvia	...	...	...	...	...	28.1	36.4	36.5	37.6	38.3	40.6	43.9
Lithuania	...	...	...	...	...	32.0	30.2	31.7	32.3	29.6	32.6	33.8
Moldova	...	...	...	...	...	30.3	22.8	31.3	33.9	32.1	36.3	34.6
Russia	...	...	...	...	...	39.5	36.2	34.6	33.5	33.0	36.4	31.5
Tajikistan	...	...	...	...	...	35.2	37.3	56.0	10.8	12.1	12.2	12.0
Turkmenistan	...	...	...	...	...	42.2	12.8	8.1	10.7	16.6	25.4	23.1
Ukraine	...	...	...	...	...	34.2	42.7	41.9	37.8	36.7	38.0	34.0
Uzbekistan	...	...	...	...	...	31.5	35.3	32.3	34.6	34.2	30.1	31.1
Average	...	...	41.0	...	...	32.1	31.5	31.3	26.4	26.1	27.3	27.5
Central and Eastern Europe												
Albania	49.2	53.2	48.2	46.8	31.4	22.5	24.9	23.3	23.9	18.3	16.9	20.3
Bulgaria	60.2	55.2	57.4	52.8	40.4	38.4	37.2	39.9	36.1	32.6	31.6	34.8
Croatia	...	...	...	...	31.5	32.2	34.2	45.6	47.4	49.5	43.7	...
Czech Rep.	61.0	61.2	62.4	58.9	59.1	45.0	45.9	44.7	43.5	42.5	41.3	40.3
Hungary	...	...	...	47.1	48.5	46.2	45.7	43.5	42.5	44.4	43.7	42.1
Macedonia, FYR	...	...	...	...	...	39.3	40.2	46.4	42.0	41.0	38.9	37.2
Poland	...	...	...	45.3	42.0	43.8	47.6	46.8	45.7	45.0	44.4	42.9
Romania	50.2	44.8	50.9	39.8	41.9	37.4	33.9	32.1	32.1	30.1	30.7	30.1
Slovak Rep.	47.6	47.6	48.3	46.7	50.7	46.1	44.3	46.4	48.7	47.7	44.9	42.8
Slovenia	...	40.5	42.0	48.7	43.7	45.9	47.0	45.9	45.3	44.8	44.0	45.3
Average	53.6	50.4	51.5	48.3	43.2	39.7	40.1	41.5	40.7	39.6	38.0	37.3

Source: Data provided by the national authorities and Fund staff estimates.
Note: BRO = Baltics, Russia, and other former Soviet Union countries; . . . = no data.
[1]Averages are unweighted.

thorities have to rely on unorthodox methods for cutting expenditure, such as across-the-board freezes, sequestration, and cash rationing. Such actions may help preserve macroeconomic balance but at the cost of corrupting the budgetary process. This raises an important question: If the government does not abide by its legal obligations, how can it expect that others will?

**Table 6. General Government Expenditure and Net Lending in
25 Transition Economies[1]**

(In percent of GDP)

Economy	1987	1988	1989	1990	1991	1992	1993	1994	1995	1996	1997	1998
Average for all countries[2]	...	...	...	...	...	47.2	44.9	41.4	36.8	35.9	35.4	35.0
BRO												
Armenia	...	...	...	...	...	64.3	68.6	37.8	31.0	26.9	25.5	24.8
Azerbaijan	...	...	...	...	...	80.0	55.8	45.9	22.4	20.4	22.5	18.8
Belarus	...	...	...	...	...	46.0	56.1	50.0	44.6	42.6	32.1	41.7
Estonia	...	...	...	...	...	33.6	39.2	40.0	41.7	37.4	39.7	43.3
Georgia	...	...	...	...	...	55.7	50.0	33.2	17.6	20.9	23.4	21.5
Kazakhstan	...	...	...	...	...	31.9	25.2	26.2	20.1	18.5	20.7	25.8
Kyrgyz Rep.	...	...	...	...	...	31.4	39.8	32.4	34.0	26.5	25.1	28.1
Latvia	...	...	...	...	...	28.9	35.8	40.5	41.1	39.7	39.2	43.9
Lithuania	...	...	...	...	...	31.5	35.4	36.5	36.8	34.1	34.4	39.6
Moldova	...	...	...	...	...	56.0	30.4	40.8	39.7	38.7	43.1	37.6
Russia	...	...	...	...	...	57.9	43.6	45.0	39.6	41.7	44.3	39.5
Tajikistan	...	...	...	...	...	65.7	60.7	61.0	18.7	17.9	15.3	15.8
Turkmenistan	...	...	...	...	...	28.9	13.1	9.2	12.1	16.9	25.4	25.8
Ukraine	...	...	...	...	...	57.4	54.5	50.6	42.7	39.9	43.6	36.7
Uzbekistan	...	...	...	...	...	42.8	54.9	36.4	38.1	39.8	32.5	34.5
Average	...	...	49.5	...	...	47.5	44.2	39.0	32.0	31.0	31.5	31.9
Central and Eastern Europe												
Albania	50.9	54.4	56.8	62.1	61.9	44.3	40.2	36.3	34.3	30.3	29.4	31.0
Bulgaria	59.0	60.8	58.8	65.6	55.0	43.6	48.1	45.7	42.4	45.2	34.1	33.3
Croatia	...	...	...	...	36.3	36.1	35.0	44.1	48.9	51.1	46.3	...
Czech Rep.	56.1	59.8	61.1	61.1	54.2	47.1	45.4	45.8	45.3	43.6	43.4	39.4
Hungary	...	...	...	46.0	52.1	53.7	54.6	52.1	48.7	47.5	48.5	46.4
Macedonia, FYR	...	...	...	...	...	49.1	53.6	49.3	43.1	41.4	39.4	38.6
Poland	...	...	...	42.1	49.1	49.5	50.5	49.2	48.0	47.5	47.5	45.7
Romania	43.5	39.1	42.8	38.7	38.7	42.0	34.2	33.9	34.7	34.1	34.3	33.7
Slovak Rep.	55.8	59.3	60.3	61.7	59.3	58.0	51.3	47.8	48.3	49.0	50.1	48.2
Slovenia	...	39.6	41.7	49.1	41.0	45.6	46.7	46.1	45.7	44.9	45.7	46.3
Average	53.1	52.2	53.6	53.3	49.7	46.9	46.0	45.0	43.9	43.5	41.9	40.3

Source: Data provided by the national authorities and Fund staff estimates.
Note: BRO = Baltics, Russia, and other former Soviet Union countries; . . . = no data.
[1]Including identified expenditure arrears.
[2]Averages are unweighted.

Conclusion

We began with a brief discussion of the role of government in the old system. This role was overwhelming. We also argued that major changes need to occur to complete the transition. Some of these

Table 7. Overall General Government Balance in 25 Transition Economies[1]

(In percent of GDP)

Economy	1987	1988	1989	1990	1991	1992	1993	1994	1995	1996	1997	1998
Average for all countries[2]	...	...	...	...	...	−12.0	−10.5	−6.0	−4.6	−4.4	−3.7	−3.7
BRO												
Armenia	...	...	...	...	...	−37.6	−39.7	−10.1	−11.1	−9.3	−5.8	−4.2
Azerbaijan	...	...	...	...	...	−29.0	−15.3	−12.1	−4.8	−2.8	−2.8	−1.7
Belarus	...	...	...	...	...	0.0	−1.8	−2.5	−1.9	−1.7	−0.7	−2.7
Estonia	...	...	...	...	...	−0.3	−0.6	1.3	−1.2	1.6	−0.1	−3.9
Georgia	...	...	...	...	...	−45.5	−40.3	−25.5	−6.9	−6.7	−5.6	−5.1
Kazakhstan	...	...	...	...	...	−7.4	−4.1	−7.7	−3.2	−5.3	−7.1	−7.6
Kyrgyz Rep.	...	...	...	...	...	−14.7	−14.7	−11.6	−17.3	−9.9	−8.9	−10.0
Latvia	...	...	...	...	...	−0.8	0.6	−4.0	−3.5	−1.4	1.4	0.0
Lithuania	...	...	...	...	...	0.5	−5.2	−4.8	−4.5	−4.5	−1.8	−5.8
Moldova	...	...	...	...	...	−25.7	−7.6	−9.5	−5.8	−6.6	−6.8	−3.0
Russia	...	...	...	...	...	−18.4	−7.4	−10.4	−6.1	−8.7	−7.9	−8.0
Tajikistan	...	...	...	...	...	−30.5	−23.4	−5.0	−7.9	−5.8	−3.1	−3.8
Turkmenistan	...	...	...	...	...	13.3	−0.3	−1.1	−1.4	−0.3	0.0	−2.7
Ukraine	...	...	...	...	...	−23.2	−11.8	−8.7	−4.9	−3.2	−5.6	−2.7
Uzbekistan	...	...	...	...	...	−11.3	−19.6	−4.1	−3.5	−5.6	−2.4	−3.4
Average	...	...	−8.5	...	...	−15.4	−12.7	−7.7	−5.6	−4.7	−3.8	−4.3
Central and Eastern Europe												
Albania	−1.7	−1.2	−8.6	−15.3	−30.5	−21.8	−15.3	−13.0	−10.4	−12.0	−12.5	−10.7
Bulgaria	1.2	−5.6	−1.4	−12.8	−14.6	−5.2	−10.9	−5.8	−6.3	−12.6	−2.5	1.5
Croatia	...	...	...	...	−4.8	−3.9	−0.8	1.5	−1.5	−1.6	−2.6	−0.8
Czech Rep.	4.9	1.4	1.3	−2.2	4.9	−2.1	0.5	−1.1	−1.8	−1.1	−2.1	0.9
Hungary	...	...	...	1.1	−3.6	−7.5	−8.9	−8.6	−6.2	−3.1	−4.8	−4.3
Macedonia, FYR	...	...	...	...	...	...	...	−2.9	−1.1	−0.4	−0.5	−1.4
Poland	...	...	...	3.2	−7.1	−5.7	−2.9	−2.4	−2.3	−2.5	−3.1	−2.8
Romania	6.7	5.7	8.1	1.1	3.2	−4.6	−0.3	−1.8	−2.6	−4.0	−3.6	−3.6
Slovak Rep.	−8.2	−11.7	−12.0	−15.0	−8.6	−11.9	−7.0	−1.4	0.4	−1.3	−5.2	−5.4
Slovenia	...	0.9	0.3	−0.4	2.7	0.3	0.3	−0.2	−0.4	−0.1	−1.7	−1.0
Average	0.6	−1.8	−2.1	−5.0	−6.5	−6.9	−5.0	−3.6	−3.2	−3.9	−3.9	−2.8

Source: Data provided by the national authorities and Fund staff estimates.
Note: BRO = Baltics, Russia, and other former Soviet Union countries; . . . = no data.
[1]Data are on a cash basis. Negative numbers represent deficits.
[2]Averages are unweighted.

changes—essentially those visualized by the shock therapy approach—are superficial. Others—such as the creation of many new institutions, changes in incentives, changes in processes, changes in the role of government, and so on—are deep. The latter are much more

Table 8. Corruption Perception Indices for 15 Transition and
Socialist Economies

Economy	Index[1]	Variance
Albania	1.02	2.89
Russia	2.27	0.87
Belarus	2.38	1.15
Ukraine	2.61	0.78
China	2.88	0.82
Romania	3.44	0.07
Cuba	3.45	0.46
Yugoslavia	3.46	0.01
Slovak Rep.	3.65	0.12
Bulgaria	3.94	1.78
Poland	5.08	2.13
Latvia	5.11	0.05
Hungary	5.18	1.66
Czech Rep.	5.20	0.22
Estonia	6.16	0.10

Source: Compiled by Johann Graf Lambsdorff, Göttingen University.
[1]Data are averages of several subsidiaries. An index of 10 denotes the absence of corruption, and an index of zero denotes maximum corruption.

difficult and time-consuming because they involve profound structural reform and major changes in attitudes, incentives, and relations.

In the new world of market economies, the role of government must change dramatically. Government will no longer seek to achieve its objectives through direct controls, but rather mostly through the tax system, the budget, and a few essential regulations. The tax system should be totally reformed to make it efficient and equitable and to provide a reasonable level of taxation. Expenditure policies should be changed to bring them more in line with reduced public resources. At the same time, regulations must be fundamentally modified. New essential regulations will have an important role to play, for example in setting the rules of the game, regulating private pensions, and enforcing competition, but most permits, authorizations, and other things that lend themselves to the extraction of bribes must disappear. It is a known fact that these regulations promote corruption, which for many of these countries remains very high (Table 8).

Given what has happened to Gini coefficients in these economies, and given the experience with privatization, it is reasonable to expect that governments will be asked to play a more positive role in income redistribution. It is not unthinkable to expect that those who made fast money by raiding the public treasuries will be singled out for special attention in future years.

Policymakers should work hard at harmonizing the conception of the role of the state that seems to prevail in many legislatures with one that is feasible, given existing macroeconomic conditions and the level of institutional and economic development in these countries. A campaign to educate the public and legislators on what the state is expected to do in a market economy and the limits to what it can do would be useful. However, those who take on this function will have to be persons of great credibility.

A fuller realization is needed that, although large fiscal deficits are often a macroeconomic problem, they also become fundamental problems when they force governments into reneging on their legal contracts by imposing across-the-board expenditure freezes and sequestrations. These actions represent a form of corruption of the whole budgetary process and, more generally, of a market economy. When a public employee puts in a day's work and is not paid, or when pensioners do not receive the pensions to which they are legally entitled, there is something fundamentally wrong with the whole political budgetary process.[11]

Bibliography

Bokros, Lajos, and Jean-Jacques Dethier, eds., 1998, *Public Finance Reform During the Transition: The Experience of Hungary* (Washington: World Bank).

Cangiano, Marco, Carlo Cottarelli, and Luis Cubeddu, 1998, "Pension Developments and Reforms in Transition Economies," IMF Working Paper 98/151 (Washington: International Monetary Fund).

Cheasty, Adrienne, and Jeffrey Davis, 1996, "Fiscal Transition in Countries of the Former Soviet Union: An Interim Assessment," *MOCT–MOST: Economic Policy in Transitional Economies (Netherlands)*, Vol. 6, No. 3, pp. 7–34.

European Bank for Reconstruction and Development, 1998, *Transition Report 1998* (London).

Havrylyshyn, Oleh, Ivailo Izvorski, and Ron van Rooden, 1998, "Recovery and Growth in Transition Economies 1990–97: A Stylized Regression Analysis," IMF Working Paper 98/141 (Washington: International Monetary Fund).

Kolodko, Grzegorz W., 1998, "Equity Issues in Policymaking in Transition Economies," paper prepared for a Conference on Economic

---

[11]On the other hand, when macroeconomic difficulties lead to inflation, which reduces the real value of what some individuals receive, at least the legal obligations have been met.

Policy and Equity, June 8–9 (Washington: International Monetary Fund).

Kornai, Janos, 1997, *Struggle and Hope, Essays on Stabilization and Reform in a Post-Socialist Economy* (Northampton, Massachusetts: Edward Elgar), pp. 239–54.

Nagy, Piroska Mohacsi, 1997, "The Meltdown of the Russian State" (unpublished; Washington: International Monetary Fund).

Saving, Jason, L., 1998, "Privatization and the Transition to a Market Economy," *Economic Review*, Federal Reserve Bank of Dallas, 4th Quarter, pp. 17–25.

Shleifer, Andrei, 1996, "Government in Transition," Harvard Institute of Economic Research Discussion Paper Series No. 1783, pp. 1–43, October.

Staff team led by Liam Ebrill and Oleh Havrylyshyn, 1999, "Reforms of Tax Policy and Tax Administration in the CIS Countries and the Baltics" (Washington: International Monetary Fund).

Tanzi, Vito, 1992, *Fiscal Policies in Economies in Transition* (Washington: International Monetary Fund).

_____, 1994, "Reforming Public Finances in Economies in Transition," *International Tax and Public Finance,* Vol. 1 (October), pp. 149–63.

_____, 1998, "Essential Fiscal Institutions in Selected Economies in Transition," Collegium Budapest, Institute for Advanced Study, Discussion Paper No. 53 (November).

United Nations Development Program, 1996, *Human Development Report* (New York; Oxford: Oxford University Press).

Inequality During the Transition: Why Did It Increase? 12

Branko Milanovic

The countries that we still, somewhat lazily, call the transition economies are becoming more diverse by the day. This increase in diversity is reflected in their incomes per capita: some countries have turned the corner on economic recession and are growing again, while others, most notably the two most populous transition countries, Russia and Ukraine, remain mired in depression.

Figure 1 illustrates the growing divergence in incomes by showing the coefficient of variation[1] of GDP per capita in constant 1987 dollars for the countries of Central and Eastern Europe (CEE) and the countries of the former Soviet Union. Before the transition, this coefficient for the republics of the Soviet Union was about 0.3. Ten years later it exceeded 0.5. The increase started as soon as the Soviet Union disintegrated. Similar if less dramatic are the developments in CEE. If the same calculation were done using GDP per capita in current dollars, the divergence between the countries would be even greater.

A similar phenomenon is observed if one looks at income inequality. Inequality has increased everywhere in the region, as shown in Figure 2 by the number of countries above the diagonal. But the dispersal of the Gini coefficients among countries is now also much greater than before the transition. In the past Gini coefficients ranged from 21 (in Czechoslovakia) to about 26 to 28 (in the Central Asian republics and Poland). Now, however, Ginis in the region span the range from the mid-20s to 40, and a few outliers (Kyrgyz Republic, Russia, and Ukraine) have Ginis about or even above 50, reflecting a level of inequality often associated with Latin American and African countries.

Figure 3 shows for each transition country the loss in GDP between 1987 and 1997 and the increase in inequality, as measured by the Gini coefficient, over approximately the same period. Countries are arranged from left to right by the percentage of their income loss: the farther a country is to the right, the more it has lost relative to its pre-transition GDP. By 1997 only Poland's GDP had actually risen, by 20 percent compared with 10 years before. Four other Central European

---

[1]The coefficient of variation is the ratio between standard deviation and the mean.

Figure 1. Coefficients of Variation of GDP per Capita in Transition Economies

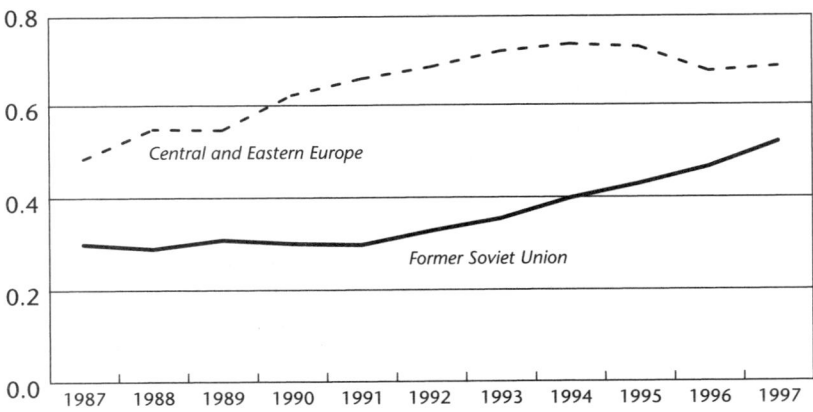

Source: World Bank DEC database.

countries (Czech Republic, Hungary, Slovak Republic, and Slovenia) and Uzbekistan had relatively small losses ranging from 2 to 9 percent of GDP compared with 1987.

Figure 3 also shows that although the Gini coefficient has risen in all of the countries for which data are available, except the Slovak Republic, it has generally increased more in those that have suffered larger declines in incomes. This is not, of course, to assert a causal relationship. Many other factors might have driven inequality up, and GDP down. However, the fact of large GDP losses and large increases in inequality has very important implications for what happened to the percentage of people in poverty. This set of countries was therefore hit with a double whammy: large income losses and large increases in inequality. Both, of course, pushed poverty up. This again implies a rising disparity among the transition economies, this time in terms of poverty head counts.

The five Central European countries known as the Visegrad countries (Czech Republic, Hungary, Poland, Slovak Republic, and Slovenia) display features that are very different from the other transition economies. Their GDP losses, as we have seen, have been smaller. Their income inequality has increased less than elsewhere. Social spending as a share of GDP has risen more significantly than in the other transition economies. These differences make it increasingly in-

Figure 2. Gini Coefficients Before the Transition in 1994–95 in 18 Transition Economies

Gini in 1994–95

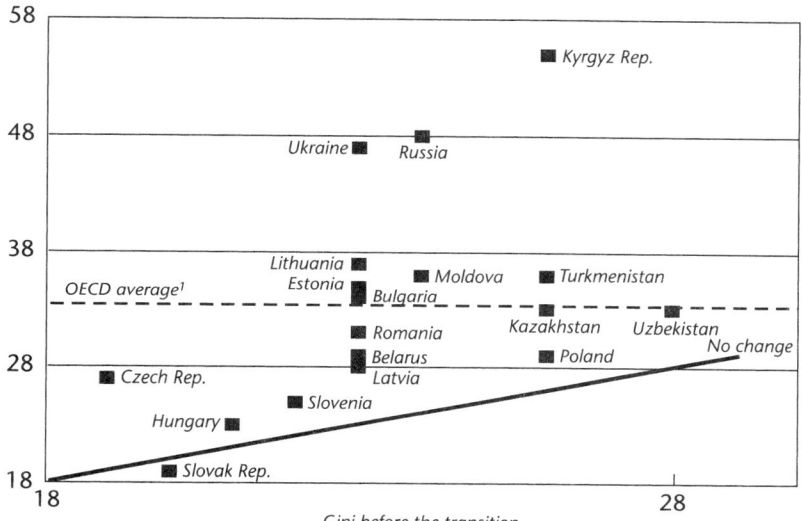

Source: Milanovic (1998, p. 41); Luxembourg Income Study data.
Note: "No change" means no change compared with inequality before the transition. Gini coefficients are calculated on the basis of income per capita.
[1]Gini coefficients for 18 market economies based on disposable income.

appropriate to generalize across all transition economies. But when we discuss the transition economies, the situation becomes much more varied, and it is not easy to identify groupings that share distinct common features.

Rapidly Rising Inequality: The Example of Russia

The general increase in inequality in the transition economies no longer comes as a surprise. What is surprising, however, is how large and fast the increase in inequality was in some of these countries.

Figure 4 shows Gini coefficients from 1980 until the mid-1990s for Brazil, Russia, and the United States. The Gini coefficient is a sluggish measure. What was, in historical perspective, a large increase in inequality in the United States in the 1980s shows up as a gently upward sloping line. But that increase pales in comparison with Russia's. In the 1980s, inequality increased in the United States by about ½ a Gini point per year.

Figure 3. Changes in Gini Coefficients and GDP Loss for 26 Transition Economies

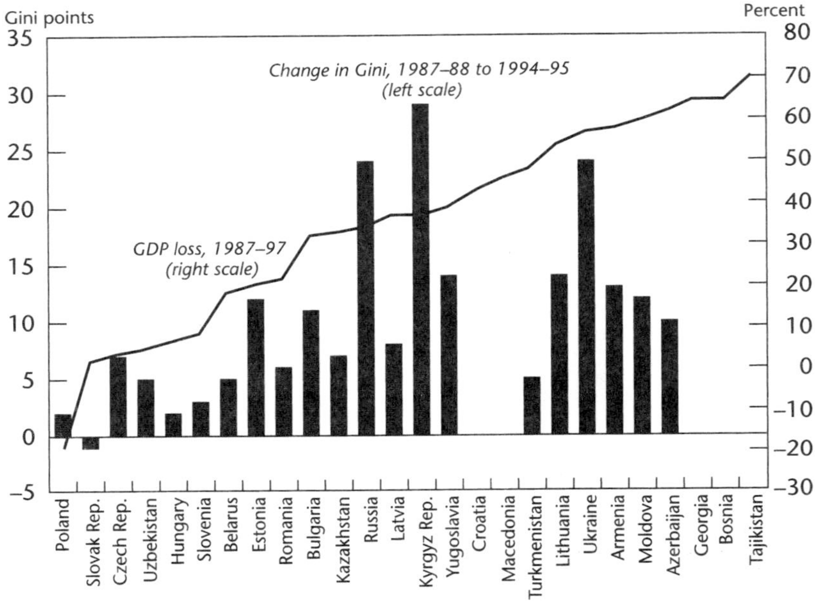

Source: World Bank data.

This is about one-fourth or one-fifth the pace of the recent increase in the Gini coefficient in Russia. The speed with which inequality has increased in Russia is, indeed, probably unique in recorded world history. Of course, one needs to take into account that inequality was underestimated before the transition. But even if one revises the pretransition Ginis upward by a few points (as suggested by the difference in the Gini values calculated by the *Goskomstat* (State Committee of the Russian Federation of Statistics) and by the Russian Longitudinal Monitoring Survey in the years for which both are available), one still observes an extremely steep increase.

The increase in Russia's Gini is even more remarkable when set against the fact that, when Gini coefficients for many countries are combined in a pooled cross section, more than 90 percent of the variability is explained by the differences in cross-country Ginis (Li, Squire, and Zou, 1998). In other words, changes in inequality within countries over time are typically small. But this is not the case in Russia and a number of other transition economies.

It is also interesting, and puzzling, that this remarkable increase in inequality took place as Russia became more democratic. Empirical research and some theory have generally tended to argue that more au-

Figure 4. Gini Coefficients for Brazil, Russia, and the United States

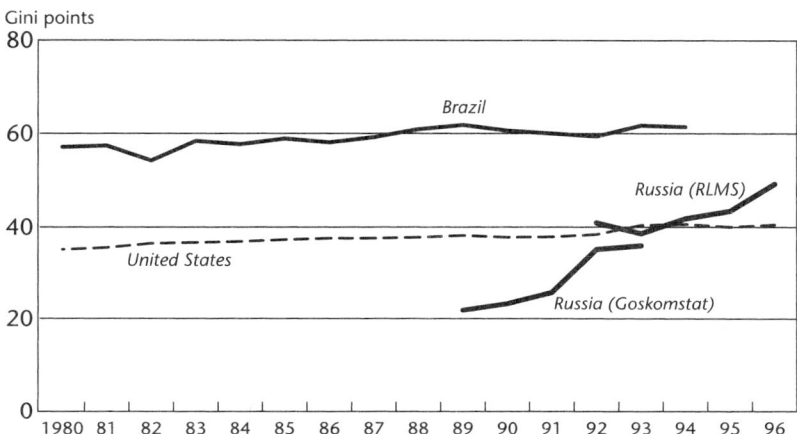

Sources: Data for Russia: 1989–93 from Goskomstat Rossii; 1992–96 from Russian Longitudinal Monitoring Survey data; U.S. data from Current Population Survey; Brazilian data calculated from PNAD Survey (supplied by Francisco Ferreira).
Note: Gini coefficients are calculated on the basis of disposable income per capita.

thoritarian societies, characterized by a high concentration of both political and economic power, will tend to display high inequality (Hewitt, 1977; Muller, 1988). Thus, if anything, we would expect democratization to reduce inequality.

How To Account for Increasing Inequality: Looking at the Recipients

How can we account for the increase in inequality in the transition economies? Can we disaggregate the factors that pushed inequality up? If we can point to the factors that, at least in some accounting sense, raised inequality, this might provide us with some direction for further research and allow us to say something meaningful about the economic forces behind the increase.

I will start with a simple model that is discussed more extensively elsewhere (Milanovic, 1999). Let us assume that, before the transition, the economy was composed of a small private sector and a large state sector. I assume that the private sector consists mostly of self-dededdemployed labor and that its growth is blocked by legal restrictions on its size. (For example, in a number of socialist countries, nonagricultural private businesses were limited to 5 or 10 hired workers.) The state sector employs everybody else. There is no unemployment. Wages in the private sector are higher than in the state sector. Obviously, if labor could freely flow from the state to the private sector, the two wage rates would be equalized. But the restrictions on hiring in the private sector allow the two wage rates to remain different. In addition to the state sector workers and the self-employed, there are pensioners, who are paid out of tax revenues. The mean income of pensioners is the lowest of the three groups.

The social structure before the transition thus looks as follows. By far the largest percentage of household heads are working in the state sector, where wage differentiation is relatively small and wage levels are moderate (the state sector wage can be taken as a numeraire). Some household heads (say, 10 percent) are self-employed. Their average income is higher than that in the state sector, and the distribution of their incomes is more unequal. Finally, some household heads (say, 10 to 20 percent) are pensioners with relatively low income per head and very low income differentiation.

During the transition, the large group of state sector workers, with incomes intermediate between those of the other two sectors, bifurcates. Some workers remain in the state sector. But others transfer into the private sector, and still others lose their jobs. So whereas before the transition 60 or 70 percent of household heads were state sector employees, with a fairly moderate income differentiation, after the transition there is a hollowing out of that sector, with some people moving into highly paid private sector jobs and others joining the unemployment rolls.

Having thus briefly sketched the changes that have occurred during the transition, we can consider how this might translate in terms of the Gini coefficient. The overall Gini coefficient can be broken down into sectoral Gini coefficients as in equation (1):

$$\text{GINI} = Gy \, \pi y \, py + Gw \, \pi w \, pw + Gt \, \pi t \, pt + \qquad (1)$$
$$+ \frac{1}{\mu} \left[(y - ws) \, py \, pw + (y - t) \, py \, pt + (ws - t) \, pw \, pt \right] + L,$$

where the Gi's are the Gini coefficients of *recipients only* of private sector employees (Gy), state sector employees (Gw), and transfer recipients (Gt). The last of these groups includes pensioners and the unemployed (the latter, of course, only after transition has begun), because they are both paid out of tax revenues. The πs and ps are weights attached to these sectoral Gini coefficients: the πs are income shares and the ps population shares. The variable μ is average overall income. In addition, the expression includes terms showing the differences in mean incomes between these three categories. For example, $y - ws$ shows the difference between average private sector income and the average state sector wage. Finally, because the Gini coefficient is not exactly decomposable by recipients, there is also an extra, "overlapping" term, L. This term accounts for the fact that someone in a sector with a higher average income (say, a private sector employee) may have a lower income than someone from a "poorer" sector (say, a pensioner). Of course, if all private sector workers were richer than all pensioners or state sector workers, there would be no overlapping, and L would equal zero.

How would the transition be reflected in equation (1)? There are three possible ways. The first is through movement of labor. We know that, by definition, the transition is about people leaving the state sector and moving into better-paid private sector jobs. But there are also state sector workers who have lost their jobs and have joined the unemployed. If, initially, $Gy > Gw$, the movement of workers into the private sector will increase overall inequality (the weight attached to a higher G will increase). Note that, according to this first scenario, the overall Gini is affected through movement of labor alone; the sectoral Ginis (Gw, Gy, and Gt) as well as the mean sector incomes stay the same. This is the mobility explanation.

Another scenario through which the overall Gini might change involves increases in individual ("inherent") sector inequalities—that is, Gw, Gy, and Gt might go up. In this scenario, people do not move between the sectors, and mean incomes do not change, but inequality (income dispersion) within each sector becomes greater: wages, private sector income, and even pensions become more unequally distributed. This, too, is a possible definition of transition: widening income differences within sectors.

The third possibility is that labor stays where it was before the transition, and within-sector inequalities do not change (so that the sectoral Ginis stay the same), but mean sectoral incomes change in such a way that the rich (private) sector becomes richer, and the poor transfer recipients become even poorer. In other words, all pensioners remain pensioners, and inequality among them stays as before, but all pensions are, for example, simply cut in half. Then, obviously, the mean pension declines relative to the mean wage or mean private sector income, and because the differences between the mean sector incomes in equation (1) rise, the overall Gini rises, too.

We do not expect to find in real life a country in which one of these "pure" scenarios occurs to the exclusion of the others. The real-world change in the Gini will be the product of complex interactions in which each of these three scenarios occurs to some degree.

Table 1. Composition of Gross Income Before Transition and Several Years Later in Selected Transition Countries

(In percent of total household income)

Country and Years	Wages Before	Wages After	Nonwage Private Income Before	Nonwage Private Income After	Pensions Before	Pensions After	Other Social Transfers Before	Other Social Transfers After
Central and Eastern Europe								
Bulgaria, 1989–95	57	47	22	31	17	18	5	4
Hungary, 1987–93	60	50	14	16	19	19	7	15
Poland, 1987–95	55	34	24	30[1]	17	30	5	7
Slovenia, 1987–95	67	57	20	18	17	22	2	4
Regional average[2]	60	47	20	24	17	21	5	8
Former Soviet Union								
Russia, 1989–96	74	49	5	27	8	18	7	6
Latvia, 1989–96	82	50	12	23	8	18	3	9
Regional average	78	50	9	25	8	18	5	7

Source: Authors' calculations using data from the countries' annual household budget surveys. See Milanovic (1999).

Note: Totals may not sum to 100 because of rounding.

[1]Includes private sector wages.

[2]Unweighted average of the countries listed.

How To Account for Increasing Inequality: Looking at Income Sources

Next we look at how different income sources (as opposed to income recipients) have changed during the transition. When we look at sources of income, we no longer consider individuals to be either pensioners or state or private sector workers, but simply people who draw their income from different sources. In the Gini disaggregation by sector of recipient, people belonged either to one category or another (they were either pensioners, private sector workers, or state sector workers). In the Gini disaggregation by income source, in contrast, a person can, for example, be a pensioner who has an extra job, or a state sector worker with some property income.

Consider the income composition data from six countries: Bulgaria, Hungary, Latvia, Poland, Russia, and Slovenia. The data come from successive annual household budget surveys covering approximately the period 1987–96. Table 1 shows the results for each country for the two years (first and last) for which data are available. Total income is divided into four sources: labor income (wages), private nonwage income (including home consumption, self-employment income, property income, remittances, and gifts), pensions, and other cash social transfers.

Consider first the share of labor income. Before the transition, labor income was almost entirely derived from state sector employment. Now, obviously, labor may be employed in either the private or the state sector. The share of labor income has decreased throughout. It fell from 60 percent to 47 percent in the four CEE countries in Table 1 and from 78 percent to 50 percent in Russia and Latvia.

Second, the importance of nonwage private sector income has increased in all six countries except Slovenia. This increase may be deemed either a positive or a negative development. It is positive if there has been a shift toward higher-value-added activities. These include, for instance, workers who decide to leave the state sector and start their own businesses (for example, architects or lawyers who open their own offices). But nonwage private sector growth might also reflect a negative development: people may return to the countryside and try to eke out a meager existence working on their own plot of land or engaging in subsistence agriculture. In one case, self-employment is a promodern, positive strategy; in the other, it is a demodernizing survival strategy. In addition, nonwage private income has traditionally been distributed rather unequally. This is inevitable because it includes people who are very diverse: some are at the top of the income pyramid, and others at the bottom. Thus the growth in the relative importance of this source of income (in the four CEE countries it rose from 20 percent of total income to 24 percent, and in Russia and Latvia much more sharply, from 9 percent to 25 percent) places upward pressure on the overall Gini coefficient.

Third, pensions have generally increased as a share of total income. The pretransition data for Latvia and Russia are not very reliable because of systematic underrepresentation of pensioner households in income and expenditure surveys (Milanovic, 1999). So the increase in the pension share from 8 percent to 18 percent of total income is probably an overestimate. However, the trends are unmistakable for CEE, where one can be much more confident in the comparability of the pre- and posttransition data, and where the proportion of pensioners in the total population has significantly increased.[2]

Finally, other cash social transfers were small before the transition and have remained so. However, they, too, have increased from 5 per-

---

[2]Between 1987 and 1997, the proportion of pensioners in the population increased from 25 percent to 30 percent in Bulgaria, from 22 percent to 31 percent in Hungary, from 17 percent to 24 percent in Poland, and from 22 percent to 26 percent in Russia and Estonia. It stayed at 23 percent in Slovenia (World Bank DEC database).

cent of total income to 7 or 8 percent now. Thus, the shares of each of the three income sources (nonwage private sector income, pensions, and other cash social transfers) have increased at the expense of the declining share of labor income.

What has happened to the concentration coefficients, that is, to the distribution of each of these income sources? The concentration coefficient, denoted C in equation (2), measures both the inequality with which a source is distributed and its correlation with overall income— that is, whether it is a pro-poor or a pro-rich source. Social assistance is, of course, distributed very unequally, because very few people receive it. Capital income is distributed very unequally as well. However, we need to distinguish between the two: whereas one is a pro-poor source (since mostly poor people get it), the other is a pro-rich source. So instead of looking at the Gini coefficients (which may be the same for both), we use the concentration coefficient, which is equal to the Gini coefficient multiplied by the correlation of that source with total income. In the case of capital income, the correlation will be positive, and the concentration coefficient will be positive, too. The opposite is true for the concentration coefficient for social assistance. A high positive concentration coefficient therefore means that the source strongly contributes to overall inequality; a negative concentration coefficient means that the source reduces inequality. Of course, the importance of each source is weighted by its share in total income, where the subscripts w, y, p, and o stand, respectively, for wages, nonwage private sector income, pensions, and other transfers:

$$\text{GINI} = Cw \ Ww + Cy \ Wy + Cp \ Wp + Co \ Wo. \tag{2}$$

Table 2 shows the values of the concentration coefficients before the transition and in 1995–96 for the same six countries as in Table 1. We see that the concentration coefficient of labor has increased significantly in all the countries, from a range of 20 to 25 before the transition to an average of 32 in CEE, and much higher in Latvia and Russia. The cause of this increase has been the increase in the Gini coefficient of wages.

Similarly, nonwage private sector income has become much more unequally distributed in Russia and Latvia, whereas in CEE the increase in inequality has been small or nil. However, before the transition, nonwage private sector income was the most unequal source in the four CEE countries (Table 2). What has happened now is that wage inequality has caught up with the inequality of nonwage income sources.

The concentration coefficient of pensions has not changed very much. In the case of Poland and Russia, pensions have, paradoxically,

Table 2. Concentration Coefficients Before Transition and Several Years Later in Selected Transition Countries

(In percent)

Country and Years	Wages Before	Wages After	Nonwage Private Income Before	Nonwage Private Income After	Pensions Before	Pensions After	Other Social Transfers Before	Other Social Transfers After
Central and Eastern Europe								
Bulgaria, 1989–95	21	34	38	37	11	13	–6	2
Hungary, 1987–93	25	35	30	26	14	21	–13	–16
Poland, 1987–95	25	40	37	40	17	37	–10	–10
Slovenia, 1987–95	20	26	18	21	22	21	–4	–19
Regional average[1]	23	32	31	31	16	23	–8	–11
Former Soviet Union								
Russia, 1989–96	28	60	18	56	–20	27	8	42
Latvia, 1989–96	23	41	16	43	34	9	–7	7
Regional average	25	50	17	50	. . .[2]	18	. . .[2]	25

Source: Authors' calculations using data from the countries' annual household budget surveys. See Milanovic (1999).
Note: Individuals are ranked by gross income per capita.
[1]Unweighted average of the countries listed.
[2]Country differences are so large that averaging is meaningless.

contributed to the increase in the overall Gini. As for the other cash transfers, their concentration coefficients have been, and remain, negative in most cases: they are clearly pro-poor. The problem is that they have not become *more* pro-poor—that is, their concentration coefficients have not decreased by much (in CEE the average value went down from –8 to –11). So a very slight improvement in their pro-poor targeting could hardly have made a dent in other forces that were pushing inequality up, namely, greater wage income inequality and the rising share of private sector incomes.

But we need to decompose the overall increase in inequality in order to identify the key factors more exactly. Table 3 does this for the two end years (1987–89 and 1995–96). Except in Russia, the change in the composition of income did not have much to do with the increase in the overall Gini. What was driving inequality up was, in the first place, the increasing concentration coefficient of labor. This measure has a positive sign for all countries and explains increases in the Gini of between 3.6 points in Slovenia and 23.6 points in Russia. For three countries (Hungary, Latvia, and Slovenia), the rising concentration coefficient of labor explains more than 100 percent of the overall increase in

Table 3. Decomposition of Changes in Gini Coefficients During Transition in Selected Transition Countries

Country and Years	Gini Coefficient In initial year	Gini Coefficient In final year	Change in Gini	Components of Change in Gini (in Gini points) Change in income composition	Wages	Change in concentration Social transfers Total	Pensions	Non-pension transfers	Nonwage private sector	Interaction term (in Gini points)
Bulgaria, 1989–95	21.7	31.7	+10.0	+1.6	+7.8	+0.9	+0.4	+0.4	−0.4	+0.3
Hungary, 1987–93	20.7	22.9	+2.2	−2.7	+5.5	+1.2	+1.4	−0.2	−0.6	−1.1
Poland, 1987–95	25.0	35.6	+10.6	−1.3	+7.9	+3.3	+3.4	−0.1	+0.6	−0.1
Slovenia, 1987–95	19.8	22.3	+2.6	−0.3	+3.6	−0.5	−0.1	−0.4	+0.4	−0.7
Russia, 1989–96	21.9	51.8	+29.9	−6.2	+23.6	+6.0	+3.7	+2.3	+4.3	+2.2
Latvia, 1989–96	22.6	32.6	+10.0	−1.8	+15.0	−1.5	−2.0	+0.5	+1.4	−3.1

Source: Authors' calculations using data from the countries' annual household budget surveys. See Milanovic (1999).

Figure 5. Poland: Distribution of Pensions, Family Benefits, and Unemployment

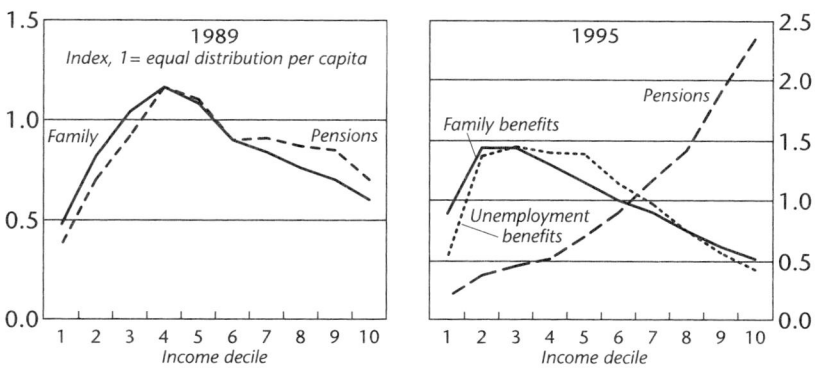

Source: Author's calculations from Polish Household Budget Surveys.
Note: Deciles are formed according to gross household income per capita.

inequality (other sources reduced inequality). For the other three countries it explains between 75 and 80 percent of total Gini increases.

Turning now to the efficiency of social transfers, the key question is, To what extent do these transfers reach the poor and thus offset the increasing inequality driven by the strong forces of greater differentiation of wages and private sector income? Unfortunately, on that score the changes in the transition economies do not present a very bright picture. On the one hand, pensions have not really had much of an impact in reducing inequality. Indeed, in some countries (Poland and Russia) pensions actually contributed to increasing inequality. This has happened as the ratio between the average pension and the average wage went up, and pensioners moved up the income ladder. Figure 5 shows this change very clearly for Poland. Before the transition (left panel), the distribution of pensions followed almost exactly the same pattern as the distribution of family cash benefits: the modes of the distributions for both pensioners and children (in respect of whom the family benefits are paid) were in the fourth income decile. But by 1995 the situation had changed (right panel). The mode for family benefits has shifted downward, to the second decile. (Note that this distribution of family benefits follows very closely that of unemployment benefits.) But the distribution of pensions has turned strongly pro-rich. The people in the top decile receive 2.4 times as much in the form of pensions as the average Pole, whereas before the transition people in the top decile received only 70 percent of the average. Clearly, the reason is that many more pensioners in Poland are now among the "rich," whereas in the past only a few pensioners made it to the top income decile. Only in Latvia, because of the Latvian pension reform of 1992–93, which introduced pensions that depended almost solely on the length of service, and not on previous earnings, do we notice a strong pension compression. There the concentration coefficient fell from 34 before the transition to 9 in 1996 (Table 2).

However, in general the lack of a substantial impact of pensions on inequality is not surprising. The primary role of pensions is not to reduce inequality or to fight poverty but to smooth income fluctuations. Pensions are only marginally different from labor income—and then only to the extent that most publicly funded pension schemes (as exist in transition economies) include an element of redistribution in favor of lower-earning households.

The primary onus of the fight against poverty (and against widening income disparities) falls on nonpension transfers. These include family benefits, unemployment allowances, and social assistance. However, as Table 3 shows, their role in that respect has not really expanded to any significant extent. These transfers have become only slightly more pro-poor than they were 10 years ago. This improvement in targeting is principally due to unemployment benefits, which, of course, did not exist in the previous system. However, the amounts of these benefits are very modest (Boeri and Edwards, 1998), and they reach only a part of the unemployed. This is because only the registered unemployed are entitled to benefits, and there is a large difference, particularly in the former Soviet Union, between registered and actual unemployed. For example, registered unemployment rates in Russia and Latvia in 1998 were 3 and 8 percent, respectively, whereas unemployment rates estimated from labor force surveys, using the standard definition of unemployment adopted by the International Labor Organization, were 12 and 15 percent, respectively.

What Has Really Happened: Some Preliminary Conclusions

We can conclude that, of the three possible "pure" mechanisms that might have brought about the increase in inequality (labor mobility, increases in individual sector inequalities, rising differences in mean sector incomes), the first, that is, mobility out of the state sector, must have been very important. The share of labor earnings in total income fell in all countries (by 13 percentage points on average in CEE, and more than 25 percentage points in Russia and Latvia; Table 1), whereas

Table 4. Average Pension as a Fraction of the Average Wage in Selected Transition Countries

Country	1987	1997
Central and Eastern Europe		
Bulgaria	44	32[1]
Hungary	55	56
Poland	51	64
Slovenia	55	66
Regional average[2]	51	55
Former Soviet Union		
Russia	37	34
Latvia	40	35
Regional average	39	35

Source: World Bank (DEC) database.
Notes: The regional means are unweighted averages.
[1]Data are for 1996.
[2]Unweighted average of the countries listed.

the ratio of the average wage to average income changed little, or even increased (Milanovic, 1999). These two facts imply that the number of employees decreased (something we also know from labor surveys). As we assumed initially, some of these employees went into self-employment, others became unemployed, and still others (mothers of small children, for example) withdrew from the labor force.

The second possible cause, an increase in individual sector inequalities, is an even better candidate, because we find that in all countries the concentration coefficient of wages went up. This factor is important because wages represent a large share of total income (between 60 and 80 percent before the transition). Even if we were to use today's wage share in the Gini decomposition analysis, this component would still be the largest. In contrast, increasing inequality in the nonwage private sector was significant only in Russia.

The third possible "pure" scenario is widening differences in mean incomes. The evidence for this scenario is rather weak. Of course, we lack information on average income in the private sector (and even its meaning is unclear, given the very heterogeneous composition of the sector), but we know that the ratio of the average pension to the average wage was stable in most countries or even increased (Table 4). This contradicts the third scenario, which assumes widening disparities—that is, that the poorest sector (transfer recipients) has fallen behind the middle sector (wage earners).

Having concluded that most of the huge increase in inequality is due to increased inequality among wage earners, the next question is whether this is good or bad. Unfortunately, there is no clear-cut answer to this question. We know from a number of studies of CEE (see Rutkowski, 1996, for Poland; Vecernik, 1994, and Chase, 1977, for the Czech and Slovak Republics; Orazem and Vodopivec,1995, for Slovenia; and Rutkowski, 1995, for Bulgaria) that the returns to education have uniformly increased, from about 4 percent per additional year of schooling to 7 or 8 percent. This is, in principle, a good development because we know that one of the socialist system's inefficiencies was a lack of sufficient reward to education and a "leveling off" of wages. However, the situation in Russia, and perhaps in most of the former Soviet Union, is not so clear: the variance of earnings for a given level of education has exploded: an institute mathematician can end up a dollar billionaire (as Boris Berezovsky did) or as an unpaid state employee. Similarly ambiguous is the fact that a larger share of overall earnings than in the past is left unexplained by the usual regressors (education and experience). Again, to the extent that there are individual elements that the regressions cannot capture, such as drive, ambition, or entrepreneurship, this may be a positive development. But it may be that what is behind these residuals is the ability of some people, thanks to their political connections or corruption, to capture huge economic rents.[3]

This opens a promising avenue for further research into what really underlies the increasing wage inequality. What are the relative contributions of education, entrepreneurship, and political connections? And in a deeper sense, it opens the question of what kind of capitalism these large increases in inequality point to. Is increasing inequality the result of better returns to education and of "primitive accumulation of capital," where eventually the new capital owners will, to legitimize their ownership, generate demand for the rule of law? Or is it the manifestation of what Max Weber called "political capitalism," where political connections and political power are the necessary requirements for the accumulation of wealth?

Bibliography

Boeri, Tito, and Scott Edwards, 1998, "Long-Term Unemployment and Short-Term Unemployment Benefits: The Changing Nature of Non-Employment Subsidies in Central and Eastern Europe," *Empirical Economics*, Vol. 23, No. 1–2, pp. 31–54.

Boone, Peter, and Boris Fedorov, 1997, "The Ups and Downs of Russian Economic Reforms," in *Economies in Transition: Comparing Asia and*

---

[3]For example, Boone and Fedorov (1997, p. 186) report the results of a study by Treisman that shows that the only variable that explains who gets credit in Moscow is "director's connections."

Eastern Europe, ed. by Wing Thye Woo, Stephen Parker, and Jeffrey D. Sachs (Cambridge, Massachusetts: MIT Press), pp. 161–88.

Chase, Robert, 1997, "Markets for Communist Human Capital: Returns to Education and Experience in the Czech Republic and Slovakia," Yale University, Economic Growth Center Discussion Paper No. 770 (New Haven, Connecticut: Yale University), pp. 1–37.

Hewitt, C., 1977, "The Effect of Political Democracy and Social Democracy on Equality in Industrial Societies: A Cross-National Comparison," *American Sociological Review*, Vol. 42, pp. 450–64.

Li, Hongyi, Lyn Squire, and Heng-fu Zou, 1998, "Explaining International and Intertemporal Variations in Income Inequality," *Economic Journal*, Vol. 108, pp. 26–43.

Milanovic, Branko, 1998, *Income, Inequality, and Poverty during the Transition from Planned to Market Economy* (Washington: World Bank).

———, 1999, "Explaining the Increase in Inequality during the Transition," *Economics of Transition*, Vol. 7 (May–June), pp. 299–341.

Muller, E.N., 1988, "Democracy, Economic Development, and Income Inequality," *American Sociological Review*, Vol. 53, pp. 50–68.

Orazem, Peter, and Milan Vodopivec, 1995, "Winners and Losers in Transition: Returns to Education, Experience and Gender in Slovenia," *World Bank Economic Review*, Vol. 9, No. 2.

Rutkowski, Jan, 1995, "Labor Markets and Poverty in Bulgaria," Background paper for the World Bank poverty assessment (unpublished; Washington: World Bank).

———, 1996, "High Skills Pay Off: The Changing Wage Structure during Economic Transition in Poland," *Economics of Transition*, Vol. 4, May, pp. 89–112.

Stanovnik, Tine, and Nada Stropnik, 1998, "Impact of Social Transfers on Poverty and Income Inequality in Slovenia: A Comparison between the Pre-transition and the Post-transition Period," SOCO Program, Ljubljana, September.

Vecernik, Jiri, 1994, "Changing Earnings Inequality under the Economic Transformation: The Czech and Slovak Republics in 1984–92" (unpublished; Prague: Czech Academy of Sciences).

Concluding Remarks 13

Shigemitsu Sugisaki

On behalf of the Managing Director and the three departments that jointly organized this conference, I would like to thank you, the participants, for the valuable contributions you have made to a better understanding of the transition record and the challenges that lie ahead. Let me try to highlight some of the themes that emerged from the papers and discussions of the conference.

First, fiscal and monetary prudence is an essential priority and a continuous requirement for recovery and sustained growth. Indeed, there has been no instance of sustained growth in the transition economies without macroeconomic stability. The empirical evidence presented during this conference pointed to the positive correlation between lower inflation rates and economic growth in the transition countries. I was also impressed by the finding that rapid disinflation had not involved output costs once other factors had been taken into account.

Second, macroeconomic stabilization needs to be complemented and supported by a broad spectrum of institutional and structural reforms. Participants noted the crucial role played by progress on these two fronts in fostering growth and attracting foreign capital flows, particularly foreign direct investment. There was also considerable agreement that a market-friendly environment is still missing in many countries and needs to be fully developed even in countries that are more advanced in the transition process. As the Managing Director noted in his opening statement, this means, in particular, enforcing the rule of law and property rights and putting in place the institutions and incentives required for the proper functioning of markets. This will help discipline the newly privatized entities into being efficient profit-seekers. But it will be equally important to shrink the underground economy and open the door to new private enterprises, a key source of dynamism and innovation in these economies. The positive effect of the changing role of government—played mostly through the tax system, the budget, and a few simplified and transparent regulations—was stressed.

Third, privatization, which for the general public may be the most important symbol of transition, generated the greatest amount of debate. The issue at hand was not whether to privatize—this was viewed overall as being the preferred option in dealing with the problems of state enterprises—but rather how best to privatize; in other words, whether to do so through rapid mass privatization programs or through a gradual, case-by-case approach. While this question still eludes a definitive answer, the participants at this conference were unequivocal in stressing that a strong institutional framework is critical to the success of privatization, and that privatization must proceed in an open and transparent manner. The examples of successful privatization in a number of transition countries should serve to guide those countries still grappling with privatization problems.

Fourth, banking sector reform is an essential component of the reform agenda. The task at hand is a dual one—to develop a modern system of financial intermediation and to ensure sound behavior by banks. Progress in carrying out this task will require a stable macroeconomic environment, a competitive system open to foreign financial institutions, strong prudential regulation, and, here too, an appropriate incentive structure.

Fifth, the sharp income inequalities that we see emerging during the transition must be addressed, not only to redress the growing inequalities but also because public perceptions of unfairness can eventually undermine support for the reform process. Institutional change and increased competition can contribute to reducing economic rents and income inequalities. In the interim, however, governments need to do more to provide a well-targeted social safety net for the most vulnerable segments of society.

These are the five key themes that have come out of your deliberations. Perhaps all may be captured under one umbrella, namely, the role of government. Under central planning, the administrative control by government was all pervasive, and transition has meant dismantling and changing its massive and intrusive operations. But much remains to be done in all transition countries to redefine the role of government, to build up new government structures, and to establish proper incentives. The transition from an omniscient provider overseeing all aspects of the command economy to an agent supportive of an environment conducive to private sector growth is indeed a historic one.

This conference has addressed the most fundamental issues in transition, taking stock of the achievements and shortcomings of the transition process so far. The exchange of views and the experiences of the participants from the transition countries have provided a most valuable menu of ideas on which we all need to reflect, and which, I hope, will provide a basis for better answers to the challenges in the coming years.

List of Participants

Titles and affiliations were those in effect at the time of the conference in February 1999.

Åslund, Anders
   Carnegie Endowment for Peace

Avanessian, Vahram
   Minister of Economic and Structural Reform, Office of the Prime Minister, Republic of Armenia

Babaev, Guylamjon
   State Economic Advisor for the President, Office of the President, Republic of Tajikistan

Blanchard, Olivier
   Massachusetts Institute of Technology

Bokros, Lajos
   Director, Private and Financial Sector Department, Europe and Central Asia, World Bank

Camdessus, Michel
   Managing Director, IMF

Cani, Shkelqim
   Governor, Bank of Albania

Cottarelli, Carlo
   Assistant Director, European I Department, IMF

Cseres, Akos
   Advisor to the President, Office of the President, National Bank of Hungary

Cuddington, John
   Georgetown University

Daianu, Dan
   Official, National Bank of Romania

Doyle, Peter
   Deputy Division Chief, European I Department, IMF

Fernald, John
   Federal Reserve Bank

Frydman, Roman
   New York University

Gaidar, Yegor
    Director, Institute for the Economy in Transition
Havrylyshyn, Oleh
    Senior Advisor, European II Department, IMF
Hrncir, Miroslav
    Chief Executive Director, Czech National Bank
Imashev, Chorobek
    Deputy Minister, Ministry of Finance, Kyrgyz Republic
Johnson, Simon
    Assistant Professor, Assistant Director, MIT Entrepreneurship
    Center
Jusko, Marián
    Vice Governor, National Bank of Slovakia
Kalra, Sanjay
    Economist, Asia and Pacific Department, IMF
Kaufman, Daniel
    Manager, World Bank
Khoubanov, Vadim
    Vice Governor, National Bank of Azerbaijan
Levine, Ross
    University of Virginia
Löhmus, Peter
    Deputy Governor, Bank of Estonia
Milanovic, Branko
    Lead Economist, Development Research Group, World Bank
Murrell, Peter
    University of Maryland
Nellis, John
    Senior Manager, Private Sector Development Department, World
    Bank
Nenova, Mariella
    Director, Agency for Economic Analysis and Forecasting
Nsouli, Saleh M.
    Deputy Director, IMF Institute
Portes, Richard
    University College of London
Riecke, Werner
    Deputy Governor, National Bank of Hungary

Rosati, Dariusz
  Member of Monetary Policy Council, National Bank of Poland,
  Professor of Warsaw School of Economics

Saidenov, Anvar
  Chairman, Kazakh Investment Agency

Selowsky, Marcelo
  World Bank

Shleifer, André
  Harvard University

Škreb, Marko
  Governor, Croatian National Bank

Sløk, Torsten
  Economist, Research Department, IMF

Stavreski, Zoran
  Director, Research Department, National Bank of the Republic of
  Macedonia

Steinbuka, Inna
  Director, Economic Analysis and Fiscal Policy Department,
  Ministry of Finance, Latvia

Stern, Nicholas
  Chief Economist, European Bank for Reconstruction and
  Development

Sturza, Ion
  Deputy Prime Minister and Minister of Economy and Reforms,
  Ministry of Economy and Reforms, Republic of Moldova

Sugisaki, Shigemitsu
  Deputy Managing Director, IMF

Tanzi, Vito
  Director, Fiscal Affairs Department, IMF

Tsibouris, George
  Senior Economist, European II Department, IMF

Urbsiene, Laima
  Vice-Minister, Ministry of Finance, Lithuania

Viyugin, Oleg
  Deputy Minister, Ministry of Finance, Russian Federation

Wolf, Thomas
  Assistant Director, European II Department, IMF